STATISTICS FOR THE 21ST CENTURY

STATISTICS FOR THE 21ST CENTURY

PROPOSALS FOR IMPROVING STATISTICS FOR BETTER DECISION MAKING

Joseph W. Duncan
Andrew C. Gross

IRWIN
Professional Publishing

Chicago • Bogotá • Boston • Buenos Aires • Caracas
London • Madrid • Mexico City • Sydney • Toronto

This publication is designed to provide accurate and authoritative information in regard to the subject matter covered. It is sold with the understanding that neither the author or the publisher is engaged in rendering legal, accounting, or other professional service. If legal advice or other expert assistance is required, the services of a competent professional person should be sought.

From a Declaration of Principles jointly adopted by a Committee of the American Bar Association and a Committee of Publishers.

Executive editor:	Ralph Rieves
Project editor:	Beth Yates
Production supervisor:	Lara Feinberg
Designer:	Mercedes Santos
Compositor:	Precision Graphics
Typeface:	11/13 Times Roman
Printer:	Quebecor/Fairfield

Library of Congress Cataloging-in-Publication Data

Duncan, Joseph W.
    Statistics for the 21st century : proposals for improving statistics for better decision making / by Joseph W. Duncan and Andrew C. Gross.
        p. cm.
    Includes index.
    ISBN 0-7863-0328-X
    1. United States—Statistical services. 2. Statistical services.
I. Gross, Andrew C. II. Title. III. Title: Statistics for the twenty-first century.
HA37.U55D84 1995
353.0081'9—dc20   94–36893

PREFACE

Responsible decisions—whether they are made by businesses, governments, or individuals—have this central element in common:

They are based on information that comprises the basic input required for the successful analysis of current conditions, the evaluation of proposed strategies, and the assessment of actions to be taken.

When it comes to the evaluation of economic and social decisions, there is a second area of often-overlooked commonality. Much of the common understanding flows from official statistics produced by the federal government.

During the past two decades, the concepts and definitions used in federal data collections have become increasingly less adequate in measuring the pace of social and economic changes. This problem is not limited to the United States. It is also seen in the international organizations, such as the United Nations, World Bank, and International Monetary Fund; and in the regional organizations such as the Organization for Economic Cooperation and Development and the European Union. Indeed, the problem exists in most countries around the globe as they seek to reduce the role of government, especially in the collection of data from people and institutions.

This study looks at the challenges posed by the need to bring the federal statistical activity up to speed with the changing realities. It is based upon over 25 years' experience of one of the two authors, Joseph W. Duncan—first, as a board member of the former Federal Statistics Users Conference; second, as a government official with responsibility for setting federal statistical policy; and, most recently, as a user of government statistics in business. This report is equally based on the experience of the second author, Andrew C. Gross, who has written a major text on using information in marketing, a text based on his work in several industries and on his role in founding Predicasts, Inc., a market research and publishing firm. Dr. Duncan is Vice President, Corporate Economist, and Chief Statistician of The Dun & Bradstreet Corporation, and Dr. Gross is Professor of Marketing and International Business at

Cleveland State University. Both authors have been assisted by many specialists, but they are solely responsible for the content of this report.

This is not a committee report, but a particular perspective designed to initiate further discussion, debate, and action on an important and critical challenge. Designing a statistical system that will meet the needs of the 21st century is an enormous undertaking. Unfortunately, current developments lag in fully resolving the needs that are clearly evident. This report is intended to present one view of some important future needs, some current deficiencies, and some ongoing improvements that need to be accelerated. Thus, this document is not intended to be the expert's final word in summarizing a definitive solution; rather, it is *a sentinel's early signal of a growing challenge.*

The objective is to focus attention on future needs and to challenge others to join the effort to bring about the changes that are clearly needed. The Dun & Bradstreet Corporation, as the world's leading marketer of information, software, and services for business decision making, is pleased to sponsor this report in the interest of stimulating further research toward improving official statistics as the foundation for decision making in the future.

Charles W. Moritz, Chairman
Robert E. Weissman, CEO & President

The Dun & Bradstreet Corporation
New York, New York, U.S.A.

October 1994

ABOUT THE AUTHORS

Joseph W. Duncan is Vice President, Corporate Economist, and Chief Statistician of The Dun & Bradstreet Corporation. He is the corporation's chief economist and is responsible for interpreting global economic trends to assist management of the corporation and its divisions in developing business strategy. As Chief Statistician, he oversees the quality of the databases maintained at all Dun & Bradstreet divisions. He works with the extensive information resources of the corporation to develop new products and services.

Dr. Duncan served as President of the National Association of Business Economists (1992–93). His presidential address in September 1993 featured material presented in the first edition of this book. A long-time student of official statistics, he served as Deputy Associate Director in the Office of Management and Budget from 1974–1981, with responsibility for policy oversight of the federal government's statistical agencies. He was appointed by President Nixon to be the U.S. representative to the Statistical Commission of the United Nations, serving as Chairman of the Commission in 1981.

He is the Executive Editor of *Dun & Bradstreet Looks at Business* and *Dun & Bradstreet Comments on the Economy,* bimonthly newsletters on economic statistics. He is the section editor of "Statistics Corner" in *Business Economics.*

He is coauthor of *Revolution in United States Government Statistics, 1926–1976,* published by the U.S. Government Printing Office in 1978, and was editor of two other books. He holds a Ph.D. in Economics from Ohio State University, an M.B.A. from Harvard University, and a B.S.M.E. from Case Institute of Technology.

Andrew C. Gross is currently professor of marketing and international business at Cleveland State University, where he has been a member of the faculty for the past 25 years. During this time he has served as a visiting professor at the University of New South Wales in Australia, and also at McGill University and McMaster University in Canada. Prior to coming to CSU, he was on the faculties of Ohio State and Lehigh.

Dr. Gross was a Fulbright Senior Scholar in Hungary in 1989 and again in 1992 at the Budapest University of Economic Sciences. In 1989 he was the first faculty lecturer at the newly established International Management Center in Budapest. He has been visiting Eastern Europe since 1971–1972, when he held an International Research and Exchanges Board fellowship at the Hungarian Institute for Market Research.

Dr. Gross has also worked in government and industry, beginning his career as an engineer with Ohio Edison and Standard Oil of Ohio. He served on the staff of Statistics Canada, the Science Council of Canada, and Battelle Memorial Institute. He was a founding partner of Predicasts, Inc. (now a division of Information Access) and served for many years on its board of directors. Currently, he is an active consultant to large and small companies in the United States as well as abroad.

Dr. Gross has published 15 monographs, over 50 articles, and two books, *Business Marketing* and *Education and Jobs*. He is on the board of several marketing and international business journals; he also serves as section editor of "Industry Corner" for the journal, *Business Economics*. He holds a PhD from Ohio State University, an MBA from Western Reserve University, and a BSEE from Case Institute of Technology.

The views expressed in this publication are the sole responsibility of the authors and do not reflect policy views of The Dun & Bradstreet Corporation or Cleveland State University.

CONTENTS

LIST OF FIGURES

ACRONYMS

ABI	Automated Broker Interface Program
ADB	Asian Development Bank
AEO	Annual Energy Outlook
AERP	Automatic Export Reporting Program
BEA	Bureau of Economic Analysis
BIS	Bank for International Settlements
BJS	Bureau of Justice Statistics
BLS	Bureau of Labor Statistics
CDC	Centers for Disease Control
CEC	Commission of the European Union
CERN	European Organization for Nuclear Research
CES	Current Employment Statistics
CIS	Congressional Information Service
CNN	Cable News Network
CPEs	Centrally Planned Economies
CPI	Consumer Price Index
DRI	Data Resources, Inc./McGraw Hill
ECE	Economic Commission for Europe
ECPC	Economic Classification Policy Committee
EDI	Electronic Data Interchange
EFTA	European Free Trade Association
EIA	Energy Information Administration
EPA	Environmental Protection Agency
ERS	Economic Reporting Service
ESCAP	Economic and Social Commission for Asia and the Pacific
ESOMAR	European Society for Opinion and Market Research
EU	European Union
Eurostat	Statistical Office of the European Union
FAO	United Nations Food and Agriculture Organization
FRB	Federal Reserve Board
GAO	General Accounting Office
GATT	General Agreement on Tariffs and Trade
GDP	Gross Domestic Product
GEMS	Global Environment Monitoring System
GNP	Gross National Product

GRI	Gas Research Institute
HMOs	Health Maintenance Organizations
HS	Harmonized Commodity Description and Coding System (Harmonized System)
IADB	Inter-American Development Bank
IAEA	International Atomic Energy Agency
ICAO	International Civil Aviation Organization
IEA	International Energy Agency
IIS	*Index to International Statistics*
ILO	International Labour Office
IMF	International Monetary Fund
INS	Immigration and Naturalization Service
IRS	Internal Revenue Service
LAFTA	Latin American Free Trade Association
MNCs	Multi-national Companies
NABE	National Association of Business Economists
NASS	National Agricultural Statistics Service
NATO	North Atlantic Treaty Organization
NCES	National Center for Education Statistics
NCHS	National Center for Health Statistics
NGOs	Nongovernmental Organizations
NICs	Newly Industrialized Countries
NIPA	National Income and Product Accounts
NMES	National Medical Expenditure Survey
NOAA	National Oceanic and Atmospheric Administration
NPIs	Nonprofit Institutions
NSF	National Science Foundation
NTDB	National Trade Data Bank
NTIS	National Technical Information Service
NYSE	New York Stock Exchange
OBE	Office of Business Economics
OECD	Organization for Economic Cooperation and Development
OFCs	Offshore Financial Centers
OMB	Office of Management and Budget
OPEC	Organization of the Petroleum Exporting Countries
PLO	Palestine Liberation Organization
QFR	Quarterly Financial Report
SAM	Social Accounting Matrix
SEC	Securities and Exchange Commission
SEDs	Shippers' Export Declarations
SIC	Standard Industrial Classification System
SIGs	Special Interest Groups

SIPP	Survey of Income and Program Participation
SISCIS	*Subject Index to Sources of Comparative International Statistics*
SNA	United Nations System of National Accounts
SRI	Stanford Research Institute
TICS	U.S. Department of the Treasury International Capital Reporting System
U.N.	United Nations
UNCTAD	United Nations Conference on Trade and Development
UNEP	United Nations Environment Programme
UNESCO	United Nations Educational, Scientific and Cultural Organization
UNSO	United Nations Statistical Office
UNSTAT	United Nations Statistical Division
USDA	U.S. Department of Agriculture
USDL	U.S. Department of Labor
USDOE	U.S. Department of Energy
USGS	U.S. Geological Survey
USTTA	U.S. Travel and Tourism Administration
WB	World Bank
WHO	World Health Organization
WMO	World Meteorological Organization

CHAPTER 1

THE NATURE OF THE PROBLEM

Imagine for a moment what a "perfect"—perfectly complete, perfectly accurate—system of statistics might look like; for example, a perfect system of world economic statistics. Such a system would capture the economic significance, expressed in a constant and universal currency, of every economic transaction anywhere in the world, as well as all stocks and holdings having economic value. It would register not only the substance of each of those transactions, but their effects, in terms of augmenting or depleting the economic "stocks" of the participants and the larger communities of which they are a part.

There is a deceptive simplicity about such a model. It seems to suggest the core of what any system of economic statistics seeks to capture. It suggests that the economic reality lies waiting to be measured, if only the physical means were at hand to do it. If only we had resources and time enough to register every transaction; if only we had a lens strong enough to see into every corner where economic activity takes place; if only we had computers that could register and analyze all the data from every transaction. Since we don't, we take certain scientifically justified shortcuts, such as sampling techniques.

But our perfect model, while clear and straightforward, is deceptive. The economic—or demographic, or topical (environment, ecosystems, education, health care, etc.)—realities we seek to describe in statistical systems do not simply lie there waiting for us to come up with instruments to measure them. We see that the moment we descend from the high level of abstraction in our model and begin to define its constituent terms—particularly the term "having economic significance."

Consider two real-life cases. In one case, a domestic worker cleans, cooks, tends children, and generally manages the house. In the second case, a spouse cleans, cooks, tends children, and generally manages the house. The first person is a domestic worker, who is paid wages and who pays income and social security taxes. The second worker is the spouse of an employed worker, who receives no wages and pays no taxes. Should the work of both those "domestic workers" be recorded in our "perfect" system of economic statistics? Do they both engage in actions that have economic significance, or only the one who is paid wages and submits taxes?

A range of arguments could be—and has been—mustered about whether the second person's work has "economic implications." The point here is not to decide that issue. It is to demonstrate that deciding the question—that is, defining the terms so that we know what to include and what to exclude—is not a matter of finding more time to describe the activity or a stronger lens through which to view it or a stronger computer with which to record and analyze it. *It is a matter of making very basic theoretical assumptions—assumptions that determine which data are to be collected and how data are to be analyzed.*

Those assumptions underlie any system of statistics in any field. (Just think of the definitional assumptions that must be made for a demographic study of ethnicity, for example.) Until definitions have been formulated, the object to be measured does not exist. Furthermore, those assumptions usually follow from the uses to which the system of statistics will be put.

Capturing economic reality with a statistical system is much like representing a physical landscape with a map. The map a geologist wants is very different from the map a taxi driver wants. The mapmaker who has no audience in mind has no principle or set of principles on the basis of which to exclude any aspect of the terrain. Without such principles to exclude some aspects as irrelevant, such a map would have to be just the terrain itself. As the philosopher Wittgenstein once said, "that would be like putting your hand on top of your head and saying, 'I know how tall I am.'"

Systems of economic statistics, like maps, are devised to serve purposes, and those purposes—more or less explicit, more or less well understood—dictate the assumptions and the principles that govern which data are collected. They also shape how data are analyzed.

What if we simply decide on a set of purposes and then build the system of statistics upon it? A moment's reflection shows that would not work either. The fact is that different systems of statistics serve different purposes almost as varied as their users, which are likely to change over time.

Moreover, while it is certainly true that statistical systems have to be constructed with purposes in mind—otherwise there would be no way to rule data "in" or "out"—most of the statistical systems many of us use most of the time have been inherited. While they were originally constructed to serve certain functions, those functions are likely not to be completely congruent with our own, because they were constructed under different circumstances and using means different from our own. Simply put, we were not present at the creation of the system of statistics, whether in economics, demography, health care, or whatever.

Even if we could, we would not want to create the system of economic statistics from the ground up. Much of the purpose of any system of statistics is to show trends over time, to compare the past with the present in order to try to assess the future. Without the statistics we inherit, that would be impossible.

So for better or worse, we start midstream, in a world overflowing with information and data, but also *too often suffering a shortage of useable knowledge and understanding.* In part, that is precisely because we live in the midst of the so-called information age. In a sense we stand thirsty in front of Niagara Falls, with only a thimble to catch the flow.

The purpose of this book is to encourage more useful systems of statistics. We live in a world in which information has a larger role than ever before, in which the changes wrought by technological, demographic, and political revolutions have radically changed everything we seek to measure.

All our efforts to reform these systems must start with the recognition of our continued dependence on the inherited system. To borrow a metaphor, it is a boat within which we must stay afloat even as we repair it. Accordingly, we must start from several points of departure simultaneously and from a variety of angles of attack. Quite unapologetically, we will swing from sweeping suggestions for overhaul in some areas to suggestions for simply tinkering at the margins in others.

Before we look at a more detailed preview of the chapters to come, let us consider two overarching realities that stand as the background for all of the discussion in this book: the nature of the so-called information age and the changes in the global realities that call for new statistical systems.

THE INFORMATION AGE

The concept of the information age suggests that there is more information now than ever before, which is indisputable. It also implies that more people spend more time producing and using more information than ever before, which is also indisputable. Beyond that, the concept of a new information age suggests that the role of information is more important in the economy than ever before and that information is replacing some earlier "fuel" of the American economy. These last two propositions are forcefully debated and disputed.

Here is a famous, and fairly typical, formulation from Peter Drucker:

> Three hundred years of technology came to an end after World War II. During those three centuries, the model for technology was a mechanical one: the events that go on inside a star such as the sun. . . . Since the end of World War II, however, the model of technology has been the biological process, the events inside an organism. And in an organism, processes are not organized around energy in the physicist's meaning of the term. They are organized around *information*.[1]

The extended theory founded on this core belief divides U.S. economic history into different eras, depending on the primary economic activity during the period. From colonial times until late in the 19th century, according to this theory, the American economy was agrarian. Most Americans worked the land, and agriculture was the basis of the economy. Roughly from the dawn of the 20th century through the end of World War II, the U.S. economy was predominantly a manufacturing economy. Industry—especially heavy industry—was the motor that drove the entire economic engine. After World War II, according to this concept, the American economy became increasingly dominated by its services sector; by the mid-1950s more than half of all U.S. employment was in providing services rather than in fabricating goods.

Then, more recently, as Peter Drucker and others have averred, a fourth stage can be distinguished: The American economy has come to be increasingly dominated by *information*—the gathering, analysis, and distribution of data and knowledge. In one sense, of course, the infor-

---

[1] Peter Drucker, *Innovation and Entrepreneurship*. New York: Harper & Row, 1985, pp. 3–4.

mation industry is a part of the service sector. Nevertheless, there are good reasons for distinguishing information services from the rest of the services sector as a fourth separate component or stage of the economy.

For one thing, information is different from the noninformation services in that the latter are generally *tangible* in a way that information is not. Think of such noninformation services as transportation or public utilities. Yet, it is clear that the historical progression has been not only a movement through different economic eras, but also a movement from relative simplicity to daunting complexity. The transition from an economy based on agriculture to one based on manufacturing was essentially straightforward, unlike the subsequent transitions—first to a service-based, then to an information-based, economy.

One source of confusion is the fact that the movements from manufacturing to services and then to information were of a different character from earlier transitions. In the first place, while the transition from an agricultural to a manufacturing-based economy was marked by a decline in the number of jobs in agriculture, there has been no such diminution in the number of manufacturing jobs after the shift to a service economy. Moreover, American manufacturing currently accounts for roughly the same percentage of U.S. gross domestic product (GDP) as three decades ago.[2]

As a further complication, many argue that the services sector of the economy simply cannot be seen as a separate segment or an economic subsystem. Such observers instead insist that it "serves" precisely the manufacturing sector it is supposed to have replaced, remaining dependent—even parasitic—on manufacturing. Here is a succinct statement of that argument from the book *Manufacturing Matters:*

> At the heart of our argument is a contention that tight linkages tie a broad range of service jobs to manufacturing. . . . These services are complements to manufacturing, not potential substitutes or successors. . . . Were America to lose mastery and control of manufacturing, vast numbers of service jobs would be relocated after a few short rounds of product and process innovation, largely to destinations outside the United States, and real wages in all service sectors would fall, impoverishing the nation.[3]

---

[2]Stephen S. Cohen and John Zysman, *Manufacturing Matters: The Myth of the Post-Industrial Economy.* New York: Basic Books, Inc., 1987, p. 60.

[3]Ibid., p. 7.

Moreover, coming up with clear definitions and boundaries for the information industry is, on reflection, a considerably complicated undertaking for a number of reasons:

- Most information products or services are provided free of charge or substantially below cost, with most of the cost borne by government, philanthropies, or corporate advertisers.[4]
- In one sense, virtually every corporation or business is at least partly in the business of providing information, at least insofar as they engage in advertising.
- Each of the two primary ways of defining and delimiting the information industry has weaknesses. The first definition includes all those firms that produce, gather, or disseminate information products. This definition would include many individuals—the paper delivery person, the custodian in a library—whose jobs are much more in the nature of physical labor than of "knowledge work." The second definition defines the industry in terms of individual occupations rather than companies, thereby excluding the library's custodian but including the consulting engineer for an automobile firm. Of course, measuring the size of the industry becomes, by that definition, a virtually impossible task.
- Another complicating factor is the fact that there is no very reliable way to assess the exact impact of any particular unit of information input on economic output. It is not certain, for example, that an increased investment in information as a percentage of GDP will result in more knowledge being provided. For example, if the U.S. expenditure for books increases, that could be because more books are being purchased and read (more knowledge consumed), or it could be because *fewer* but more expensive books are being purchased.

These complications in defining and measuring the information industry underscore some of the complexities in speaking of an "information age." From one point of view, information has always been so much a part of the whole economy that it makes little sense to speak

---

[4]Fritz Machlup, *The Production and Distribution of Knowledge in the United States.* Princeton, NJ: Princeton University Press, 1972, p. 28.

of a "new" information age. In fact, classical economic theory has always assumed the presence of information and has given it a central role. As economist Fritz Machlup has pointed out, the mechanisms of the marketplace—supply, demand, competition—are all founded on the assumption that sellers know the highest price at which they can sell their products, while buyers know the lowest price at which they can purchase them.

Moreover, the classical theory always assumed that producers know the available technology of their era and, thus, the lowest cost of producing those goods. Such close observers of capitalist economic arrangements as Karl Marx and Joseph Schumpeter both remarked on the central role that statistical information plays in free market economies.[5]

In his landmark dissertation, *The Information Economy*,[6] Marc Porat discusses at great length what share of the economy has become "information-laden." Following in the footsteps of Fritz Machlup, he argues that information goods and services accounted for about 25 percent of the GNP in the United States in 1967. He is able to show the information portion of the GNP by major categories such as (1) personal consumption, investment, net exports, and government purchases; (2) durable goods, nondurable goods, services, and structures; (3) industry by industry categories; and (4) occupations. A good example of his research can be seen in Figure 1.

Recently, a cover story in *Business Week*[7] that criticized government statistics suggested that the information sector be broken out in a fashion similar to that advanced by Porat. According to that article, about 70 percent of the U.S. economy is in services, 15 percent in goods, and 15 percent in information. We think this is a conservative estimate and the likely share of the information sector is closer to the 25 percent cited by Porat.

The pace of change has been accelerating for many years. Major events in just the past six years would have been considered major revolutions in earlier periods. A listing of some of the major events of the past six years is provided in Figure 2.

---

[5]Ibid., pp. 3 and 4.

[6]"The Real Truth about the Economy," *Business Week*, November 7, 1994, pp. 113–118.

[7]M. U. Porat, *The Information Economy*, Vol. I, unpublished Ph.D. dissertation, Stanford University, 1976, pp. 90–102.

FIGURE 1
Four Sector Aggregation of the U.S. Work Force by Percent 1880–1980
(Using Median Estimates of Information Workers)

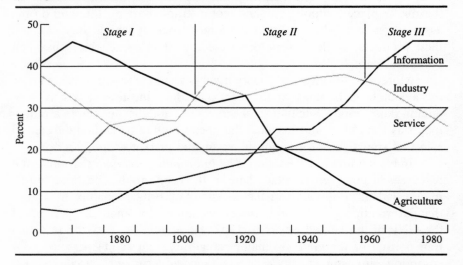

Source: M. U. Porat, *The Information Economy,* Vol. I, unpublished Ph.D. dissertation, Stanford University, 1976, p. 189 (available on demand from University Microfilms and published in 1977 by U.S. Department of Commerce, Office of Telecommunications).

FIGURE 2
Major Events 1989–1994

1989

The collapse of the Berlin Wall—a symbol of the end of the Cold War.
Tiananmen Square riot in China—an emergence of popular power in a dictatorial society.
Growth in Europe accelerates based upon the proposed 1992 program of unification.
Japan announcement of first commercially available high definition television (HDTV).
Congress passes legislation to rescue the savings and loan industry (signed into law on August 9).

1990

West Germany begins effort to absorb East Germany; it opens its borders to immigrants from Central Europe.
Start of shock treatment in Poland to move from command economy to market economy.
In August, Iraq overruns Kuwait and takes control of disputed oil resources.

(continued)

FIGURE 2 *(continued)*

President Bush signs bill designed to reduce budget deficits by nearly $500 billion over five years (November 15).

1991

The coup in Russia ends the leadership era of Gorbachev.
War with Iraq to retake Kuwait begins and ends with unprecedented United Nations joint action.
The Conservative government of the U.K. overthrows Prime Minister Margaret Thatcher after $11^{1}/_{2}$ years.
Bank mergers (Chemical and Manufacturers Hanover, and Bank of America and Security Pacific).
Iran/Contra charges dropped against Oliver North.
Charles Keating convicted of securities fraud as part of savings and loan failures.

1992

Election of President Clinton—end of Republican administration after 12 years.
Near collapse of the European rate mechanism (ERM); concern about European unification.
Environmental summit in Brazil signals worldwide sensitivity to emerging conflicts between economic development and the protection of the environment.

1993

Collapse of IBM is recognized with selection of new chairman and drop in street value from $80 billion in early 1991 to under $30 billion late in the year.
War in Bosnia continues as sign of the inability of U.N. and European Union to deal with internal problems and with historic tensions in a sovereign state.
Fall of the Liberal Democratic Party (LDP) in Japan and growing sense that Japan has lost direction in internal consensus and in economic policy.
Agreement in the U.S. among competing designs for HDTV, yielding a new dimension to the redesign of that industry (see 1989 above).
Corporate downsizing expands to include healthy companies.
U.S. stock market hits all-time high.
Europe struggles with growing unemployment.
President Clinton signs bill to cut deficit by nearly $500 billion over five years (see 1990).
Israel and PLO sign mutual recognition treaty.

1994

Japan forms third government—an unexpected alliance of Socialist and LDP— after four decades of stability.
The European Union has difficulty choosing a new president.
China is granted most favored nation trading status despite human rights issues.
North Korea challenges nuclear proliferation treaty; President Kim dies unexpectedly; Kim Jong II rises to power.

(concluded)

Even from this incomplete list, it is obvious that *the framework for designing social policy, for stimulating economic growth, and for planning business and personal decisions has been upset by the emergence of totally new conditions in the United States, Japan, Europe—indeed, in the world.*

Throughout this period, world trade has increased significantly, even as economic conditions have weakened. This underscores the economic interdependence of nations around the globe. As shown in Figure 3, trade measured as the sum of global imports and exports has increased at a rapid rate in recent years. The result is a growing recognition today of the interactions among countries.

The so-called jobless recovery is a problem that transcends national borders. Unemployment in Europe has been at a high level, even during the 1980s when employment in the United States increased by 20 million jobs following the 1982 recession. Technological development, global outsourcing, excess world capacity, and intense international competition are converging in international debates about trade policy, national fiscal policy, and industrial organization—including the role of the global corporation. Economic policy makers and corporate decision

FIGURE 3
World Trade and Output

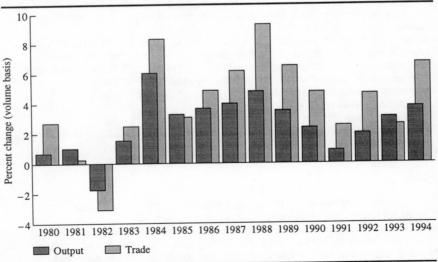

Source: GATT, Dun & Bradstreet Projections

makers are struggling to make sound decisions in this environment of far-reaching change.

In the midst of these dramatic changes in only the past five years, the basic data we collect to measure economic and social progress have been essentially unchanged. As will be discussed in this book, there have been some important improvements, such as:

- International agreement on an improved United Nations System of National Accounts (SNA) for measuring national economic activity.
- Implementation of a common system of commodity classification—the Harmonized Commodity Description and Coding System, known as the Harmonized System (HS) concepts.
- An international program to help redesign the statistical systems of the formerly planned economies.

These changes take a long time. The SNA revision began in 1983 and was finally adopted by the United Nations in July 1993.[8] As will be discussed later in this report, the United States is now in the process of moving the U.S. national accounts toward that system. Work on developing the Harmonized System began in 1970 by the Customs Cooperation Council. It was finally implemented in 1988. Implementing statistical program changes in the former command economies will take many years, but the new and improved frameworks, such as the SNA, should be the basis for fundamental improvement in those countries.

THE PACE OF CHANGE IN STATISTICS

The loosely interlocking system of statistics can be seen as a sort of conceptual net thrown over rapidly changing economic, social, demographic, and other realities in an effort to bring them into closer focus, to assess their size and meaning, and to try to determine their future direction. *As the 21st century approaches, it is increasingly clear that our current conceptual net, designed for earlier realities, does not cover current realities very well.*

---

[8]United Nations Statistical Office, *The System of National Accounts—1993*, United Nations, 1994.

Reforming the statistical network is immeasurably more complicated than simply redesigning it to bring it up to date. The reality is that there are very good reasons—beyond, say, institutional inertia—for taking a conservative approach to changing statistics. Whereas there are several sound reasons for this slow evolution, sluggish change also creates certain problems, as will be discussed later.

What are the arguments for keeping the pace of change in statistics moderate? First, official statistics are most valuable as a reference point for measuring progress or lack of it. Thus, an important characteristic of official statistics is the development of a time series of consistent measures over an extended period of time so that comparisons can be made. For example, in economic terms, it is especially important to compare developments at different points in the business cycle. In an industrial sense, many businesses want to have a consistent history of their marketplace so they can gauge their relative progress and evaluate the changes in their marketplace in relation to other parts of the economic system.

Therefore, there is a strong bias among both producers and users of statistics to keep the definitions, concepts, and classifications consistent over time. This is well illustrated by the Standard Industrial Classification (SIC) system, developed in the 1940s when the U.S. economy was essentially focused on manufacturing activities. Despite revisions over the last four decades, the SIC system is still focused on industrial concepts, with particular detail on specific manufacturing activities.

A second factor restricting change in statistical series is the recognition that current developments are often short-term. Thus, a revision of statistical concepts to reflect a new tendency, or perhaps a fad, risks being labeled capricious in the sense that such short-term developments are only transient changes in the structure, so that focusing on them can ultimately distort analysis of fundamental conditions.

A third reason for sticking with old definitions is that such stability avoids the dangers of changing the measurement system in response to shifting political objectives. The resistance to change in the definition of poverty, for example, reflects a natural political resistance to avoid creating additional demands on the budget even though the older measures may be outdated in terms of current social and economic conditions, as discussed below.

There are some good reasons for the official statistical system to evolve slowly. Nevertheless, we must recognize that failure to change the statistical system over a long period of time results in distortions of our measurements and our ability to understand current economic and social conditions. In effect, the statistics lose touch with reality.

The difficulties with not making changes are illustrated by both the Standard Industrial Classification and the poverty definition mentioned above. Currently, U.S. economic data are inadequate for services sector activities. In the Standard Industrial Classification coding system, employment data exist for 192 four-digit subclassifications in the manufacturing sector, which had 17.9 million employees as of June 1993. In contrast, data exist for only 36 SIC codes in the nonfinancial services areas, which covers 30.4 million employees. This illustrates the fact that we have much less detail and therefore much weaker understanding of the services sector.

The definition of poverty also illustrates this point. The current poverty level definition originated in the 1960s when Molly Orshansky analyzed food consumption and determined that one-third of the typical family budget was devoted to food expenditures. Then, using a minimum nutrition standard to determine the market basket needs for a family, the food component was defined for the poverty level as a minimum sustained budget. This number was multiplied by three, since food accounted at that time for one-third of total household expenditures. Today, however, compelling arguments have been made that food accounts for only one-fifth, rather than one-third, of family expenditures. This would argue for multiplying the food component by five rather than three, resulting in the difficult political decision of whether to increase the budget for maintaining poverty-level income. On the other hand, governmental programs to deal with poverty now include many payments in kind, which are not reported in received income. These include the earned income tax credits, food stamps, and housing allowances. Thus, the definition of poverty in the 1990s is a much more complex concept than in the 1960s. The countervailing political powers, however, make it virtually impossible to undertake, at this time, an objective analysis of how to redefine the statistical dimensions of poverty.

Another problem resulting from the failure to change statistical concepts is that, by the time the change is adopted, it takes additional time to develop a sufficient time series. For example, in the revision of the Consumer Price Index (CPI) in 1978, there was initially a six-month period of overlap between the unrevised CPI and the new CPI. Thus, while we can point out anomalies in the official statistical system that do not reflect existing conditions, it is important to recognize the built-in control systems that avoid unnecessary change and dampen the risk of political manipulation.

ENVIRONMENT FOR STATISTICS

In a book published in 1978,[9] Sir Claus Moser, then the director of the Central Statistical Office of the United Kingdom, offered the following comment on the role of official statistics. His observations hold true more than 16 years later:

> The enormous increase in the demands of governments for more and better statistics has reflected the increase in government itself. Wherever one looks, governments have tended to govern more, and it is a basic question whether this trend is likely to continue. There are two contradictory streams of demand. People and organizations call for more intervention and services from government and they also express growing concern about the extent of government intervention in their lives; many take the view that governments should govern less. It is anyone's guess to what extent the cries for less government and less interference will carry the day against the opposite view. The chances are that the pressure for less *central* government will have some success though perhaps not enough to affect the central government appetite for official statistics; but there is no doubt it will make the climate in which we work tougher, with more public resistance to requests for data, and thus threats to reliability. At the same time, the activities and importance of regional and local government is likely to increase, and with it the demand for small area statistics.
>
> But even if one assumes that the central government environment ten years hence will be such as to require at least as much statistical support as today, this is not to imply an unchanged official environment for statisticians. Far from it: I believe that the continued government demand for statistics will be set in a *very* changed context.
>
> First, *resources* will not grow in parallel with demands. Public expenditure will come under increasing scrutiny and the size and growth of civil services in particular will be kept more in check, including the statistical activities. Yet the demands are certain to increase, and partly because governments themselves will need good data for setting their own priorities. An increasing conflict between demands and resources is likely, and this will mean:
>
> a) A greater emphasis on *efficiency* in statistical organization and production and on cost reduction generally, and a greater reliance on cheaper (e.g., administrative) sources.

---

[9]Joseph W. Duncan, ed., *Statistical Services in Ten Years' Time.* New York: Pergamon Press, 1978.

b) A much greater need for rational setting of statistical *priorities,* with strictly structured medium-term statistical programmes becoming the norm—related to policy needs, and with the more sophisticated use of cost-benefit techniques applied to statistics . . .

Second, the *nature of government demands* for statistics is likely to change. This is meant in several senses:

a) Governments attempt to steer economies—and, up to a point, social developments—with the aid of statistics . . .

b) Government users of statistics will look for greater simplicity . . .

c) Policy-makers will increasingly want to supplement general background statistical information, with data bearing on specific problems—to help them in making particular decisions and in monitoring their consequences . . .

d) Above all, policy-makers in government will expect from their statistical offices not so much the production of more data as, increasingly, their analysis and interpretation . . .

In sum, the government environment ten years hence will be tougher as regards resources and more critical about what official statisticians produce. The magic of numbers may be less seductive than now. Ministers and top administrators will be sophisticated enough about statistics to want guidance about the accuracy of the figures, as well as greater timeliness and relevance in the figures themselves; they will want more help in analysis and interpretation. Priorities and statistical programmes will have to be explicit, with *user*-orientation (for users outside and inside government) dominating their choice. Regular routine statistics may become less important, one-off surveys and analyses more so.[10]

This similarity in the environment for statistical programs today, compared with 1978, has been used by some to suggest that change is not possible. We believe it is possible, and this book is a statement of that belief. *What is needed is aggressive leadership and the development of a better understanding of both the needs for change and the benefits to society of having statistics that do an improved job of measuring economic and social conditions.* That is the reason for our discussion in the next few chapters and for the recommendations made later.

THE LONG-TERM ELEMENTS OF GOVERNMENT DECISION MAKING ABOUT STATISTICS

The nature of government decisions concerning the budgets for statistical activities results in a long time frame for implementation of new programs. In order to develop a new statistical program (or make

---

[10]Ibid., pp. 6–8.

fundamental changes to existing ones), it is necessary to undertake research to define appropriate concepts, classifications, and standards, and to determine feasible data collection methodologies.

Too often, there are no research funds to support these preliminary investigations. New concepts may originate in universities or in special contract projects related to specific governmental programs. Rarely are these concepts initiated in statistical agencies studying long-term issues related to social and economic measurement. *Lack of funding for fundamental conceptual research at the National Science Foundation and other agencies also restricts the amount of attention given to these questions.*

Once a proposal is developed for improving statistical measurement, other difficulties arise in trying to implement them. First, in the normal budgeting process, it is important to get support in the agency that is the home for the statistical activity. In the executive process, the home agency is required to submit the budget request, and inevitably there are many competing demands with all major cabinet departments. Thus, during budget-setting time, the proposals to improve statistical programs compete with other major activities within the host agencies and departments.

After the departmental hurdle is overcome, Office of Management and Budget approval is required as part of the budget process. Competing demands among all aspects of governmental activities make it difficult for long-range statistical improvements to gain attention within the executive branch, regardless of the political party in power. It is a natural tendency for every administration to seek programs that will have immediate political benefit. Thus, long-term programs that may not yield results for several years (often well beyond the tenure of the decision makers) are not often undertaken. In fact, it is remarkable that any proposals emerge from the executive branch to deal with improved statistical activities.[11]

The next barrier in initiating a new statistical program is the congressional appropriations process. As is well known, the interests of congressional representatives and senators are relatively short-term, and they

---

[11]A notable exception is the program initiated by Michael Boskin, chairman of the Council of Economic Advisors, during the last three years of the Bush administration. While all funding requests were not approved, this effort serves as an illustration of how executive branch leadership has resulted in building a concrete program for long-term improvements. See Figure 6A for program increases associated with this initiative.

are often driven by the interests of key constituents. Thus, it is difficult to gain support for proposals that originate in the executive branch and which will have little direct benefit to the congressional leadership. The record is full of congressional rejection of statistical initiatives for that reason.

Once the proposal for improvement has cleared the hurdles of departmental, administration, and budget analysis; executive branch approval; and congressional review, we are only at step one. The next part of the process is also lengthy.

The implementation of authorized improvements in official statistics also requires a long time period. First, there is a requirement to test and implement the design that was envisioned. Second, there is a need to improve the processes used for data collection. The record-keeping practices of firms, the development of electronic transfers, and changing definitions have made old methods of reporting obsolete. Then there is the development of a time series, which takes several years. Under the most optimum of circumstances, it is clear there is at least a five-year gap between identifying a need for statistical programming innovation and useful output. In reality, the change is likely to be more than a decade. This overall process is outlined in Figure 4, which generalizes the time line for statistical program improvement.

FIGURE 4

A Decade of Decisions (Time Line for Statistical Program Improvement in the U.S. Government)

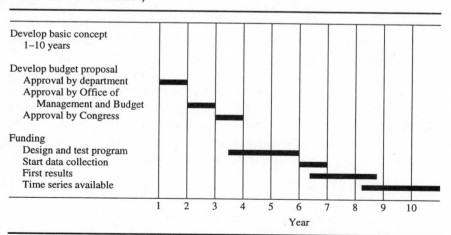

Source: Estimates by the authors.

These delays are illustrated by the development of the Survey of Income and Program Participation (SIPP). Initial proposals to measure "income-in-kind" with other income measures were officially addressed in the early 1970s. After major efforts to secure modest funds for research on SIPP, the survey was finally approved by Congress, and data collection began in 1983. Today, the evolution of the program continues, though the time series data are relatively weak.

THE ULTIMATE TRADE-OFFS

Statistical programs generate data users. These users then become part of the justification for the program, but, in turn, they bring their own demands. Users of statistics quickly identify deficiencies. They push for improvements in the timeliness of the series, seeking efforts to speed up data processing and reporting so that early results are available. Sometimes this conflicts with their second concern, which is accuracy. The conflict between accuracy and timeliness is most evident in the National Income and Product Accounts, but it is also characteristic of virtually every series where people seek early estimates so they can make current decisions. Finally, as time passes, the users discover more and more applications for the data, and there is a call for more comprehensive measures. Comprehensiveness, of course, brings with it additional costs and additional reporting burdens.

Government statisticians have long been concerned about minimizing the burden of providing information required by statistical inquiries.[12] In the 1930s, the Central Statistical Board studied statistical reporting burdens at the request of President Franklin D. Roosevelt. Other studies of the paperwork burden include the Mills-Long Report (1948), the Federal Paperwork Jungle Hearings of the Subcommittee on Census and Population (1965–66), the Kaysan Committee (1966), and the President's Commission on Federal Statistics (1971). However, the most thorough study was undertaken by the congressionally established Commission on Federal Paperwork, which undertook its study during the

---

[12] A detailed discussion of this topic is found in Office of Federal Statistical Policy and Standards, *A Framework for Planning United States Federal Statistics for the 1980s.* Washington, DC: U.S. Government Printing Office, 1977, pp. 337–347.

period 1975–1977. During this time, it issued 36 separate reports on many topics, such as statistics and reporting burden. Its final report was issued on October 3, 1977. The Commission's findings led to the Paperwork Reduction Act of 1980, which is the current legislative basis for statistical policy coordination and reporting burden control in the federal government.

The preceding section has outlined a number of positive and negative reasons why evolution of the statistical system is slow. These range from the nature of statistical activities themselves to the difficult process of achieving budget authority and program implementation. This report is written with specific recognition of these inhibiting factors. However, in the judgment of the authors, it is indeed time for a full-scale approach to the redesign of statistical systems. As noted earlier, the pace of change in social and economic institutions is dramatic at this time in history. The need for better information in the "information age" is increasingly recognized. Therefore, this report is developed to build a case for more attention to the issues of defining the information required for decision making in the years ahead. The 21st century is only five years away. The time frame presented earlier suggests that it is unlikely that, even if action is taken today, significant changes will be available as we enter the new millennium. If we do not begin to address these questions, we will never get to the point of having adequate information to handle the difficult questions posed by our rapidly changing social and economic conditions.

DESCRIPTION OF CHAPTERS

Chapter 2 contains an analysis of the strengths, weaknesses, opportunities, and threats (called a SWOT analysis) presented by the statistical information emanating from four separate sources. Chapter 3 considers the three primary dimensions of statistical information: uses and users; products and producers; and collection, presentation, and dissemination.

It was the philosopher Plotinus who once said, "Knowledge, if it does not determine action, is dead to us." That is perhaps especially true of statistical knowledge: Its purpose is to shape policies and determine action. For that reason, the next three chapters of this book are quite specific, seeking to seize concretely how current statistical systems either are or are not adequately determining action: Chapter 4 looks at how information is used in a specific policy area (health care)[13] and it presents some comments on education and demographic statistics, with special attention to the planning for the next Census of Population in the year 2000. Chapters 5 and 6 discuss policy issues and resulting statistical needs in the areas of energy and the environment. Chapter 7 looks at the ways statistical systems are being revamped to provide greater adequacy for measuring the national economic income (the System of National Accounts). Chapter 8 examines the needs for global financial information, an area that particularly calls out for more attention and better statistics as globalization increasingly affects all nations.

Chapter 9 presents a series of specific recommendations[14] for improvements in areas affecting the System of National Accounts and the critical measures of the international economy. Chapter 10 contains some brief concluding remarks.

Appendices provide additional material on errors in GDP estimates, budgets for statistics, and some detailed problems with data on international services, as well as voluminous bibliographic materials.

---

[13]Presently, the National Center for Health Statistics is preparing a major review called Health 2000. Some materials from this review are used in Chapter 4.

[14]There have been a number of reviews of the U.S. Statistical System in recent decades. All statistical agencies have encouraged outside review panels. Often, detailed studies of individual data series have led to important improvements. The present report takes a more global perspective. Similar studies in the past included: The President's Commission on Federal Statistics, 1970; The Bonnen Committee report for President Carter's Statistical Reorganization Project, 1977; and the recent report from the Committee on National Statistics, entitled "Principles for Statistical Agencies." Also see U.S. Department of Commerce, Office of Federal Statistical Policy and Standards, *Gross National Product Data Improvement Project Report.* U.S. Government Printing Office, October 1977.

CHAPTER 2

"SWOT" ANALYSIS FOR STATISTICS

The acronym SWOT—Strength, Weakness, Opportunity, and Threat—is a standard method of case analysis used to size up a company's situation in the marketplace. Strength and weakness are factors internal to the organization; opportunity and threat are external factors. One way of sizing up what is happening, SWOT serves as a basis both for analysis and for developing recommendations for action.

SWOT can also be applied to the realm of statistics: public or private, local or international, longitudinal or cross-sectional. We are going to review the strengths and weaknesses of existing data in four different types of organizations: international agencies, national governments, business firms, and statistical/information industry firms including nonprofit agencies. The discussion will illustrate the type of analysis that can be done and highlight opportunities and threats, focusing on how the statistical output from various sources are used by the customers. This chapter is intended to illustrate the type of review needed to plan for the future.

The United States is a statistical society. Statistics are news. Statistics make the news. Consider the front page of the business section of the July 10, 1993, edition of the *New York Times*. Stories with statistical information are shown in Figure 5.

Or, consider another widely read daily newspaper, *The Wall Street Journal,* specifically, the "Outlook" column on July 26, 1993. The headline reads: "Likeliest Forecast: More Weak Growth." Writer A. L. Malabre, Jr., concluded that the economy will continue to expand, but at a subdued pace. On what did he base his evidence? Consider the sources cited in the article:

FIGURE 5
Statistics in the News

Headline/Topic	Underlying Concepts/ Statistics	Sources (actual and/or implied)
1. Global joblessness, jobless recovery, job creation, etc.	Unemployed, underemployed, underutilized workers, payrolls, new entrants, etc.	Governments, especially Western, especially USDL/BLS
2. Early retirees	Retirement age benefits	Foster Higgins
3. Asian airlines fear U.S. airlines (cabotage)	% boarding each type, landing rights, transfers, discounting, frequent flyers	ICAO, IATA, AIA, governments, individual airlines
4. Federal Reserve Board policy on interest rates, etc.	Interest rates, past and present, other economic data policy implications	FRB, individual banks, nonbank financial institutions
5. Jack in the Box food poisoning incident	Fast-food service, customer loyalty, nutrition, competitors' market share	Fuddruckers, NYSE, news agencies, etc.

- *Blue Chip Economic Indicators,* a private newsletter that summarizes the views of economists who fearlessly forecast up to 18 months ahead. (It may be noted that the consensus of their forecasts is generally superior to any individual's record.)
- "The U.S. Department of Commerce's index of leading indicators recently has been wobbly . . . but that does not mean a recession is imminent . . . [but] it does behave in an erratic fashion after the economy has been expanding for a considerable time."
- Columbia University's Center for International Business Cycle Research publishes a "long-leading index," which provides an appreciably longer lead time than the Commerce Department's. "This index has been climbing steadily, with little interruption, since the 1990–91 recession."

Similar examples could be chosen from the *Financial Times* and the *Economist,* from Japanese journals or bank newsletters, and many other financial publications—all of which tend to rely on a vast mix of sources (government, private, and nonprofit sectors) for their own analyses.

What do the above examples reveal about the underlying data, specifically about the SWOT aspects of the statistics?

Simply stated, the strength of statistics is their wide availability. There are thousands of sources, producing millions of data bits. But this is also their weakness, because there are too many numbers to absorb, too much data to interpret. Also, there are questions about every source, such as:

Can we be sure the producers of data used the same definitions and classification?

What methodologies and procedures were employed to collect the data?

What is the likelihood of revisions in the numbers, and whom should we believe?

Businesses of all sizes and users of every description are hungry for good data and are willing to support organizations and programs that provide them. With the advent of on-line computer databases and CD-ROM type delivery, statistics can be put into users' hands easily and quickly. Sophisticated software packages and other "interfaces" facilitate the comparison and analysis of available data. The threat is also real, however; with too many revisions, too many sources, contradictory information, and lack of analysis, the users may become less confident and the data less useful. The following is a brief SWOT analysis of four different categories of data-producing organizations.

DATA FROM INTERNATIONAL AGENCIES

Many international agencies issue statistics on a regular basis. Others gather data for internal use and publish only an occasional report. Our emphasis will be on the former. In this category are the United Nations (U.N.), the Organization for Economic Cooperation and Development (OECD), the International Monetary Fund (IMF) and its sister institution, the World Bank (WB), the Statistical Office of the European Union (Eurostat), and the various regional banks, for example, the Inter-American Development Bank (IADB) and the Asian Development Bank

(ADB). Other agencies encompass a wide variety of fields, ranging from air transport (the International Civil Aviation Organization [ICAO] in Montreal, Canada) to atomic energy (the International Atomic Energy Agency [IAEA] in Vienna, Austria).

While the larger organizations focus on broad economic/business data gathering, others emphasize more narrow areas. Regional data will likely expand, for example, to include developments in Eastern Europe or the North American Free Trade Area.

Strengths

The U.N. is almost 50 years old and has developed statistical series and publications encompassing all member nations no matter what their level of economic development. The U.N. has also developed statistical standards and classifications to facilitate the international comparison of national data. The OECD is the prime statistical agency for data on the industrialized, developed countries. As such, it has done good work in both gathering and publicizing its data bank. Some of the OECD information is available in computer-readable format; other data are subjected to analysis and interpretation. The World Bank has developed an impressive set of world indicators that are published in over 30 tables as an appendix to its *World Development Report.*[1] Statistics in this volume go beyond economic/business data, encompassing a wide variety of social and cultural indicators. The regional and industrial agencies have become experts in their fields. The ADB publishes data on the countries in its region, and the ICAO has kept a good time series on air transport and even on airport size.

The statistical databases of these international agencies can be considered the starting point for any global or regional research undertaking. Any major departure from them would require justification. They have collected long time series, and on occasion they can marshal good cross-sectional data. They have well-defined categories and have established meaningful classifications. In short, comparison is possible both over time and across countries—up to a point. The narrower the scope

---

[1]The World Bank, *World Development Report (1993),* published for the World Bank by Oxford University Press, New York; and *World Tables 1993,* published for the World Bank by the Johns Hopkins University Press, Baltimore.

of the agency's work (e.g., ICAO and IAEA), the more likely it is to be an expert on that topic. While some agencies guard their data bank holdings zealously, others, such as the OECD, have learned to profit handsomely from the sale and distribution of their data.

Weaknesses

International organizations ultimately depend on the cooperation of member nations, special interest groups, and individuals for the data they collect. No matter how good the definitions and classification systems are, they are interpreted differently by their member constituencies. Further, countries may not have the resources to implement revisions of international classifications and will continue to produce data using the old version. Few organizations have the means of a large independent staff dedicated to worldwide surveys. International organizations publish data reported by their members, and there is a reluctance to pass judgment overtly on the quality of these data. Furthermore, these agencies are not quick to adjust to new conditions and to start new categories and new time series. For example, like national governments, they have been slow to recognize the need for gathering data on the services sector.

Oskar Morgenstern[2] wrote about the accuracy of economic observations three decades ago. Using his own research as well as that of S. Kuznets and E. J. Russell, he estimated that worldwide economic data had a range of error of 5–20 percent, depending on country and product category involved. To put it bluntly, he said, "Economics is a one-digit science."

More important than the question of definition, revised figures, and subsequent disagreement (which is often labeled "range of error") is the matter of continuity and of reporting. Here, the situation seems better but is certainly not always encouraging. As one key example: The U.N.'s publication, *National Accounts Statistics: Main Aggregates and Detailed Tables,* was last issued in 1992, but the reference period for the data was 1990. Certain capital-spending time series available earlier from the U.N. also have not come to light in recent years. The IMF and WB have finally

---

[2]Oskar Morgenstern, *On the Accuracy of Economic Observations,* 2nd ed. Princeton, NJ: Princeton University Press, 1963, pp. 279, 286.

realized that the gross national product per capita is not meaningful in terms of exchange rates and began publishing GNP per capita on a purchasing power parity basis. For developing nations, the latter shows a two- to fivefold increase in this key number. To some readers, this will be useful; to others, it will certainly seem rather confusing.

As for the disagreements among the data issued by the various international agencies, these have not been resolved, as each one clings to its own established routine. Finally, some nations are unwilling to provide figures to international agencies even on their most basic statistics (e.g., Saudi Arabia), while others are unable to do so due to internal turmoil (e.g., Eastern Europe).

Opportunities

The major international data-gathering bodies have succeeded in obtaining funding through much of their existence and have published statistics that provided a certain degree of continuity. There is, however, fraying at the edges and even in the center. *The world has changed rapidly, and they have been slow to adjust. The opportunities lie in recognizing which portion of their output is valued highly and in marketing those statistics.*

A good example is the OECD, which is now aggressively selling its database in various formats. Some of the specific agencies are responsive to requests, but others are not willing to share the information with commercial or academic audiences. *The "parent" organization or the policy-making board must see to it that these agencies begin the most elementary market research: Who uses data? How and why? How can we cater better to their needs and wants?*

Creating and then delivering millions of data bits in print or electronic format is by no means easy. The international agencies, however, have a definite opportunity in this regard as the prices of small computers and workstations drop. Providing appropriate hardware and software to both those who provide the data (member nations and organizations, but ultimately individuals) and users who "massage" the numbers will result in a more efficient collection. At the dissemination end, in a similar fashion, the data should be available in not just print form and on-line, but also in a CD-ROM format, as is the case now for the National Trade Data Bank of the U.S. Department of Commerce and the global trade data of Statistics Canada.

While new time series and new formats can be encouraged, it is crucial for these organizations to maintain continuity. Justification must be provided for sudden departures in definitions, and new series should be linked with old ones. It seems also wise to provide a band or range rather than point estimates. Early figures should be so defined and be visible as such, not just marked with a footnote or a small "e" (for "estimate") after the number. Instead, bold letters, "estim," should be put in front of the preliminary numbers.

Revisions should have explanations and should state the percentage difference from the previous values. Readers can be directed to alternative sources for comparison. The marketing of the data ideally should be entrepreneurial. Institutions can choose a range of options, from being a manufacturer or wholesaler of statistics to negotiating a system of incentives, quantity discounts, multiyear subscriptions, and so forth. Customer responsiveness and customization have not been the hallmarks of delivering data in the case of international agencies, but the opportunity exists for reform in this regard.

Threats

The biggest threat to the international statistical bodies is the sharp cutbacks in their budget allocations (from member nations and/or other supporting bodies). Some agencies, including the U.N., have discontinued gathering and/or publishing certain statistics. These budget and program cutbacks can be overcome by placing emphasis on

1. Publishing data that are relevant to users.
2. Aggressive marketing to actual and potential clients.

These steps also imply an "in-touch" policy with users of the data.

There are other threats as well. Some nations object to transborder data flow; others complain about issues of workload, secrecy, privacy, security, data exchange, access, and so forth. Any international agency must reassure those who provide it information that it will not cause them undue burdens. It must also stress its objectivity and equal treatment in its data-gathering and disseminating activities. If its sale of the data results in much income, part of the gains can be distributed back to the membership who supplied them. Ultimately, as is the case for national government bureaus, the international agencies must think and act in an entrepreneurial fashion.

STATISTICS FROM GOVERNMENT AGENCIES

In 1989, Henry Kelly and Andrew Wyckoff of the U.S. Office of Technology Assessment wrote an article entitled "Distorted Image" in The Massachusetts Institute of Technology's *Technology Review,*[3] in which they argued that:

1. The ability of government statistics to tell us what we most need to know has become more questionable than ever.
2. It takes so long to create some statistics that by the time they are published, they no longer accurately reflect reality.
3. Modernization of government statistics must begin with managerial reform.
4. New technologies could increase the timeliness of government statistics and reduce the burden on firms.

Criticisms along these lines are unique neither to the U.S. government nor to the present time. Consider the following excerpt from a book review by N. Virts of A. Friedberg's *The Weary Titan:*

> When faced with the task of measuring such complex phenomena as economic and military power . . . officials relied extensively on easily computed measures, trade statistics for economic power and number of battleships and infantry reinforcements for military strength. Unfortunately, such statistics often hid more than they revealed.[4]

The place and time? Britain from 1895 to 1905.

Overall, the points of the 1989 article by Kelly and Wyckoff have been echoed in many places, ranging from I. Kaminow's article on "Statistical Stagnation"[5] to M. Hillman's review, "Uses and Abuses of Transportation and Road Safety Statistics."[6] Writing in the same year as Kelly and Wyckoff, H. Stout focused on the constant revision process of government data.[7]

---

[3]Henry Kelly and Andrew Wyckoff, "Distorted Image," *Technology Review,* February/March 1989, pp. 53–60.

[4]*The Wall Street Journal Europe,* May 30, 1989, p. 6.

[5]*Government Executive,* July 1, 1992, p. 48.

[6]*Policy Studies,* July 1, 1992.

[7]H. Stout, "Shaky Numbers/U.S. Statistics Mills Grind Out More Data That Are Then Revised/Fed, Companies and Markets Can Be Seriously Misled; One Cause: Budget Cuts/Alan Greenspan Prefers Speed," *The Wall Street Journal,* August 31, 1989, p. 1.

More recently, in a one-page "Call-to-Arms," an article by Walter Wriston in *Forbes*[8] argues that "economists cannot measure economies and if you cannot measure how can you manage?" He cites the IMF's drastic revision of China's output (fourfold upward), then goes on to castigate the U.S. Department of Commerce for its constant revision of economic growth, and refers to four differing definitions of the deficit. Finally, Wriston echoes the two often-stated points: that the U.S. federal government is not using an accrual basis (that is, counting infrastructure monies as an expense rather than as an investment), and that there is a lack of emphasis on services sector industries.

We agree with the general thrust of all the articles cited above, although the tone is somewhat overstated. We especially applaud the call for more timely data, reform, and upgrading. We also hold that integrity, accuracy, timeliness, and interpretability of data are crucial, and we believe that the current situation reflects the high level of professionalism among governmental statisticians.

However, we are not certain that a new independent statistical agency is needed to regulate government data collection, agency coordination, and dissemination, as advocated by Kelly and Wyckoff. There is much strength in the existing agencies. It is quite possible that streamlining policies and mandating public-private sector cooperation may accomplish the same thing as centralization. *There is little doubt, however, that major changes are needed and, when instituted, will result in both better government policies and better private sector decisions.*

Strengths

Possibly the greatest strength of U.S. and other national government statistics is their uniqueness. There is only one sovereign government in each nation, and it has a monopoly on government data. Governments are in the unique position to provide continuity and stability in statistical services. Policies and regulations can be established to ensure compliance and cooperation. In short, a leadership role can be asserted, and with gentle or firm arm-twisting, collaboration can be assured.

The second major positive feature of government statistics stems from the first. With continuity and stability, government bureaus are able

---

[8]*Forbes,* June 21, 1993, p. 88.

to provide a long-run perspective of the economy. Thus, for example, historical time series in the United States, the United Kingdom, and Canada provide an excellent overview of trends during decades and even centuries, as can be found in *Historical Statistics of the United States, Colonial Times to 1970* and *Historical Statistics of Canada*. Economic and business historians have relied on these two volumes in their research of a variety of economic conditions.

A third strength (which some observers view as a weakness) is the duplication of data collection by various agencies. In our view, it is an advantage that the Bureau of Economic Analysis (BEA), the Bureau of the Census, and the Bureau of Labor Statistics (BLS) gather price, productivity, and other measures of economic activity. *In effect, this provides a system of checks and balances, though it takes a skilled analyst to make sense of what may seem at first contradictory information.* The BEA has developed detailed input-output tables. No one else would have been able to perform this pioneering work on the structure of the U.S. economy. Dozens of other government bureaus are hard at work collecting program and administrative data, supplementing the work of the key statistical agencies.

Yet another strength is the willingness of government bureaus to listen to their audiences and to make changes as warranted. For example, as the U.S. economy became more and more integrated in the global economy, the U.S. Department of Commerce made numerous adjustments and has developed various ways of accessing data. An example of this is the downloading of consultant reports onto CD-ROM diskettes in the case of trade data. Known as the NTDB, the National Trade Data Bank is an easy way of looking at market opportunities abroad for U.S. goods and services. (A major shortcoming of NTDB will be noted in the next section.)

Moreover, there is a gratifying ability and willingness of U.S. government statisticians to discuss the data with users over the phone, via mail, or even in person. Our experience over three decades indicates that statisticians are approachable. A concrete example of this is the listing of specialists' phone numbers in the annual *U.S. Industrial Outlook,* a key tool used by almost all business researchers.[9] In a similar fashion,

---

[9]Such directories are available from all major statistical agencies. Contact the public affairs offices for further details.

our interaction with chief statisticians and members of their staff in many other nations provides further strong evidence that the "keepers of the data" are willing to discuss problems that arise from assumptions, definitions, and matters of classification.

Last, but certainly not least, one of the major strengths of U.S. federal statistics (true also for many other Western nations' data) is their integrity. Indeed, the July 1993 issue of *Business Economics*[10] is devoted largely to this topic. These articles, by staff of the General Accounting Office (GAO), the Bureau of Economic Analysis, and the Bureau of Labor Statistics, all marshal impressive evidence that such vital integrity has been safeguarded and will continue to be observed. This means that the task of gathering, processing, and disseminating data remains free of political interference. *The credibility of official economic and social statistics is truly crucial for the proper functioning of a democratic, diverse society. Without it, trust and usage would be quickly lost!*

In this volume, we cannot explore in detail the strengths and weaknesses of the output of other nations' central statistical bureaus. According to a panel of statisticians, Canada had the most accurate and Italy had the worst set of statistics among 10 OECD nations.[11] Canada had the smallest number of revisions between the first and final set of published figures. The panel judged the agencies on three criteria:

1. Coverage and reliability.
2. Methodology.
3. Integrity and objectivity of the statistical agency.

Centralized systems, such as those in Australia and Canada, avoid duplication, display more integrity, and show better response to the shift toward services. Since only a single entity collects the data, interference from the political process is minimized. The panel was concerned that in decentralized systems, such as in the United States, the numbers are more exposed to political interference. While the integrity of U.S. sta-

---

[10]*Business Economics,* Vol. XXVIII, No. 3, July 1993: Joseph W. Duncan, "Integrity in Official Statistics," pp. 8–11; Bruce Johnson and Lori Rectanus, "The Integrity of Federal Statistics: A Case Study From the GAO Perspective," pp.12–17; Carol S. Carson, "Assuring Integrity for Federal Statistics: Focus on GDP," pp.18–24; Janet L. Norwood, "Perception of Reality: Can We Trust Federal Statistics?" pp. 25–28.

[11]"The Good Statistics Guide," *Economist,* Sept. 7, 1991, p. 88. See also "The Good Statistics Guide," *Economist,* Sept. 11, 1993, p. 65.

tistics has been upheld, this does remain a danger. As noted below, duplication also occurs in a decentralized system, but this can be a point of strength (see above) or one of weakness (see below).

Weaknesses

There is no shortage of criticism aimed at federal (as well as state or provincial and local) statistics. The charges leveled include faulty assumptions, along with old-fashioned definitions and classification; long time delays in the publication of data, especially in regard to censuses, coupled with revisions; outright errors, discrepancies, and data gaps; overflow of information along with duplication; and, finally, competition with the private sector, including charges of too much and too little rivalry. The list could easily be expanded and could include the flip side (e.g., some charge there is too little information and interpretation). Let us briefly examine each of these alleged weaknesses, with special reference to U.S. federal statistics.

Government statistics trace their ancestry back many decades, even centuries. The data-gathering bureaus, by definition, bring stability and continuity to their tasks. It is not surprising that early assumptions, classic definitions, and initial classification schemes that worked well in the past are no longer valid. Critics often point to the way government treats expenditures on highways and other structures (as well as research, education, etc.). Such spending is counted as an expense; there is a lack of accrual accounting. In short, public investment is not recognized as such; this makes for poor policy decisions. The GAO and others recommend changing the situation, but old ways prevail. Similar criticism is aimed against the Standard Industrial Classification system, whose categories focus far too much on old-line manufacturing, far too little on high-tech products and service industries. The various branches of the U.S. government need to settle a host of similar problems; for example, defining the budget and trade deficits in a more precise manner.

Delays in the release of government data adversely affect decisions in both the public and private sectors. Many observers commented on delays that range from months to years; a newly formed input-output benchmark, based on 1982 census data, was released in 1989. Portions of censuses of population, manufacturing, services, agriculture, and so on, dribble out in bits and pieces, with full volumes available only after excruciating waits of several years. What infuriates users of the data even more are the constant revisions that occur not just for the gross domestic product, but for other series as well. Changes in housing statistics (new starts, etc.) are especially frequent and leave users wondering when final/correct figures will arrive. Needed revisions in industrial production and capacity utilization indices are just now being done by the Federal Reserve Board.

Errors, discrepancies, and data gaps in government statistics do occur despite the best efforts of the staff. Notable in this regard is the 1990 Census of Population and Housing, which undercounted by about 5.3 million people. According to an authoritative GAO report, there was a far bigger problem: The census missed between 9.7 million and 15.5 million people and double-counted between 4.4 million and 10.2 million people. On the estimation front, the Central Intelligence Agency has vastly overestimated the economic and military strength of the former Soviet Union and underestimated China's.

Because each government agency has its own mandate, it is not surprising to find a certain amount of duplication and information overflow. Up to a point, this may even be desirable, but recent evidence indicates that the current arrangement also results in waste and confusion. For example, Kelly and Wyckoff, as well as others, note that food consumption data are available from both the Department of Agriculture and BEA. While both track money spent on food eaten outside the home, each agency defines food consumption differently. Enterprise and labor statistics also originate from various sources, with the result again being duplication and information overload. Though each agency has good reasons for its methodology, to outsiders—even those experts at interpreting data—the results can be confusing.

The U.S. government, as well as state and local bodies, have been criticized for being in the information-gathering and dissemination business. Remember that the U.S. Constitution mandates the population census. The track record and integrity of the agencies also argue in favor of their continuing the collection of information. Thus, it is more at the dissemination end that we find criticism and strong recommendations for commercialization. The pros and cons of this have been explored in *The Politics of Numbers*.[12] Good arguments are marshaled on both sides of the issue, which has not been resolved to date.

---

[12]William Alonso and Paul Starr, eds., *The Politics of Numbers*. New York: Russell Sage Foundation, 1987.

An example is the 1993 debate over the way in which the Securities and Exchange Commission (SEC) shares data with the public.[13] The SEC plans to allow Mead Data Central to offer the SEC electronic database of 15,000 publicly traded corporations on-line at about $160,000 per year. Librarians and individuals object to this commercial involvement in the electronic distribution of public records. In contrast, Mead and others defend the practice by saying, "You need to be careful not to pre-empt the market vision" and by arguing that competition among on-line firms will hold down the price to final users.

A possible resolution of the above debate can be seen in the deal that the SEC has struck with another contractor, Disclosure, Inc. This firm is in charge of releasing corporate reports (annual, 10K, and other filings) to the public at a charge; for example, it charges $25 for an annual report. It also resells the information in CD-ROM format and via on-line electronic databases. And it maintains public reference rooms in Washington, New York, and Chicago, where the same information is free (but more cumbersome to assemble).

Opportunities

The following avenues are open to government statistical agencies to enhance their relationship with individual users and user groups:

1. Improve the existing statistics (fewer errors, minimal revisions, less delay, etc.).
2. Create new series, sharpen sampling, possibly at the expense of censuses.
3. Coordinate with other sources, eliminate duplication.
4. Become user-friendly in terms of getting the data in and out; that is, soliciting advice, speeding delivery, reducing pricing, and streamlining operations overall.

It would be foolhardy to enumerate at this point all the existing series of federal and other government statistics that are in need of improvement and/or to cite all the new time series and cross-sectional data that should be created. Figures 6 through 8 present abstracts of articles that address these concerns. The first is an abstract of "Reviv-

---

[13]"Trove of SEC Data Available by Computer—for a Price," *Washington Post,* July 26, 1993.

FIGURE 6
Reviving the Federal Statistical System

Title:	"Reviving the Federal Statistical System: The View from Academia"
Authors:	Jeffrey A. Miron and Christina D. Romer
Journal:	*American Economic Review* (AER) ISSN: 0002-8282 Vol: 80 Iss: 2 Date: May 1990 pp: 329–332 Illus: Reference
Companies:	Federal Reserve Board
Subjects:	Economics; statistics: statistical methods; consistency; consumer spending; revisions; recommendations
Codes:	9190 (United States); 1110 (Economic conditions & forecasts); 9550 (Public sector)
Abstract:	Academic researchers are concerned about assumptions and consistency over time of official government statistics. To address the first concern, the government might: 1. Try to derive series based on more actual data and fewer assumptions, 2. Provide both the final series and the actual base data to researchers, 3. State assumptions more clearly, and 4. Present data without seasonal adjustments. Government statisticians might mitigate the inconsistencies resulting from the very different ways long time series are constructed in the prewar and postwar eras by: 1. Using additional resources and effort to improve existing prewar estimates of many economic aggregates, 2. Documenting the existing prewar series more thoroughly, and 3. Flagging inconsistencies more diligently. Inconsistencies within the postwar era might be minimized by not undertaking date revisions lightly, by taking revisions as far back as possible, and by providing a period of overlap between old and new procedures when revisions cannot be taken back in time.

See also the following in the same issue of AER: "Reviving the Federal Statistical System: A View from Industry," by R. Cole, pp. 333–336; "Reviving the Federal Statistical System: International Aspects," by R.E. Lipsey, pp. 337–340; and "Reviving the Federal Statistical System: A View from Within," by J.E. Triplett, pp. 341–344.

ing the Federal Statistical System: The View from Academia"[14] by J. Miron and C. Romer, which, while four years old, is still valid in its concern about the consistency over time of official government data series. The second is an abstract from a sequence of articles by co-

[14]J. Miron and C. Romer, "Reviving the Federal Statistical System: The View from Academia," *American Economic Review,* May 1990.

FIGURE 7
The Statistics Corner

Title:	"The Statistics Corner"
Authors:	Joseph W. Duncan
Journal:	*Business Economics* (BEC) ISSN: 0007-666x Vol: 24 Iss: 1 Date: Jan 1989 pp. 48–50
Subjects:	Economics; statistics; reliability; poverty; merchandise; international trade; data; errors
Codes:	1110 (Economic conditions & forecasts)
Abstract:	Substantial evidence indicates that government statistics are sub-ject to large revisions and are not reliable enough for business and government to use in making informed decisions about what is happening with the economy. Much of the data can even result in wrong decisions. Five main problem areas need to be addressed. First, the goverment must use more timely methods for sampling and measurement. Such methods are widely avail-able and are used daily by the private sector. Second, new sec-tors of the economy must be measured. The process of change in the economy has not been matched with change in the statisti-cal base and statistical methods. Third, new directions in statistics are needed instead of relying on concepts. Fourth, the statistics must be made more reliable. Finally, the apparent antagonism between the business community and the data gath-erers must be eliminated.

author Joseph W. Duncan, which addresses the inadequacies of official statistics for decision-making purposes.[15] The abstract in Figure 8 dis-cusses a local government's view of statistical policy and its relation-ship to federal data.[16]

Possibly the most significant issue in any economy is economic growth, and the most watched variable is gross domestic product (GDP) or GDP per capita. These series are tied, by definition, to other key eco-nomic variables, including employment and unemployment numbers. Several analysts and legislators think that the GDP of the United States has been consistently inflated. One of the critics, Alan Sindlinger, claimed in a rather exhaustive analysis that the Department of Commerce misled both the public and government leaders by using data that yielded

---

[15]Joseph W. Duncan, "The Statistics Corner," *Business Economics,* January 1989.

[16]J. Bozeman and B. Bozeman, "How to Lie with Statistics," *Public Productivity & Management Review,* Fall 1989.

FIGURE 8
How to Lie with Statistics

Title:	"How to Lie with Statistics"
Authors:	J. Lisle Bozeman and Barry Bozeman
Journal:	*Public Productivity & Management Review* (POP) ISSN: 1044-8039 Vol: 13 Iss: 1 Date: Fall 1989 pp. 13–26
Companies:	Bureau of the Census
Subjects:	Local government; statistics; statistical methods; factors; improvements; state government
Codes:	9190 (United States); 9550 (Public sector)
Abstract:	A local government view of statistical policy is provided, and some steps local government officials can take to enhance the utility of federal statistics are suggested. Problems cited include: 1. The incompatibility of data obtained from multiple sources, 2. The dissimilarity of data collection methods between local, state, and federal agencies, and 3. A reduction in funds and an increase in responsibilities. Improvements in local government statistical policy can be made, for example, by acquiring available indices, setting policies and procedures for consultants, and deciding on a small body of strategic data. Steps that the federal government can take include: 1. Providing resources and technical assistance to local governments to answer questions about data structure, 2. Working toward maximum uniformity in definitions and procedures, 3. Devoting more resources to small areas and categories, 4. Considering a quinquennial census, and 5. Providing assistance for the implementation of geocoded systems.

too high a figure for employment. According to him, there was a discrepancy of about 1.4 million workers between the BLS's household survey and its establishment survey.[17]

The almost identical issue surfaced again in 1991–92 when the BLS discovered an atypically large difference between the employment levels as measured by its monthly survey of a sample of business establishments, and as measured by unemployment insurance reports gathered from the universe of the same businesses about a half year later. (The two series are called Current Employment Statistics [CES] and Unemployment Insurance.) A discrepancy of 650,000 was found between the two, with the CES reporting the higher numbers.

[17]His studies were reported in several issues of his regular subscription letter service.

An analysis by the authors is shown in Figure 9. This shows the total impact of the revisions from January 1989 to May 1991. The 12-month moving average is a good indicator of the cumulative impact of the revisions. The BEA used the CES employment data to issue its GDP estimates.

In light of the above, government statisticians have an opportunity to take a rather aggressive approach to defend both the integrity of the federal statistical system and the general accuracy of the underlying data. Others have used the situation to call for an advisory committee, and still others want to establish a new, centralized statistical agency. Certainly, a window of opportunity exists now to strengthen the federal statistical system. One good way of accomplishing the task is to rethink which surveys and which series are needed, which censuses can be reformed, and which can be eliminated in favor of samples. An effort must be made to get beyond the census approach and recognize that well-designed samples can do the job in many cases.[18]

FIGURE 9
U.S. Labor Force—Change in Monthly Estimates

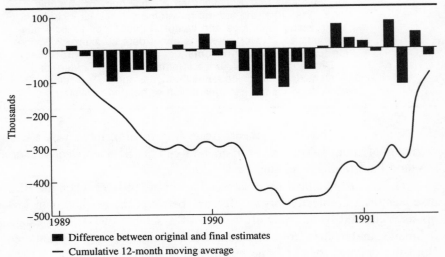

■ Difference between original and final estimates
— Cumulative 12-month moving average

See also, R.D. Hershey, Jr., "Jobless Rate Underestimated U.S. Says, Citing Survey Bias," *The New York Times,* November 17, 1993, pp. A-1 C-2.

Source: Haver Analytics, from BLS data file

[18]Joseph W. Duncan, "The Numbers Are Starting to Lie: Restructuring Economic Statistics," *Leaders Magazine,* Vol. 15, No. 3, July, August, September 1992, pp. 44–45.

How can government agencies do more with less? According to many experts, the key lies in information technology for improving both the quantity and the quality of their work. Simply put, modern electronic and optical devices are ready to assist government statisticians in doing a better job of collecting, analyzing, and disseminating the data.[19] The imperative is to move away from the mountains of paper and into electronic filing, CD-ROM storing/retrieving, and a vast array of other electronic, optical imaging, and networking systems, which will assist in the task. Evidence is at hand that information technology has finally come of age and that it can aid in handling the billions of data bits.

Threats

The gravest threat to government statistical systems would be the refusal to cooperate in the provision of information on the part of individuals and businesses. This is a distinct possibility if the forms and questionnaires get longer and if there is more invasion of privacy. While government authorities could rely on the stick (lawsuits, regulations, etc.), the carrot (shorter forms, electronic filing, sampling rather than census/universe count) will always work much better. A well-designed marketing program showing tangible benefits may range from the serious (feedback, appeal to patriotism, promise of no callbacks, etc.) to the light (specialty promotions; e.g., stickers, coins, pamphlets, etc.). Certainly, shorter questionnaires, fewer surveys, and electronic filing will go far in this regard.

A second threat is the possibility of further budget and staff cuts in government agencies as taxpayers balk and as legislators look for easy ways of holding the line. There is a sense, however, that like certain other categories of public service (e.g., customs, immigration, drug licensing, air traffic control), data collecting is a proper activity for government and has definite benefits for all sectors of the economy. No other body is as well equipped for gathering statistics, and the process is of much benefit to enterprises and individuals.

Members of major data collection agencies, such as the Bureau of the Census, BEA, BLS, and others, do need to step forward, however, and begin to do a better job of marketing themselves to Congress, the

---

[19]See, for example, Henry Kelly and Andrew Wyckoff, "Distorted Image," *Technology Review,* February/March 1989, pp. 53–60.

private sector, and the public at large. This means not only defending the accuracy and integrity of the data, but also patiently explaining the nature and the value of surveys undertaken. Pruning outdated censuses, starting new ones, switching to sampling, instituting new ways of filing, and so forth, also require publicity and indeed a "selling job" in specific terms. The responding organizations and individuals will be especially receptive to simpler forms and the elimination of duplication. Automation can go a long way toward easing the burden and may even allow more frequent surveys.

Those providing the data to government statistical agencies are often concerned with issues of privacy and secrecy. The concerns can extend from the way a census enumerator introduces himself or herself to a reminder phone call from a staff member of a regulatory commission, from the way a question is formulated to the manner in which reassurance is given that the answers will not be shared with other authorities. Both the human element and the design of the paper/electronic format must reassure the participants that strict privacy and secrecy will be observed. *Whole surveys and individual questions must be rethought along two lines: Are they really necessary? Will they offend the participant in any way?*

Setting up a "proper" system of social statistics that probes sensitive areas is fraught with more danger than is the case for economic data systems. Included here are such topics as education, ethnicity, race, religion, health, aging, disability, and welfare. Each of these topics is treated at some depth in the excellent volume already mentioned, *The Politics of Numbers.*

DATA FROM THE PRIVATE SECTOR (THE INDIVIDUAL FIRMS)

There are two major categories of data coming from profit-making enterprises. Both are important, and both are useful in their own rights and as complementary statistics to those gathered by the international, governmental, and nonprofit agencies. The categories are:

1. The statistics about the organization itself, usually published in its own annual and quarterly reports, news releases, and the like.
2. The facts and figures gathered about organizations by outsiders, such as information service companies, market research firms, think tanks, or trade/industry associations.

We will deal with the former here; the latter will be discussed briefly in the next section of this chapter and in the following chapter.

Strengths

Corporate data, which are often complex and multifaceted, can be highly useful. The macrodata of any national economy really rest on the foundations of microdata. It can be argued that the quality of statistics is an important part of the civic responsibility of corporate officials and ordinary citizens.

The business economist and others concerned about the quality and reliability of government data should work with accountants, controllers, and others in the company to make sure that the internal data are in order and that government forms submitted provide an accurate picture and a sound estimate of the information being requested. A well-designed database can help communication with employees on the inside and with suppliers and customers on the outside. And it allows for comparison with competitors.

In the electronic age, even the smallest company can have good records available on instant notice. Cost, price, product shipment, and other figures should be accessible to the relevant employees. Many firms in the United States and elsewhere practice solid accounting standards and have meaningful information systems. The advent of desktop computing and networks allows the interchange of information within the company and even, as and when appropriate, with vendors and customers through dedicated tie-lines (known as EDI, or electronic data interchange). The central issue within a company is usually about proper cost allocation, especially in regard to overhead, rather than (as is the case for public agencies) about accuracy and integrity. The challenge is to have a data environment that provides easy access, pertinent data, and user-friendly devices or interfaces.

Weaknesses

While some small firms are confronted with gaps in their database, others struggle with statistical and information overload. A major weakness of both small and large organizations—reminiscent of government agencies—is inertia manifested by continuing bookkeeping, accounting, and maintaining old-line time series—much as they have done in the past.

Once-a-year spring cleaning may be a great idea for corporate data. Companies, like government agencies, struggle with inaccurate data that will require revisions sooner or later.

Opportunities

Small and large firms have a veritable statistical gold mine on their hands—if they will only use it wisely. Quite often consultants who undertake a task for a company find that the necessary data for managerial decisions are already present, but that they are partly hidden or scattered in a variety of forms and locations. Organizations that keep streamlined statistics on their production costs, sales, purchases, or payroll are far more effective and competitive.

Enterprises should have good data on their employees, suppliers, and customers. This is not an invasion of privacy; this is sound business practice. In this fashion, they can analyze major alternatives in human resource allocation, purchasing, and selling. A detailed database on employees can result in far better policies in regard to promotion, transfer, retirement, rotation, and so on. As firms do more and more outsourcing, knowledgeable vendors will be even more crucial. Statistics should include delivery records, fulfillment rates, refund records, etc. The customer base can yield insights on where they are, what they buy or do not buy, how often and how much they buy, how they react to price promotions, and the like. Farsighted companies know not only their customers, but also their customers' customers.

Certainly, any company's key edge comes in serving its client base and watching out for its customers' customers. Enterprises have developed two kinds of reporting systems for analytical purposes: macro and micro. Corporate data play a large role in both. Macro reports provide an overview of total business operations and act as general monitoring devices, alerting management to changes in the firm's environment. Micro reports are used to narrow the analytical focus to the specific areas of operation in order to identify causes of problems and to assist in day-to-day functions. An example of each, using data for decisions, is shown in two short accompanying exhibits. Figures 10 and 11 show in general terms the manner in which data input levels can be organized and the way in which such data input serves as a base for macro and micro report generation.[20]

---

[20]Andrew C. Gross, et al., *Business Marketing.* Boston: Houghton-Mifflin, 1993, pp. 618–623.

FIGURE 10
A Macro Report Pinpoints Sales Problem

A large U.S. multinational active in Canada noticed a decline in its central division current-month sales, when in fact the commodity market in which it sold was known to be expanding rapidly. An investigation down to the branch and customer group levels discovered that a number of the retail customers in specific branch trading areas were being offered extremely favorable prices by another U.S. producer attempting to gain a foothold in the central division. Because the market threat was quickly pinpointed by geographic trading area and customer group, the multinational was able to respond immediately by instituting price cuts that countered the market-penetration strategy of the potential invader. The report system in this instance told management which customers and trading areas were most vulnerable to competitors, thus allowing the firm to undertake specific price cuts without generally depressing margins throughout its national distribution system.

Source: Andrew C. Gross, et al., *Business Marketing*. Boston: Houghton-Mifflin, 1993, p. 622.

FIGURE 11
Use of Micro Report Could Have Saved Company $47,000

The sales analyst of an integrated forest product producer became suspicious when reviewing the purchasing profile of one of the branch's largest customers. Historically, the industrial user bought only the vendor's premium quality products for remanufacture in his plants. The purchasing pattern changed dramatically, and the client suddenly began to concentrate on the vendor's poorest and cheapest grades of lumber. Branch and head office personnel ignored this change because sales volumes continued to remain large, and current credit checks indicated no financial problems. The sales analyst's requests for further investigation were ignored. With virtually no warning, the customer was placed in receivership by a competitor, and the vendor suffered a bad debt in excess of $47,000. The sales analyst's company now routinely reviews marked changes in customer purchasing behavior, having discovered that even relatively current credit checks can provide dated information.

Source: Andrew C. Gross, et al., *Business Marketing*. Boston: Houghton-Mifflin, 1993, p. 623.

Threats

The most vital step a company must take with respect to its corporate database is to protect it from physical destruction. Elaborate electronic protection is normally required for files on computers, along with physical protection for print format. Backup tapes and backup files, sometimes at a remote location, can serve this function. Companies must be on guard against both employee pilferage of data and outside intrusion. Passwords may need changing frequently.

Since most organizations realize how valuable their statistical database is, there is little danger of budget cuts threatening the existence of such foundations. As the number of files grows, even in electronic format, it will cost more and more to keep them orderly and to make the data readily available to those needing access to them.

While many firms recognize the need for both physical protection of data and for streamlining the statistical system, relatively few have a good handle on how statistics and information in general should be managed. The reason? They cannot manage the politics. In the words of authors who analyzed the situation at length in several companies: "As information becomes the basis for organizational structure and function, politics will increasingly come into play. The most information-oriented companies are least likely to share the information freely."[21]

DATA FROM STATISTICAL/INFORMATION INDUSTRY FIRMS AND NONPROFIT AGENCIES

In addition to statistics emanating from international agencies, national governments, and individual enterprises in the private sector, there is a fourth major category that is a rich source of business data. This is the world of information or statistical service organizations: market research companies, business consultants, not-for-profit think tanks, and a host of industry, trade, professional, and technical organizations. As is the case for individual businesses, these vary greatly in size, expertise, focus, client base, and so on.

Their common characteristic is that they collect data on a small or large scale and make that data available either on a fee basis or as a matter of course to their membership (on a request, single fee, or subscription basis). The statistics that can be obtained this way are truly extensive and varied. They can range from a single table to vast printouts containing many time series.

---

[21]J. McGee, et al. *Managing Information Strategically.* New York: Wiley, 1993, p. 152.

Strengths

The flow of figures from the profit-making information service firms and from the many nonprofit organizations is much more focused than the data emanating from international agencies or the national government bureaus. The reason is that the mandate of the former is much more specific.

For example, because of long-time tradition, Dun & Bradstreet emphasizes its vast data holdings on the creditworthiness of large and small companies. Along these lines, it developed expertise in the collection of data on a wide range of business attributes that can be analyzed by region, by industry, by size, and so on. Its subsidiaries, including Dataquest, IMS, and A. C. Nielsen, offer statistics and focused information on the electronics, medical prescription, market research, and television fields.

A host of poll takers (including news weeklies, electronic media, et al.) gather nationwide statistics on economic, social, and political patterns. In the case of nonprofit organizations, the trade/industry/technical groups have also built up impressive credentials in their specific areas— from aviation safety records to zoo attendance, from generic drug sales to oil rig fires. Often, the information is available for many industrialized countries.

Weaknesses

Like other organizations, the information service firms and nonprofit associations can lose their "agency" role (representing the interests of their clients, employees, members) and take on an institutional-type role (enhancing their own power, bureaucracy, status). Competition from the marketplace or vocal complaints from the membership should steer the organization back to its correct path. Another potential source of problems is the bias underlying the work of the enterprise. For example, consultants may give optimistic figures if they think that is what the client wants to hear or may recommend a course of action extending their time of service to generate more fee income. In the case of think tanks and nonprofit trade groups, the bias is often well known (e.g., Brookings Institution is a more liberal think tank; American Enterprise Institute is a more conservative one; the Pharmaceutical Manufacturers Association can be expected to support the interests of Merck or Pfizer).

One major weakness of an industry or a professional association may be that it is not a true cross section of the group it purports to represent. For example, only about one-half of all U.S. physicians now belong to the American Medical Association, compared to about three-fourths some decades ago. In the same way, many of the manufacturing and service/trade associations may not include a host of new and small firms, and remain representatives only of large entities. Thus, statistics coming from them may not be indicative of industry trends and may even be misleading if the new/small firms are where the innovation is taking place. In the case of the information service firms, it is advisable to be familiar with the underlying methodology and collection procedures to judge clearly if the statistics have integrity and accuracy.

Opportunities

The sky is the limit! Well, not quite, but given the thrust toward the information society, the enterprises that belong in this section should prosper and their databases should be much in demand. Large and small information service firms, left or right of center think tanks, and the various trade and professional associations will be doing well during the coming decades. Given the advent of electronic databases, networking, and existing as well as proposed "information highways," the future is assured for those organizations that provide data to their clientele, readers, or members. They have an opportunity to expand abroad and to link domestic with foreign data for an enhanced database.

The crucial aspect is the manner in which they carry out their research and the subsequent data processing. The dissemination will be relatively easy and, most likely, profitable. Validity and reliability are and will continue to be the two cornerstones. The underlying representativeness, the integrity of data gathering, and the accuracy of the figures must be assured. Above all, client needs must be paramount.

Threats

There will always be debate about whether the public or private sector, and which specific agency, is best suited to collect data. There will also be conflict about pricing, access, privacy rights, and so forth. *The pluralistic, diverse foundations of the statistical information domain should reassure that a variety of views will prevail and that negotiations will take place.*

A greater danger is that the budget constraints of government agencies and the profit-seeking nature of information service firms may result in the neglect of certain topics. Even this seems unlikely, as the many consumer, charitable, environmental, and "public interest" groups seem able to raise needed funds to gather the statistics that meet their needs.

CONCLUSION

In this chapter, we have conducted a SWOT analysis of four major categories for organizations that provide business and related statistics: international agencies, national government bureaus, the individual business enterprise, and the host of profit-making statistical service companies and both for-profit industry and professional associations. As in other chapters, the emphasis was on U.S. data and on the federal statistical system, but the broad spectrum of public and private providers of statistics was also examined.

The strengths and weaknesses of the underlying data sets were reviewed; in other words, the factors that make the existing statistics strong or weak in the eye of the users. Then the discussion moved from the question of "what is" to "what can be"—the opportunities and threats the data sets face and the manner in which their collection, processing, and dissemination are likely to unfold. While it is not always possible to separate the data from the data collector, the emphasis in this chapter was on the statistics themselves. Section 2 of the next chapter focuses more on the institutional role of the producing enterprises rather than on the characteristics of the data they publish.

CHAPTER 3

ELEMENTS OF THE STATISTICAL SYSTEM—THE STAKEHOLDERS AND INTERACTIONS

The term "statistical system" is widely used to describe the total set of institutions involved in collecting, processing, and disseminating statistical information. However, there is not a "system" in the sense of organized and integrated processes or in terms of "feedback" from one institution to another. Rather, the linkages are informal and the goals of individual institutions are independent. Nevertheless, this collection of statistical activities and the resulting statistical information serve as the cornerstone of modern decision making in public and private activities.

This chapter will focus on some of the important characteristics of the following:

1. Uses and users of statistics.
2. Products and producers of statistics.
3. Collection, presentation, and dissemination of statistics.

The purpose of this discussion is to review some of the key elements that must be considered in the development of even better and more relevant statistics for decision making in the future. The following three sections deal with the stakeholders in the development of statistical information.

SECTION 1—USES AND USERS OF STATISTICS

At one point during long congressional negotiations a few years ago, Senator Daniel P. Moynihan, Democrat from New York, said in frustration, "Look—everyone is entitled to their own opinions, but they're not entitled to their own *facts*."

Of course, as the Senator himself later ruefully recognized, the "facts" about the economy, as with other issues, are often hedged about with ambiguity, and are very much subject to quite diverse interpretation, depending on the purposes of those who need and use them. The other chapters in this report deal directly with shortcomings and needed improvements in the information provided to users. This section will review the uses and the users of economic data, including:

- Who the users of economic statistics are.
- The different purposes—therefore, the different perspectives and interpretations—that different users bring to their use of economic statistics.
- Some of the unique, inherent complexities attached to information as a "product," including the famous problem that statistics can easily—too easily—"lie."
- Some of the promises, problems, and bottlenecks of on-line technologies bringing the information "products" more quickly and conveniently to the end users.

Information Users

Whatever else the information age means, it certainly implies not only that there is more information available, but also that there are more users of information, including the quantitative information called statistics.

Interestingly, the term *statistics* did not always refer to quantitative information. Historically, statistics meant any facts or information about the state.[1] Scholars have traced its current quantitative sense back to 17th century England and William Petty's book *Political Arithmetick,* a comparison of the military and economic resources of England, France, and Holland. The purpose of the book was to show the superiority of English power in both arenas. A commentator from that time summed up the purpose of such statistics: "To help any ruler to understand fully that strength which is to guide and direct."[2]

Today, government remains simultaneously the largest producer and the largest consumer of statistics. Steven Kelman has pointed out that

---

[1]Paul Starr, "The Sociology of Official Statistics," in *The Politics of Numbers,* William Alonso and Paul Starr, eds. New York: Russell Sage Foundation, 1987, p. 15.

[2]Ibid., p. 15.

throughout our history, American legislators advanced arguments supporting statistical research that are consonant with the reasons advanced in 17th century England: First, statistical information is an important aid to the formulation of legislation and government policy; second, statistical information can serve as an important source of patriotic pride; third, information about particular groups within society can serve as an important signal to those groups of societal recognition; and fourth, information gathering by the state makes an important statement about the value of knowledge.[3]

In 1982, the chairman of the Committee on National Statistics of the National Academy of Sciences, testifying before Congress, cited political administration as the primary reason for the gathering and use of statistics by government: "The executive branch and Congress use statistical data to aid the preparation of legislation. . . . Statistics provide the infrastructure for government decision-making."[4]

While government has remained the primary user of statistical information, over time other user groups have emerged and gained greater prominence. In fact, in democratic societies, the wider spread of statistical information came to serve as a curb on the growth of governmental control. As Peter Buck put it, statistical information moved from being "a scientific prospectus for the exercise of state power" to "a program for reversing the growth of government and reducing its influence."[5]

Moreover, Kenneth Prewitt has cited research that shows, rather counterintuitively, that voters in the United States pay more attention to the economic statistics that track the economy in making political choices than they do to their individual economic circumstances.[6] (Jimmy Carter understood this point when he first fashioned the so-called misery index, which he successfully used against Gerald Ford in 1976—and which was used successfully against him by Ronald Reagan in 1980.)

---

[3]Steve Kelman, "The Political Foundations of American Statistical Policy," in *The Politics of Numbers*, William Alonso and Paul Starr, eds. New York: Russell Sage Foundation, 1987, p. 276.

[4]Ibid., p. 300.

[5]Paul Starr, "The Sociology of Official Statistics," in *The Politics of Numbers*, William Alonso and Paul Starr, eds. New York: Russell Sage Foundation, 1987, p. 15.

[6]Kenneth Prewitt, "Public Statistics and Democratic Politics," in *The Politics of Numbers*, William Alonso and Paul Starr, eds. New York: Russell Sage Foundation, 1987, p. 263.

In recent decades, the largest growth in the user base of statistical information—a growth that is both cause and consequence of the "information revolution"—has been in the sector of private companies. The uses of information vary widely in private industry, as suggested by a partial listing of some of the roles that statistical information now plays:

- Credit information used to evaluate both customers and suppliers.
- Marketing information of all kinds (about 1 million pages of scanner-based information provided each day to the customers of the world's largest market research organization, A. C. Nielsen).
- Information used for stocking shelves.
- Information for transferring funds.
- Information about passenger loads in airlines.
- Information about credit card purchases.

This, obviously, is but a short illustrative and impressionistic listing of the ways that statistical information is currently used in private industry. Drawing on work from Fritz Machlup, Mark Porat, and Andrew C. Gross, Figure 12 presents spatially both the industries and the occupations in the private sector that are the heaviest users of information.

Like all users of information, those in the private sector have differing needs, which result in differing priorities in terms of the speed with which information needs to be delivered. Those priorities, in turn, lead to different modes of information delivery. Figure 13 ranges different users' needs for speed on one axis against the speed of delivery of different modes along the other.

Information Anomalies

Different uses spur a variety of perspectives, and the object that is perceived from these different vantage points is, in any case, anomalous. After all, information is not a physical object that can be described, measured, or assessed. Also, unlike most products, information is not used up over time. In fact, the same information can be used an unlimited number of times without any deterioration in its value. On the other hand, the value of information can sometimes be very closely related to time. Knowing the winner of the Kentucky Derby 30 seconds before the race begins is exceedingly valuable; knowing the same thing three min-

FIGURE 12
Spatial Map of Information Content

High

Extent of information content — function

Research & development
Customized transactions
Marketing
Finance
Inventory
Accounting

Agriculture
Forestry
Mining
Construction
"Simple" manufacturing
Government
"Complex" manufacturing

Trade, wholesale & retail
Nonprofessional services
Financial, business services
Sophisticated, professional services

Low   Extent of information content — industry   High

Journals, newspapers
Newsletters
Abstracts, indexes
Shows, exhibits
Books, reports, mongraphs
Archives

Low

Source: Andrew Gross, "The Information Vending Machine", *Business Horizons*, January/February 1988, p. 29.

utes later is virtually worthless. The same piece of information can have very different value, depending on the persons using it and their purposes.[7] The value of a given piece of geographical information, for example, might vary, depending on whether it is used by a driller looking for oil or by a land developer assessing the stability of the land.

Because of the time sensitivity of some information, a rough-and-ready estimate delivered sooner can sometimes be more valuable than

[7]Joseph W. Duncan, "The Worth and Value of Information," in *Critical Issues in the Information Age,* Robert Lee Chartrand, ed. Metuchen, NJ: The Scarecrow Press, 1991.

FIGURE 13
Spatial Map of Information Delivery

High

Automatic alarm/response
Face-to-face
On-line
Teleconference
Videotext

Speed of delivery

Skill improvements
Retrospective search
General business news
Knowledge of industry
Information on distribution channel
New-product knowledge
Pricing decision

Promotion and campaign
Competitor's action
Market expansion or contraction
Shift in sales, inventory
Purchase transaction
Credit rating
Medical, military action

Low —————————————————————————— High
Urgency or immediacy of need

Journals, newspapers
Newsletters
Abstracts, indexes
Shows, exhibits
Books, reports, monographs
Archives

Low

Source: Andrew Gross, "The Information Vending Machine," *Business Horizons*, January/February 1988, p. 29.

exceedingly precise information delivered later. In other circumstances, inaccurate or bad information is much worse than no information at all. Indeed, that is why governments spend billions of dollars on "disinformation." Moreover, without prior purposes in mind, no information would ever be gathered for the simple reason that there would be no guiding criteria for what should be gathered.

The key point from a user's perspective is that without prior purposes that suggest the shape of the answers needed, there are no questions, no research, and no gathering of statistical or any other kind of information. Simon Kuznets noted, for example, the impossibility of measuring gross domestic product without making philosophical choices about the end purpose of economic activity.[8] This point was stressed in chapter 1.

Whose purposes, whose questions? A simple answer is: "Whoever has the power." We are familiar with the truth that "knowledge is power," that more information usually leads to more influence and greater power. It is equally true, but much less well understood, that power confers information.

Raymond Vernon has pointed out that politicians and policy makers are in charge of the technicians who gather statistics. "What such politicians and policymakers share in common is an interest in using the data—sometimes, too, in suppressing or modifying them—to promote their national or international objectives."[9] Mark Perlman stated that "economic data are constantly used in the interpretation of economic events and the formulation of economic policies by both government and the private sector. But which data are collected and how they are manipulated and analyzed depend on the underlying objectives of a statistical system."[10]

In the United States, a great deal of information is gathered about both the agricultural and the manufacturing sectors of the national economy. Not nearly as much information is collected about the services sector, despite the fact that the services sector has become the fastest-growing, and by many measures the largest, sector of the American economy. Moreover, while we have a lot of data that describe large organizations, the amount of information available on smaller companies is much less exhaustive, even though smaller companies are playing a larger role in the economy, especially in the employment picture.

The difference in information about these economic sectors follows from the historic differences in power among them. Paul Starr pointed out that different political presuppositions or commitments by users often take the form of different statistical methods: The classic dispute about

---

[8]Paul Starr, "The Sociology of Official Statistics," in *The Politics of Numbers*, William Alonso and Paul Starr, eds. New York: Russell Sage Foundation, 1987, p. 51.

[9]Raymond Vernon, "The Politics of Comparative Economic Statistics: Three Cultures and Three Cases," in *The Politics of Numbers*, William Alonso and Paul Starr, eds. New York: Russell Sage Foundation, 1987, p. 71.

[10]Mark Perlman, "Political Purpose and the National Accounts," in *The Politics of Numbers*, William Alonso and Paul Starr, eds. New York: Russell Sage Foundation, 1987, p. 133.

the national income accounts concerns the practice of not attributing any economic value to nonmarket services, such as those traditionally provided by women within the family.[11]

Moreover, as Starr indicated, "in determining the poverty rate, conservatives want to include in-kind income. . . . On the other hand, advocates of the poor want the income cutoff for poverty raised because the original basis assumed that food was one-third of income," and multiplied by three the dollar value of a subsistence level of food to arrive at the poverty level. Reformers argue, however, that food no longer consumes as much as one-third of the income of the poor, so that the multiplier should be greater than three.[12]

It is not just power in the political, economic, or social sense that guides the gathering and formulation of statistical research. It is also the power of encrusted habit and the ongoing power of assumptions that are embedded "out of sight" in procedures. For example, historically, the Consumer Price Index (CPI) has been relatively slow in adding new items to its "market basket." The CPI added cars in 1951 and pocket calculators in 1978. By the time each of these items had been added to the CPI's market basket, their prices had fallen dramatically, a price fall that was not immediately captured in the CPI.[13]

Moreover, Walter Wriston and others have pointed out that U.S. accounting methods for the deficit do not reflect "capital accounts"—that is, money spent for future investments. As Wriston put it, "everything from a 25-cent pencil to billions of dollars worth of bridges, roads and other productive assets is expensed." Who can doubt that the built-in assumptions of these statistical methods unconsciously shape national debate and, therefore, national policy making? Nikita Khrushchev is reported to have complained that in the Soviet Union it had become the tradition to produce not beautiful chandeliers to adorn homes, but the heaviest chandeliers possible. This is because the heavier the chandeliers produced, the more resources a factory got, since its output is calculated in tons. In sum, the purposes of users determine the shape of information gathered and interpreted. That information, in turn, often determines

---

[11]Paul Starr, "The Sociology of Official Statistics," in *The Politics of Numbers*, William Alonso and Paul Starr, eds. New York: Russell Sage Foundation, 1987, p. 47.

[12]Ibid., p. 48.

[13]Ibid., p. 50.

the relative power of the users and the kinds of policy that get debated and enacted—often unconsciously.

Methods of Information Delivery

The preceding section reviewed the history of the past few decades, which has seen an explosion in the uses of statistical information by the private sector. Unquestionably, private-sector use has been made possible by new technologies that have not only allowed for the convenient and compact electronic storage of enormous amounts of data, but also have allowed for the data to be downloaded easily into the customers' own systems. Customers have the option to mix and meld the data with their own proprietary information and then easily manipulate them to derive highly customized solutions to their own individual problems. This has also resulted in the formation of a number of private companies that have added value to the data that are routinely provided by the federal government for sale to customers.

In recent years, the Securities and Exchange Commission has been working on its so-called EDGAR Project, an electronic system that allows companies to file their mandated 10-K and 10-Q reports electronically. This project would also allow private firms, as customers, to download those same reports without ever having to deal with hard copy.

Through the Internet services, the National Academy of Sciences now allows its computers to be used to conduct experiments and test hypotheses. It is easy to see that a similar kind of arrangement might allow for private concerns to use powerful government computers to carry out complicated econometric studies of economic inputs and outputs—computations requiring the simultaneous solutions of thousands of equations.[14]

Other new information technologies are coming onstream virtually every day. For example, CD-ROMs now contain the most recent U.S. census results, replacing the cumbersome magnetic tapes associated with the 1960 and 1970 census distribution effort. In sum, the extraordinary increase in the technologies of information, like the increased numbers

---

[14]Paul Starr and Ross Corson, "Who Will Have the Numbers? The Rise of the Statistical Services Industry and the Politics of Public Data," in *The Politics of Numbers,* William Alonso and Paul Starr, eds. New York: Russell Sage Foundation, 1987, pp. 415–447.

of private players, is both cause and consequence of the so-called Information Revolution.

SECTION 2—PRODUCTS AND PRODUCERS OF STATISTICS

This section will focus on the organizations producing the statistics. While this review is not exhaustive, it is intended to illustrate the rich diversity that characterizes the development of statistical information.

Key agencies, companies, or institutions will be identified, and their past record and current situation will be assessed. Next, how statistics are generated and their format will be considered. Some of the data can now be produced on an automated basis; for example, from bar codes, credit card transactions, and the like. Indeed, in the future, sensors will play a key role in how data are collected. Finally, some key issues ranging from the internal politics of the statistical agencies to the manner in which users are treated will be discussed.

Generators of Business/Economic/Social Data

Both government agencies and private businesses have kept tabs on economic activities (their own and that of others) since ancient times. The rise of modern statistical bureaus in the public sector and of the library or information center in the corporation is more recent, but can still be traced over decades or even centuries. Over 200 years ago, the U.S. Constitution mandated a decennial population census. The U.S. government spent approximately $2.6 billion on the 1990 decennial census, including the full costs of planning, conducting, tabulating, and disseminating the results.

Most sovereign nations maintain a central statistical bureau for gathering data, with budgets ranging from lean to at least "moderately handsome." The trends cited by Sir Claus Moser have continued.[15] Since data gathering is not a glamorous activity, many public-sector bodies find themselves part of the effort to reduce the overhead cost of governments and, as a result, statistical agencies in most countries are working with reduced budgets compared with real levels of 10 years ago.

---

[15]*Statistical Services in Ten Years' Time,* pp. 6–8 as quoted in chapter 1.

Intergovernmental organizations that gather data are a relatively new phenomenon. In the 19th century, only a handful came into existence: the Universal Postal Union in 1874, the Metrics Union in 1875, and later the International Copyright Union. In 1930, the Bank for International Settlement was established. Most of the key data-producing agencies are products of the post-World War II period:

1944	IBRD (World Bank); IMF; ICAO
1945	U.N. and its specialized agencies, such as FAO, UNESCO
1947–49	GATT, OEEC (now OECD), COMECON, NATO
1957	EEC (now EU)
1960	OPEC, EFTA, LAFTA
1960s	UNCTAD, CARIFTA, others

Since 1960, a host of other regional and international agencies have been created, some with narrow or special missions; for example, the African Timber Organization in 1976 and the International Jute Organization in 1984. We expect there will be more such bodies reflecting commodity interests. Each of these is likely to become a repository and a publisher of its statistics. Each relies on cooperation from national and/or corporate memberships for its data collection and often for data processing and dissemination. The combined data from contributors will be only as good as its parts.

Private-sector companies and nonprofit associations constitute the final set of producers of statistics. As pointed out earlier, each company is king of its own castle and, subject to accountants, auditors, and regulators, it controls the facts and figures about itself. Often, it is in the interest of the firm to publish data sets widely; other firms, especially those whose stock is not publicly owned, prefer to release as little as possible about themselves. Groups of companies, associations, and institutes develop their own mission. At first, they are directly responsible to their membership. Later on, as observers of corporate culture note, these organizations take on a life of their own and may well become as bureaucratic as governments or large corporations.

The following quote illuminates the politicalization process that public agencies undergo over time; but, in our view, the remarks are equally applicable to the data producers in the private sector and in associations:

International bureaucrats have the same utility function as national bureaucrats . . . the economic theory of bureaucracy applies to both of them. Both try to maximize their power in terms of budget size, staff, and freedom of discretion and appreciate some leisure on the job. Both enjoy some freedom to pursue these objectives because in many respects they have acquired an information monopoly and because the politicians need their cooperation.[16]

In short, the statistical activities of organizations are as worth watching as their other undertakings. Put briefly: Consider the source. *Put differently: Who says it, when, with how much integrity and accuracy, on what basis—and do they have an ax to grind?* In Figure 14, we show an abbreviated list of producers and some of their key statistical publications. The list is a small sample, but it is representative of the three layers discussed above and below.

In the international statistical arena, the dominant producer is the United Nations, especially its Statistical Division (UNSTAT). UNSTAT gave the world the first comprehensive global set of data on both per capita national income and industrial production indices. UNSTAT also provided conversion ratios for comparing gross domestic product between market and planned economies. The UNSTAT and other agencies publish not dozens but hundreds of books and monographs, including global and regional volumes. To help users with access to the mountains of data, the UNSTAT publishes several guides, primarily its *Directory of International Statistics.*[17]

While UNSTAT and other U.N. agencies (e.g., the United Nations Educational Scientific and Cultural Organization, known as UNESCO) can be viewed as "the fountainhead," a degree of healthy skepticism should be maintained vis-à-vis U.N. data. First, the statistics are only as good as those provided to it by the national statistical offices. Independent U.N. surveys are a rarity. Second, there are problems with timeliness of the data. For example, the U.N., which is revamping its System of National Accounts, published national accounts data in 1992, but they were data for 1990. Third, comparability over time, among nations, and even for a given country is "a continuing struggle." It is not unusual to find discrepancies in data between two U.N. publications.

---

[16]R. Vauble and T. Willett, eds., *The Political Economy of International Organizations.* Boulder, CO: Westview, 1991, p. 39.

[17]United Nations, Department of International Economic and Social Affairs, Statistical Office, *Directory of International Statistics,* Vol. I. New York: United Nations, 1982.

FIGURE 14
Short List of Producers

Primary Sources

International	*U.N. Demographic Yearbook* (United Nations)
	U.N. Statistical Yearbook (United Nations)
	World Development Report (World Bank)
	IMF Statistics (International Monetary Fund)
	OECD Countries—National Accounts (Organization for Economic Development, Paris)
	EU Statistics (European Union)
	IDB Annual Report (Inter-American Development Bank)
National	*Statistical Abstract of the United States* (U.S. Department of Commerce)
	USDC Census Report (U.S. Department of Commerce)
	Census of Manufacturers
	Census of Service Industries
	Survey of Current Business (U.S. Department of Commerce)
	U.S. Industrial Outlook—Annual (U.S. Department of Commerce)
	U.S. Tariff Commission Reports
	Canada Yearbook (Statistics Canada)
	Korea Yearbook
	Statistical Yearbook of Hungary
Company and Institutional	Annual and "10-K" reports (especially in the United States)
	Bank newsletters and reports
	Filings with government agencies (export/import data, etc.)
	Trade association surveys
	Annual reports of nonprofit institutions
	Research reports from universities
	Foundation grant reports
	Scientific and technical societies

Secondary Sources

General Business Publications	*Business Week*	Newspapers	*Wall Street Journal*
	Fortune		*Wall Street Transcript*
	The Economist		*The Times* (United Kingdom)
	Forbes		*Financial Post* (Canada)
	L'Expansion		*Australian Financial Review*
Specific Trade/ Industry Publications	*Aviation Week*		*Figyelo* (Hungary)
	Computerworld		
	Coal Age		
	Datamation		
	Electronics		

(continued)

FIGURE 14 *(continued)*

Tertiary Sources and Special Publications

Indices	*Business Periodicals Index*
	Canadian Business Periodical Index
	Public Affairs Information Index
	Predicasts F & S Indexes (United States; Europe; rest of world)
	Public Affairs Information Index
Abstracts	*Dissertation Abstracts*
	Chemical Abstracts
	Employment Abstracts
Databases	On-line Databases (See Figures 16 and 17)
Directories	*Consumer Yellow Pages; Business to Business Yellow Pages*
	Dun & Bradstreet *Million Dollar Directory*
	Standard & Poor's List of Companies
	Thomas Register of American Manufacturers
	Encyclopedia of Associations
	Books in Print (United States)
	British Books in Print (United Kingdom)
	Ulrich's List of Periodicals
	Business International
	SRI International (Stanford Research Institute)
	Disclosure
	Value Line
	Standard Rate and Data Service
	Commerce Clearing House
	Euromonitor

(concluded)

Like the U.N., other international agencies with a global outlook collect, process, and publish statistics. These include the World Bank, the International Monetary Fund (IMF), the General Agreement on Tariffs and Trade (GATT), and a host of autonomous or semiautonomous agencies, such as the International Labour Office (ILO) and the International Civil Aviation Organization (ICAO). As is the case with the U.N., these agencies also rely on data from member countries.

These organizations have at least three distinct advantages: (1) their bureaucracy is somewhat smaller; (2) the subject area is more focused (i.e., labor for ILO, aviation for ICAO, finance for IMF); and (3) some primary surveys are undertaken that act as a check or balance. One of the most comprehensive statistical volumes is the *World Development*

Report.[18] In addition to excellent charts and graphs, the volume includes 33 statistical tables in the appendix, complete with technical explanations on the construction of data.

Some private-sector agencies now publish guides to the plethora of data emanating from the intergovernmental and international agencies. One such reference is the *Index to International Statistics (IIS)*, published by the Congressional Information Service (CIS). The *IIS* is usually up-to-date and comprehensive, but it is also expensive. The CIS also publishes the *American Statistics Index* and the *Statistical Reference Index* every month. Yet another reference is *SISCIS: Subject Index to Sources of Comparative International Statistics.* This volume, said to be cumbersome and often dated, is less costly than *IIS* and does offer a certain form of subject/geography index.[19]

The format for data dissemination will be discussed below. It is worth mentioning that printed media (yearbooks and other references) are complemented and often replaced by electronic media, specifically traditional magnetic tapes (for computer mainframes), electronic on-line databases (via networks or small computers with modems), computer readable databases (on CD-ROMs, available in many libraries or for purchase and use in the office or at home), and diskettes. The most comprehensive and most recent guide is the *Gale Directory of Databases,* which lists about 1,500 numerical databases.[20] See Figure 15 for details.

Among regional organizations, the Organization for Economic Cooperation and Development (OECD) is a prominent producer of data. This Paris-based organization is the umbrella group for the 25 most industrialized nations and a few associate countries. Its key statistical publications include *Main Economic Indicators* and *National Accounts of the OECD Countries.* Its country surveys are also widely followed. The OECD has developed a variety of economic time series and databases that are published in both comparative format and for individual nations. The

---

[18]Published for the World Bank, annually, by Oxford University Press, New York.

[19]Another useful publication is *International Organizations: A Dictionary & Directory.* Chicago: St. James Press, 1986. For an analysis of the agencies and the documents they produce, see another well-crafted volume, P. Hajnal, ed., *International Information: Documents, Publications and Information Systems of International Government Agencies.* Englewood, CO: Libraries Unlimited, 1988.

[20]Gale Research, Detroit, July 1993.

OECD data sets are considered among the best, which is not surprising, since, unlike the U.N., the OECD does not deal with the newly industrializing and developing nations whose data collection and processing are incomplete and untimely. Because the OECD deals with far fewer nations than the U.N., it is able to publish more readable formats; for example, the indicators are often portrayed in easy-to-read bar, line, or pie charts. The OECD also offers data on specific industries or sectors; for example, pollution control spending, health care, and education.

Statistical databases are maintained by many other international and regional organizations besides the U.N. and its affiliate institutions, the World Bank, the IMF, and the OECD. The Statistical Office of the European Union (Eurostat) collects, harmonizes, and disseminates statistical information on member countries and affiliates (e.g., the newly emerging Eastern European economies that seek association with the European Union). The data availability and formatting have become better in recent years, and access has been made easier for users outside the EU. Contents are available in both print and electronic formats. Three major statistical databases are available from Eurostat (which is headquartered in Luxembourg). They are:

- *Chronos*—economics statistics, with over 800,000 time series going back to the 1960s by 25 subject areas. Features multilingual descriptions and product codes; three subfiles are available for a number of main indicators: Eurostatus (50 series), Eurostatistics (625 series), and ICG (3750 series).
- *Comext*—offering trade statistics, organized by nomenclature, covering over 8,000 products and available by the Harmonized coding system.
- *Regio*—regional statistics, offering data on economic and social life in EU regions.

Still other sources of statistics are the Bank for International Settlements (BIS); various regional banking agencies (e.g., Inter-American Development Bank and Asian Development Bank); various energy agencies (CERN and IAEA); and dozens of major and hundreds of minor industrial or regional bodies, some of which are not governmental but semipublic or indeed industry affiliated. Budgets and staff size vary greatly, but the politics remain the same as those cited above for the international agencies.

FIGURE 15
Recent Trends in Databases

Part A: Databases by type

	1985		1992	
Class	*No.*	*%*	*No.*	*%*
Word oriented	1,926	64	4,925	70
Number oriented	1,084	36	1,533	22
Image			272	4
Audio			83	2
Electronic service			146	2
Software			39	0+
Total	3,010	100	6,998	100

Part B: Databases by medium for access or distribution

	1992	
Type	*No.*	*%*
On-line	4,519	65
Batch	320	5
CD-ROM	1,088	15
Diskette	557	8
Magnetic tape	481	7
Handheld	33	0+
Total	6,998	100

Part C: Databases by producer status

	1985	1992
Sector	*%*	*%*
Government	21	15
Commerce/industry	57	75
Nonprofits	11	9
Mix	11	1
Total	100	100

Source: K. Y. Marcaccio, ed., *Gale Directory of Databases,* Volume 1. Detroit: Gale Research, July 1993, pp. xxii–xxvii.

"Are all countries' statistics equally dodgy?" was a question posed by a leading business journal almost two years ago.[21] Its answer was No! The rankings are shown in Figure 16. What makes a good governmental statistical agency? According to the article: coverage and reliability; methodology used in collecting the data; and the integrity and objectivity of the bureau. Small countries came out on top, not simply because it is easier to collect statistics. Canada, Australia, and The Netherlands have the advantage of centralized systems whose independence is carefully guarded. The statistical agencies in these nations were able to protect themselves better against budget cuts (if needed, they would cut selectively, not across the board). The larger countries have

FIGURE 16
Number Crunchers Ranked

Country	1993	1991		
	Statisticians' Ranking	Statisticians' Ranking	Revisions Percentage Points*	Timeliness**
Canada	1	1	1.0	10
Australia	2	2	1.7	8
Sweden	5	3	2.4	5
Netherlands	3	4	1.6	9
France	4	5	1.3	6
Germany	6=	6	3.0	1
United States	6=	7	1.1	4
Japan	9	8	2.7	7
Britain	6=	9	1.7	1
Italy	11	10	1.7	1
Switzerland	10			

* Mean absolute deviation between initial estimate of GNP/GDP growth and final figure
** Average speed of publication of GNP/GDP, industrial production, consumer prices, and trade statistics: 1=fastest, 10=slowest

Source: "The Good Statistics Guide," *Economist,* Sept. 7, 1991, p. 88; and "The Good Statistics Guide," *Economist,* Sept. 11, 1993, p. 65. The more recent article has more detail on the characteristics of governmental agencies than shown above.

---

[21]"The Good Statistics Guide," *Economist,* Sept. 7, 1991, p. 88. See also "The Good Statistics Guide," *Economist,* Sept. 11, 1993, p. 65.

decentralized systems; the statisticians report to different ministers and are subject to varying political support. These agencies also find it hard to shift funding and to get extra money for surveys of new industries, such as high tech or services.

The *Economist* in the past has castigated the U.K. Central Statistical Office and labeled it one of the least independent, with "the figures often tasting of fudge."[22] This journal and others have often praised Statistics Canada. In chapter 1, we commented on the work of the Bureau of the Census and the Bureau of Economic Analysis within the U.S. Department of Commerce, and the Bureau of Labor Statistics in the U.S. Department of Labor. Basically, each of the three has a specific mandate and has carried it out quite well (see chapter 1 and the composite ranking for the United States in Figure 16). *While there is often criticism of the quality of U.S. statistical agencies, the agencies responsible for official statistics in the United States have a high degree of professionalism and integrity.*[23]

Interestingly, what the exhibit and the text above say about smaller Western countries having better statistical bureaus and numbers applies equally to non-Western nations. Specifically, in Eastern Europe, Hungary and other small nations had a better statistical collection system than the former Soviet Union. As for the former Soviet Union, here is what V. N. Kirichenko, then Chairman of the USSR State Committee on Statistics, admitted in 1990. Elaborating on statistical shortcomings with copious examples, he admitted to number padding, obvious whitewashing, the imperfection of computations, and the tendency to make the data fit the current political tasks. He called for conversion to the U.N. System of National Accounts, but admitted it would be a hard task requiring major effort and much time. Even before harmonizing with the rest of the world, he was hoping to:

> ensure the accuracy of the data . . . restore the trust in such data on the part of the Soviet and international public. The country can no longer afford to seek the right way with the help of trick mirrors.[24]

---

[22]Ibid.

[23]For a discussion of integrity, see the special issue of the National Association of Business Economists' journal, *Business Economics,* July 1993.

[24]V. N. Kirichenko, "Return Credibility to Statistics," *Business Economics,* October 1990, pp. 50–57.

A noble undertaking, indeed, but it will not happen before the 21st century. The challenge associated with building a better system of official statistics for the coming century will be to assist the former Soviet bloc countries and the developing nations in implementing new concepts and procedures more in tune with future needs. *It would be a missed opportunity if these countries simply adopted outmoded systems of the market-economy countries.*

As noted above, industry, trade, technical, and professional groups in the U.S. and around the world generate a wealth of data in areas of interest to their membership. These nonprofit organizations, like public agencies, can take on a bureaucratic role as the staff sees and seizes an opportunity and runs with it, at times without the consent of the "governed." It is not unusual to have some turmoil about the directions that an association should take.[25]

In our judgment, there are vast differences in both the quantity and the quality of the data among the various associations. *Business economists and managers need to analyze the publications, the integrity, accuracy, timeliness, and coverage of their data—just as they would for data issued by government, the private sector, and universities.* As a general rule, we find that associations that conduct ongoing surveys, with updates as needed, do a better job on data collection and data processing than those that do ad hoc or one-time studies. For example, the Association of Data Processing Service Organizations—ADAPSO, which was recently incorporated into the Information Technology Association of America—has done a fine job of collecting statistics for years from its membership (a membership drawn from computer service firms from all parts of the United States). In the pollution control field, the Water and Wastewater Equipment Manufacturers Association maintained good directories with indices, but did little data collection, leaving the task to others, such as the federal Environmental Protection Agency and another nonprofit group, the Water Pollution Control Federation.

Professional and technical groups generate some statistics, but these associations are organized much more along occupations and special interests than along industrial lines. This can be an advantage for the business researcher if the focus is on technology, which cuts across sev-

---

[25]For a good overview and running commentary on this topic, see various issues of *Association Management.*

eral industrial lines. Engineering societies maintain special interest groups (SIGs) that often generate useful statistics. Other groups publish the results of their meetings. For example, the *Chemical Market Research Association Proceedings* (annual) are for sale and constitute a treasure trove on subfields of the chemical industry. The European Society for Opinion and Market Research (ESOMAR) sponsors both an annual congress and special seminars whose *Proceedings* are available for a fee. Many other examples could be cited, but the important point is that statistics about industrial and technological trends are available from a rich set of institutions.

Think tanks, university research bureaus, scientific institutes, and foundations represent yet another source of statistical data. Various directories, such as the *Research Center Directory,* offer subject indices for the alphabetic or geographic listing of such organizations. This way, one can ascertain quickly the expertise offered. A simple phone call or fax will bring a reply as to available publications and data. For example, the Aviation Safety Institute in Columbus, Ohio, has become an independent and well-respected voice in its field, beholden neither to industry nor to government. Universities on the West Coast specialize in having excellent data on Pacific Rim nations, while those on the East Coast have developed repositories about European countries. Foreign emissaries and consulates are also willing to share data; for example, the European Union and the OECD maintain information offices in Washington, DC.

How and Where Statistics Are Generated

Quantitative information is still largely produced in traditional ways: via surveys, through observations, and occasionally from experiments. In the late 20th century and into the 21st century, data will be increasingly collected in an unobtrusive fashion—especially if safeguards for privacy and confidentiality can be provided. The Universal Product Code has made it possible for many firms to track shipments, sales, and retail outlet behavior through analysis of scanner data collected using the UPC codes printed on or attached to packages and documents. Of course, millions of transactions are already routinely recorded as a result of purchases, or even lack of purchases (e.g., a company may determine that 40 percent of their long-time clients did not place an order this past month).

"The ability to collect and analyze information about individuals is about to increase exponentially."[26] Information highways, electronic payment systems, smart buildings, and a host of sensors will ease the task of individuals but at the same time provide "grist" for the "data mill" or databases of commercial, public, or nonprofit organizations. On the positive side, the marvels of the computer-communication age will allow collection of data on millions of individuals and thousands of enterprises. On the negative side, there may be objections to close monitoring and to the sharing of data by and among the data collecting agencies. For example, several new regulations are being proposed to protect individuals from errors in their files at credit agencies. However, it should be noted that the power of the computer to increase record-keeping efficiency will as a natural by-product lead to the development of useful databases for the corporate decision maker.

As mentioned earlier, U.S. and foreign governments conduct censuses on a regular basis. The mandate to the U.S. Bureau of the Census is to conduct a decennial census of population. It also surveys businesses—including manufacturing and minerals, services, construction, retail and wholesale trade, and transportation—every five years. Other governments do much the same, such as Statistics Canada conducting its population count in years ending with 1 and also surveying Canadian industries on a regular basis. Given the high level of controversy and legal wrangle about the 1990 U.S. Census of Population, it is quite possible that the Bureau of the Census may yet turn to alternative modes of data collection; electronic filing by respondents may replace census enumerators knocking on doors. An extensive literature is being developed on alternative procedures for the census to be taken in the year 2000.

The collection, processing, and dissemination of the data in both the public and private sectors may undergo radical changes. The next section of this chapter will provide some examples of change in the area of dissemination. For example, all levels of government are dedicated to easing traffic congestion. Necessary data can now be collected via observation posts and sensors rather than asking truckers and motorists to fill out survey forms. Data banks are also being created across interstate lines on crime, weather, welfare, solid waste disposal, electric power use,

---

[26]"No Hiding Place," *Economist,* August 7, 1993, p. 16.

and so on. The challenge will be either to devise representative samples or to conduct censuses in an unobtrusive fashion.

There is also extensive literature[27] concerning the use of administrative records in the development of official statistics.[28, 29] In the private sector, credit card transactions serve as the focal point for data collection and analysis. In addition, supermarkets, drugstores, and many other large retail operations routinely collect data via optical scanning of the Universal Product Code. This is useful, but when combined with a consumer identification tag, a powerful marketing tool is born. A. C. Nielsen and other companies are using this combination to build databases about shopping habits to evaluate promotional campaigns and analyze shoppers, including those who bought and those who did not buy a product. While unobtrusive, this raises privacy issues, so cooperation via signed release forms is normally arranged beforehand, and participants in panels are often rewarded for their cooperation.

Surveys will have to be rethought, whether one-time or repetitive. The era of digital television with interactive capabilities is around the corner. Within a few years, such capabilities will be in the majority of homes. Digital television (or computer screens) in homes will be driven by games and video entertainment, but home information services will be a by-product. As a consequence, it is likely that statistical services, market research, and nonprofit groups will begin to establish ongoing but rather brief electronic survey forms for participants (print will be an option). In other words, the questionnaire will be flashed on a computer on an interactive television screen, and the respondent will be asked to enter numbers or check boxes. To make this easy on survey participants, the forms will be relatively brief because the panel characteristics will be in a related master database.[30] New questions can be added, old ones

---

[27]The bibliographic review conducted as background for this study has referenced a number of papers and reports on this topic.

[28]See William P. Butz, "The Future of Administrative Records in the Census Bureau's Demographic Activities," *Journal of Business and Economic Statistics,* Vol. 3, Iss. 4, 1985, pp. 393–395.

[29]See also Thomas B. Jabine and Frederick J. Scheuren, "Goals for Statistical Uses of Administrative Records: The Next Ten Years," in *Proceedings of the American Statistical Association,* Section on Survey Research Methods, 1984 Annual Meeting (August 13–16, 1984, Philadelphia, PA). Washington, DC: American Statistical Association, 1985, pp. 66–75.

[30]Some particularly innovative experiments on this concept have been conducted in The Netherlands.

can be dropped, but some continuity will be maintained for longitudinal comparisons. In the meantime, electronic data interchange (EDI) is gaining momentum. This requires common concepts and definitions with a common reporting format being a natural by-product. Most recently, several foundations in the New York and Philadelphia areas agreed to have a single format for grant applications. This trend is likely to spread.

Data Availability: Formats, Time Lag, Prices

The traditional output format of statistical agencies, be they large or small, public or private, has been printed matter. The U.S. government has produced massive volumes of data from the various censuses and surveys; central statistical agencies also opted for books, reports, and monographs. In the private sector, we find yearbooks, occasional reports, and so on in printed form as well. The time delay on these has varied tremendously. Some census reports are available in preliminary form in a matter of months; but it is fair to say that the final volumes often come with a lag of several years. Trade associations, institutes, and other organizations also can vary in making their survey results available in time frames ranging from one month to one year.

The move away from print is caused by the revolution in on-line and CD-ROM format. Databases became available electronically toward the end of the 1970s and early 1980s, but the growth has been especially sharp in the past 10 years. This is due largely to the advent of the personal computer, the lowered cost of telecommunications, and the resulting linking of terminals into networks. Organizations and individuals now have easy access to vast storehouses of data in a variety of formats and locations.

Figure 17 shows the recent trends in U.S. databases by producer status and by format. The role of the private sector grew, and the role of the public sector declined from 1985 to 1992. (This is in line with what has been cited above, namely, that budget and staff of the eight major statistical agencies were reduced by about 13 percent and 10 percent, respectively, during the 1980–88 period.) Much of the rise of the private sector can be attributed to aggressive marketing on the part of database vendors, such as Dialog, Mead Data Central, Reuters, and others. Now, government agencies are also taking a more aggressive stance. Both U.S. statistical agencies and Statistics Canada are actively marketing computer tapes, laser disks, diskettes, and CD-ROM, as well as mak-

FIGURE 17
Growth of Databases, On-line Services, and Subscribers in the U.S., 1980–1990

	1980	1982	1984	1986	1988	1990
Number of Databases[a]	400	965	1,878	2,901	3,699	4,465
Number of Database Producers[b]	221	512	927	1,379	1,685	1,950
Number of On-Line Services[c]	59	170	272	454	555	645
Number of Gateways[d]				35	59	88
Number of Subscribers (thousands)						
General Interest			326.1	677.0	1,018.6	
Business/Financial			377.1	558.6	726.6	
Scientific/Technical			229.2	345.8	404.5	

[a]Databases: Computer-readable collections of data available for interactive access by users from remote terminals or microcomputers. Databases can be "reference" (bibliographic or referral) or "source" (numeric, textual, numeric-textual, full-text, etc.).
[b]Database producers: Suppliers of databases, primarily publishers of print indexes and abstracts journals, but also publishers of other reports who transform and submit the data on magnetic tape to on-line vendors.
[c]On-line services or vendors: Time-sharing firms, network information services, remote computing services, etc., who provide access to databases.
[d]Gateways: Any computer service that acts as an intermediary between users and databases; several categories exist.

Sources: Lines 1–4: *Directory of On-Line Databases,* 1991. New York: Cuadra/Elsevier, 1991, p. v.; Lines 5–7: *Information Industry Factbook 89/90.* Stamford, CT: Digital Information Group, 1989, p. 229.

ing data available on-line. Statistics Canada has designed an easy-to-use volume called *The Market Research Handbook.*

These and similar steps show that government agencies are becoming user-friendly by offering their data in new and more usable formats. The most popular form for electronic retrieval is on-line, according to Figure 15. Many industrial enterprises can be expected to follow the lead of college and public libraries and acquire CD-ROM readers for their small computers (or for their information centers). Thus, CD-ROM should gain market share from on-line in the future. Here again, public agencies show some initiative; for example, the U.S. Department of Commerce's National Trade Data Bank now comes on a compact disc rather than as a lengthy printout or book. The U.S. Department of Commerce's Bureau of the Census and Bureau of Economic Analysis and the U.S. Department of Labor's Bureau of Labor Statistics offer delivery via magnetic tape, diskettes, CD-ROM, microfiche, and electronic news services.

Our experience with electronic format indicates that the time lag in publishing is far less than for the printed format. In many cases, private-sector firms and nonprofit institutions make their data available in a matter of several days or a few weeks at the most. Data from Conference Board surveys, the University of Michigan Survey Research Center's Surveys of Consumers, and the Purchasing Managers Monthly Survey are examples.[31] Typically, in the 1990s, a study can be conducted on a topic by an agency or association, and results are expected to reach all users within a few weeks. For example, shipment data obtained in a survey of machine tool manufacturers conducted by an association in the month of May is tabulated in June, and findings are reported in an article in the July 1993 issue of *Machine Design*. The abstract of the article, complete with key tables, is available to on-line users by mid-August and to CD-ROM users in September.

Some would argue that the print format is still out first. This is true, but there is a tremendous advantage to the electronic form. It affords a concise view of the data and the literature, provides a comparison with other surveys, and therefore gives a better perspective. Furthermore, in some cases the survey may not even appear in print format; it may be made available to users only on-line, on diskette, or on CD-ROM.

Although the CD-ROM format is gaining in popularity (under such names as Wilsondisc or Silver Platter), on-line remains more popular because it allows a broader access to giant databases stored in vast information warehouse files.[32] The rapid rise of databases, on-line services, and subscribers in the United States is documented for the 1980s in Figure 17. Further growth is expected. Subscribing to an on-line service is relatively simple. All the user needs is a personal computer, a modem, a phone line, and a contract. It is more difficult to choose among the many offerings and to devise an effective search strategy. Thousands of

---

[31]Indeed, as early as the late 1970s, Predicasts of Cleveland abstracted thousands of articles and tables, transferred the information to magnetic tape, and shipped them via air to Dialog of Palo Alto, which then made the abstracts available on-line. Approximate elapsed time from abstract to on-line availability was less than two weeks. By now, this has been cut in half, though there can be processing delays.

[32]For an early overview on this topic, see Andrew Gross, "The Information Vending Machine," *Business Horizons,* January/February 1988, pp. 24–33.

databases are available from hundreds of on-line firms, but not all data-bases are available from all on-line suppliers. Users must shop around. The producers of databases (e.g., Wilson for BPI, Predicasts for PTS) sell their output to the on-line services, such as Dialog, Reuters, and BRS. The most comprehensive listing currently is the *Gale Directory of Databases*,[33] which combines previous publications.

Selected Key Issues

Statistical producers should keep in mind users' needs. What are users' needs, and what can the users do to keep the producers on their toes and to get the best value from the output—the statistical system, the time series, the individual data points? To say: *caveat emptor* or *caveat vendidor* (let the buyer beware, let the seller beware) is a cop-out or a cliché. Better to say: Let both users and producers be alert, aware, and awake!

Alert and awake to what? To one another's characteristics! Users, as discussed earlier, must define or at least describe their activities, needs, desires, and preferences in rather distinct ways if they want producers to be responsive. *As a general rule, users want extensive coverage; ease of access; timeliness, not time delays; accuracy (validity, reliability); clear-cut methodology (consistency and continuity); and integrity of both the data and the source. When the producers of data keep these requisites in mind, the result should be strong demand for the figures.*

Coverage of a statistical system or database will be defined by its owner or producer—or, as we saw in the case of governments, it may well be mandated. As internal and external conditions change, however, the coverage is likely to be altered to adjust to the new situation. This is fine, but it is necessary for the producers to explain the new, and link up the new concepts with the old. Tables should highlight both the new format and the linkage to the previous set of data.

For example, the Federal Reserve Board recently revised its industrial production indices and capacity utilization figures. The coverage is similar to that of the past, basically covering U.S. manufacturing. The specific linkage with previous indices should be made clear, not hidden in footnotes. Similar rules would apply to other government agencies and

---

[33]Gale Research, Detroit, July 1993.

private-sector firms as well as to nonprofit associations. Of course, definitions can be a challenge and can affect coverage. For example, what is a computer—a mainframe, a midsize machine, a desktop unit, a portable device, or even a smart terminal? Technology does not wait (e.g., notebook computers and personal message pads), but the data gatherer must make a decision, then live by it and explain it.

Ease of access implies availability in the various formats, both print and electronic, discussed above. Ease of access, just as importantly, implies good indexing, possible use of a thesaurus, an excellent table of contents, friendly face graphics, and making the data "jump" at the user. Again, linkage with previous sets of numbers would be useful, along with methodological explanations in clear terms. On the matter of how to present statistical data, the discussion in the next section provides some suggestions. Finally, the producer should make itself accessible to users by publishing phone and fax numbers. Inquiries should be answered as promptly as possible.

Time delays in releasing data along with format and pricing were discussed in the previous section. Since the release of federal statistics is closely followed, users are now wedded to specific dates. Some reporters stand by and rush to call in the released data for next-day publication or same-day evening news on radio and television. Of course, major undertakings are often released piecemeal fashion and often require subsequent revisions, as is the case with data from the Census of Population, other censuses, or GDP estimates.

Statistics from businesses and associations are also expected on time; but, again, some delays or revisions are inevitable. In the words of the *Economist,* "By themselves, revisions are a poor gauge of statistical accuracy. If a country did not bother to revise its figures or if it delayed publication for a year until all the detailed information was in, it would have no revisions, but its statistics would be poor."[34]

As systems are designed for future decision making, the subject of accuracy should get the recognition it deserves. Once again, reference is made to the pioneer in this field, Oskar Morgenstern, in his book, *On the Accuracy of Economic Observations.*[35] Other famous economists,

---

[34]*Economist,* Sept. 7, 1991, p. 88.

[35]Oskar Morgenstern, *On the Accuracy of Economic Observations.* 2nd ed. Princeton, NJ: Princeton University Press, 1963.

such as Kendrick, Kuznets, et al., also made significant contributions. In the 1950s and 1960s, economics was truly a one-digit science, though few would admit to that. Later, as collection and processing methods became more refined, the situation improved. Even today, errors are in the range of +20 percent for developing nations and +5 percent to +10 percent for developed nations (with refinement upon revision). Causes of statistical error include poorly trained poll takers, ambiguous survey forms, misguided classification schemes, deliberate misinformation by respondents, evasion of regulators, and nonresponse.

Past data are one thing; forecasts are another. Economic and business forecasting will continue because there is much demand for it. A wide variety of qualitative and quantitative techniques are discussed in various business research, marketing,[36] and forecasting texts. In the volume written by coauthor Gross, it is stated that the best route to follow is to do composite or combination forecasting—because it considers many sources and combines the best features of qualitative and quantitative techniques. The Blue Chip indicators' track record previously cited is another testimonial endorsing this thinking. The fearless forecaster has yet another tool; that is, to combine the notion of the buildup and the breakdown method. The former calls for combining shipments of all producers; the latter means ratio analysis from GDP on downward.

For purposes here, the most interest centers on the track record of intergovernmental and international agencies and national government agencies in this regard. Figure 18 shows an interesting comparison of OECD and IMF forecast errors. The authors who analyzed these errors,[37] from Indiana University and the Canadian Bank of Commerce, conclude that while in the 1970s there was an optimism bias, in the 1980s this bias disappeared, which is encouraging. Most significantly, they conclude that there is no evidence that the published forecasts of the international organizations are superior to the national forecasts. Partly because of this and partly because some parties gain early access to confidential information, they suggest that the IMF and OECD, et al., refrain from forecasting.

---

[36]Andrew Gross, et al., *Business Marketing*. Boston: Houghton Mifflin, 1993, pp. 163–173.

[37]See M. Fratianni and J. Pattison, "International Institutions and the Market for Information," in *The Political Economy of International Organizations*, R. Vaubel and T. Willet, eds. Boulder, CO: Westview Press, 1991, pp. 100–122.

FIGURE 18
OECD and IMF Forecast Errors

Forecast Error When Forecast Was Made in the First Half of the Current Year

Mean Absolute Error

	Real GNP Growth		Inflation %		Current-Account Balance (billions of dollars)	
	OECD	IMF	OECD (Consumption deflator)	IMF	OECD	IMF
U.S.	0.54	0.83	0.26	0.51	11.44	16.21
Japan	0.71	0.56	0.43	0.79	5.81	6.58
Germany	0.91	1.05	0.39	0.28	4.42	5.18
France	0.62	0.47	0.46	0.63	2.76	3.11
U.K.	0.46	0.79	0.78	0.86	3.17	2.15
Italy	0.82	0.84	0.69	0.54	2.44	2.57
Canada	1.19	1.32	0.53	0.87	2.51	3.68
G7	0.75	0.83	0.51	0.64	4.65	5.64

Root Mean Square Error

	Real GNP Growth		Inflation %		Current-Account Balance (billions of dollars)	
	OECD	IMF	OECD	IMF	OECD	IMF
U.S.	0.54	0.83	0.26	0.51	11.44	16.21
Japan	0.71	0.56	0.43	0.79	5.81	6.58
Germany	0.91	1.05	0.39	0.28	4.42	5.18
France	0.62	0.47	0.46	0.63	2.76	3.11
U.K.	0.46	0.79	0.78	0.86	3.17	2.15
Italy	0.82	0.84	0.69	0.54	2.44	2.57
Canada	1.19	1.32	0.53	0.87	2.51	3.68
G7	0.75	0.83	0.51	0.64	4.65	5.64

Sources: OECD *Economic Outlook*, various issues; *World Economic Outlook*, IMF, various issues. Quoted in M. Fratianni & J. Pattison, "International Institutions and the Market for Information" in *The Political Economy of International Organizations*, R. Vaubel and T. Willett, eds. Boulder, CO: Westview Press, 1991, pp. 100–122.

Sound statistical methodology involves more than having extensive coverage, more than being on time, and more than trying to be accurate. At the most fundamental level, the key facets focus on integrity, consistency, and continuity. One final word here is warranted in regard to the boundary between accuracy and integrity on the one hand, and dissemination and presentation on the other. The business users, like the public at large, tend to be skeptical, and the notion of lies, damn lies, and statistics is hard to overturn.[38] One of the best ways to reassure clients is for producers of the data to make modest claims.

Producers must observe confidentiality and security. How can the producers assure those who cooperate with them that privacy and secrecy will not be violated? This is also a matter of trust, confidentiality, and collaboration. After all, government agencies, private-sector firms, and associations ultimately rely on the goodwill of various respondents, be they in the hundreds or in the millions. Sound public relations can help, but it is even more important to assure and reassure the participants that confidentiality and privacy will be strictly observed.

As more information ends up in government and corporate databases, a line must be drawn between a public or private organization's need to know and individuals' (and groups') right to privacy. Recently, Professor H. J. Smith of Georgetown University advanced the idea of the following "audit points" in regard to privacy:[39]

1. Scrutinize the sensitivity of personal data being collected. (Is it needed? Could it be obtained otherwise? etc.)
2. Avoid deception—claiming to collect data for one purpose, using it for another as well as secrecy—and collecting data by hidden means.
3. Secure the subject's permission.
4. Values and judgment play a key role in ensuring data integrity; make decisions about error levels in an explicit fashion.
5. Establish strong organizational controls.
6. Beware of automation, including automated decisions, sensors, and so on. In regard to this last point, there is merit in using anonymous procedures as opposed to those that identify indi-

---

[38]D. Huff, *How to Lie with Statistics.* New York: W. W. Norton, 1954 and W. Wallis and H. Roberts, *The Nature of Statistics.* New York: Free Press, 1956. Both enjoyed good publicity when they were published and were reprinted later in paperback editions. Their warnings are worth reading and heeding.

[39]H. J. Smith, "A Matter of Privacy," *Beyond Computing,* July/August 1993, pp. 62–63.

viduals (e.g., auditrons or keycards, rather than charge or credit cards).

This section focused on the production and the producers of statistics and statistical systems. Although these cannot be separated entirely from the underlying data, the section attempted to highlight what *is* (including what is right and what is wrong) and what *ought to be* in bringing forth the wealth of numbers and in making the output available. Producers and users must and do live together in a close relationship. As noted much earlier, producers at times become users and vice versa. On the whole, the production of statistics has occurred at a high level, though there is room for improvement.

SECTION 3—COLLECTION, PRESENTATION, AND DISSEMINATION OF STATISTICS

This section focuses on the most practical aspects of data processing: How do you collect the numbers, how do you present them, and how do you deliver them to audiences? These topics have been touched upon in other chapters, and we do not wish to compete with established textbooks in the field. The remarks here are aimed at both the practicing statisticians and business economists, to whom these may sound rather familiar, and at those who "toil in the trenches" in the form of statisticians, analysts, economists, strategists, and others who rely upon statistical input.

The thrust of these remarks can be summarized as follows:

1. Yes, censuses can be useful and at times are mandated, but consider sampling as a realistic alternative at most times and under many conditions.
2. Presentation of statistics involves several diverse facets. All are important: substantive, statistical, and artistic (graphical).
3. Dissemination must consider the publicity needs of the producer group less and the preferences of users and audiences more.

Permeating all of the above is modern technology, which holds out rich promises, and, in some cases, already delivers better sampling, clearer and more exciting presentation, and user-friendly distribution.

Collection of Data

"What do we know and what do we want to know? The two most fundamental concepts of statistics are those of a sample and a population." So begins chapter 5 of one of the classic volumes on statistics, though it was seldom used as a textbook.[40] The authors restate the obvious: A sample is not a miniature replica of the population; sample results vary by chance; and the pattern of chance variation depends on the underlying population. So why would anyone want to sample if a complete count can be obtained? There are good reasons for sampling when:

1. Complete count is impossible or impractical.
2. Gain in accuracy from a census may not be worth the cost.
3. Individual measurements may not be as accurate for a census as for a sample.
4. Underlying population or universe contains infinitely many items.
5. Population is inaccessible and no more data can be had from it.

The authors give examples and useful details. For the discussion here, point number 3 is worth elaborating, because the point is so applicable to official or government statistics. In the words of Wallis and Roberts:

> A rather paradoxical example of the effective use of samples is the Bureau of Census' use of them to check on the accuracy of the census. Although sampling error is almost absent from the census, the non-sampling errors may be considerable; that is, such errors as those arising from failure to make questions clearly understood, from misrecording replies, from faulty tabulation, from omitting people who should have [been] interviewed. In the sample census {sic}, however, these non-sampling errors may be reduced enough to offset the sampling error, for it is cheaper and easier to select, train, and supervise a few hundred well-qualified interviewers to conduct a few thousand careful interviews than it is to select, train, and supervise 150,000 interviewers to conduct a complete census of population.[41]

The authors then go on to explain why, in the light of the above, nationwide censuses are still taken. The overriding reason mentioned by them (and in a previous chapter) is the mandate of the Constitution;

---

[40]W. A. Wallis and H. V. Roberts, *The Nature of Statistics*. New York: The Free Press, 1956.

[41]Ibid., p. 138.

another is that information is often required for small groups in a large population—small towns, ethnic neighborhoods, and so on—as well as for the country as a whole.

What is true for government agencies is also applicable to private firms and to nonprofit groups. Companies must rethink whether it is necessary to poll every employee, vendor, or client when a sample would do. In the same way, associations need to ask whether a well-designed sample would serve as well. Certainly, few legal requirements exist in this area. The frequency of census or sample taking requires careful consideration as well.

Presentation of Data

The wide range of statistics that are useful for decision making is evident in the number of regular publications on the shelves of planners, analysts, and decision makers. In the past, the traditional form of presentation has been tables and text in the print media. Government censuses arrive in massive reports (hardbound or paperback), though early results are promulgated in brochures and flyers. Corporate statistics come in the form of annual and quarterly reports, news releases, and the like. These are the primary forms, while the secondary forms consist of a wealth of tables and text in journals and newspapers. Finally, the tertiary forms, indices and abstracts, give us an overview and access to the above.

These traditional forms (both their content and their style) changed relatively little until the arrival of the information age. By the 1990s, as we saw earlier, the producers of data have committed themselves to the electronic era. Today, central statistical agencies make available data to users in the form of magnetic tape for mainframes, diskettes for personal computers, on-line, and CD-ROM (compact disc). Statistics from companies are becoming available in the same way, plus, on occasion, in the form of slides, videotape, and even multimedia.

On-demand or automated delivery is also possible. It is possible to download data from large to small computers and to do desktop publishing incorporating public or private data from a variety of databases. Business data are being increasingly presented on television news, especially on such shows as the "Nightly Business Report" and the business newscasts of CNN.

Proper presentation of statistics requires attention to the media through which the figures are likely to be promulgated. Also, there are additional, equally important questions to be answered: What is or should be presented to what kind(s) of audiences(s)? How can we convey the message best? The first consideration is the actual content, the substance of the topic: Is it GDP or price indices? Is it an employment times series or a single pie chart on market share? The next question is: What is the appropriate way to deliver this set of data—tables or charts, print or electronic or both? Finally, there is an artistic element in the presentation.

We relied on several books in regard to the above points, but two have proved particularly helpful: Tufte's well-known *The Visual Display of Quantitative Information,*[42] and G. Zelazny's book, *Say It With Charts.*[43] Tufte, a Yale professor and consultant to the Bureau of the Census and large companies, has been called the guru of the information design movement. Zelazny is director of Visual Communication for McKinsey & Company. Both writers consider graphic communication crucial, and both hold the view that information is best conveyed without clutter.

In a more recent book and in an interview article, Tufte expounds on his ideas as to what constitutes good graphics and good design. He is emphasizing "ease of understanding."[44] In the words of yet another specialist, Alan Siegel, "People have the right to clarity in what they read" (quoted in "The War on Information Clutter," *Business Week,* April 29, 1991, p. 66). Still other experts are R. Wurman and N. Holmes, who create pictorial maps and infographics for popular books and magazines, as well as for organizations.

What Tufte, Zelazny, and others have done is to restate D. Huff's classic volume, *How to Lie with Statistics,*[45] except their thrust is not how to lie but how to live with (and even how to enjoy) statistics. The field of graphic design or information design has come a long way since Huff's book. Graphs and charts are being refined in layout, plotting, and overall character, while clutter and confusion are being eliminated. Simplification and removal of unnecessary elements are favored over complexity; the goal is to convey comprehension and "make every mark on

---

[42]Edward Tufte, *The Visual Display of Quantitative Information.* Cheshire, CT: Graphics Press, 1983.

[43]G. Zelazny, *Say it With Charts.* Homewood, IL: Business One/Irwin, 1991.

[44]See E. Tufte, *Envisioning Information.* Cheshire, CT: Graphics Press, 1991; and P. Patton, "Up from Flatland," *The New York Times Magazine,* January 19, 1992, pp. 29–31.

[45]D. Huff, *How to Lie with Statistics.* New York: W. W. Norton, 1954.

the page carry a meaning." Otherwise, there is no sense in going from text and tables to charts and figures. Excellent small charts can be seen in an increasing number of reports and presentations as a result of the easy-to-use graphic display packages available for desktop computers. These are precisely drawn, yet do not overwhelm; they are easy to recall, hard to forget. Indeed, they are what is called *presentation graphics*.

In today's world, one must move from the printed to other media. An in-between domain is that of slides. They are not the printed page, but they are not yet video or computer creations either. Of course, with cheaper computing power today, we are well beyond slides and into computer graphics, videotapes, and charts, even on mass media network, local, and cable television. On-line and CD-ROM formats allow featuring tables, but they are not as yet comfortable with charts and figures. Personal computers can convey graphic information quite well, with a high degree of resolution. Color is becoming almost standard both on the screen and even in printouts. Animation can be achieved in a multimedia mode. The whole area of graphics on computer screens is evolving toward more sophistication. At the same time, some graphic artists think that statistics are still best presented in print media.

The most volatile and youngest medium for statistics is television. We see graphs and charts on the news, in the political commentary or even talk shows and, of course, often on business reporting. The same rules still apply, however; indeed, even more so, because we are dealing with a moving medium. Thus, the message by definition goes by more quickly; the medium demands charts and figures that are "gee whiz." And that is both the beauty and the danger. The graphs must communicate instantly to the viewer, and only two or three points can be highlighted at the most. Line charts and simple pie and bar charts work better than complex histograms or scatter diagrams. In recent years, some cable shows are devoting more time to business news, and hence to statistical charts, with the result that an expanding audience for sophisticated graphic data presentation brings even greater demands for more accurate and timely statistics.

Dissemination (Delivery/Distribution)

How do the producers of statistics deliver their output to users? We have discussed possible formats above, but we need to do more. Audiences for data (and for the analyzed version of data; that is, information) need to be identified. After this is accomplished, the needs and preferences of users should be highlighted, including whether their favored mode for delivery is print or electronic, on-line or CD-ROM, tabular or graphical. As a general rule, we find good correlation between urgency of need and speed of delivery. In other words: Those who need statistics or information in a hurry should be and often are willing to pay for it. They need it here and now—fast! Those whose need is less pressing can and will depend on the above factors but also on prices charged (which for certain electronic media tend to drop over time, although some are high or on the rise).

As Figure 13 shows, military and medical personnel demand instant data and usually get it. In the heat of the battle and in the operating room, every second counts. In the business world, it is the realm of financial transactions that require split-second execution: deposits, withdrawals, credit checks, currency fluctuations, and exchanges. The demand for data may come from a vice president of finance or from a junior assistant executing the transaction. The next level is that of managerial, sales, and accounting personnel who need up-to-date information on their own organization, the industry (e.g., most recent competitive price changes), and the economy (e.g., producer price index changes). To get the latest, the manager—who also nowadays doubles as a researcher—may go on-line, spin a compact disc (the CD-ROM format), engage in teleconferencing, or get on the fax or phone to a distant source. Finally, in terms of in-depth, historical analysis, the business economist or market researcher may settle into the corporate information center, a college library, or the district field office of the U.S. Department of Commerce. A retrospective search may call for weeks of work, possibly in dusty archives, but this is yielding to databases that offer detailed historical data.

There is yet another audience: the citizens at large, voters, intelligent laypersons, millions eager to hear the latest unemployment figures or consumer price index changes. This is also true for a wide variety of businesspeople and for many small organizations who cannot afford a corporate information center. They will be listening to radio and television news and to special business reports. The networks, cable operators, and local stations want the data, usually in compact form, as easy-to-view tables and graphs.

What do the above remarks imply for producers, especially for generators of federal (official/government) statistics and for producers of corporate and association data? The first requirement is that the news be newsworthy. There is little doubt that a sufficient number of individuals and organizations are interested in the latest economic data, especially the key indicators (see tabulation earlier in this chapter). Beyond that, however, the releasing bureau must make a decision: How newsworthy is this set of numbers? Who is likely to ask for it, in what format, and under what conditions?

Answers to the above questions need to be thought through, for they will affect the mode of delivery (most likely, more than one format), the speed of delivery, and the prices charged. All three sectors—government, business, nonprofits—are leaning toward charging enough to cover costs, although there are currently complicated debates about what costs should be covered and how the income will fit into the overall governmental budget. Prices charged for some popular and useful volumes are on the rise. Businesses still send out annual reports gratis, but some enterprising firms or intermediaries are starting to charge for them. More valuable publications, such as the *National Trade Data Bank* (in CD-ROM format, from the U.S. Department of Commerce) or membership rosters, command much higher prices.

Beyond the audiences cited above, there are some special situations. Thus, for example, the U.S. Bureau of the Census interacts with high-profile or high-volume users of census data. In the business realm, a company may have a panel known as a user group, key accounts, or lead users. They may get information ahead of other groups. Many public and university libraries are depositories for government documents and may act as clearinghouses for certain associations in the realm of cyberspace, the interactive users who log on to America Online, CompuServe, Delphi, Genie, Prodigy, and others, and the academics who participate in Internet and other electronic networks develop into data experts who have special capabilities in their fields of interest.

Many details remain to be worked out, but automation and user fees are likely to be key features considered in the design of statistical programs for the 21st century. On-line charges are made on the basis of time used, interconnect fees, and number of "hits" achieved; CD-ROM format may also carry metering devices or sensors, with charges billed automatically when users request the "key" to release and use selected series. Versatility and flexibility will be crucial for both producers and users.

The age of multimedia and information highways is around the corner. Countless articles have appeared on the topic in the popular, business, and technical press. The notion has even been a popular topic of conversation on television and radio shows, in government buildings, and in company corridors. For the producers of statistics, what this age portends is an opportunity to disperse, share, and in some cases sell (at a handsome profit) their output. They will have to think of all the possible venues, formats, and outlets that should be approached as enumerated above. Today, statistics are widely available in print and electronic format. Tomorrow, multislide shows, videotapes, user-profile faxes, and messages beamed without wires will be the rule.

Users, however, will not want all the information, only the best. So what the producers of statistics may have to do is go beyond data and get into information. Information is data or statistics with added value through analysis, interpretation, and evaluation.

It is also possible that artificial intelligence, specifically expert systems, will take over some of this assignment. They will assess the incoming data and then dovetail the bits and pieces into a meaningful picture. The results will then be displayed on a portable computer, electronic staff aid device, or message pad. For example, several sources may have estimated the production of organic chemicals in Scandinavia, both past and forecasted. These numbers could then be brought together and displayed. The expert system may even provide an annotation as to whose numbers proved to be correct in the past. Finally, an analysis will be made contrasting such data with capacity utilization and competitors' activities, thereby providing further insights for the decision maker, whose decision will become new grist for the mill. Then, as new numbers are entered, the whole system is enriched and the process starts over again, a journey without an end.

We expect that in the new electronic age, many situations will arise that will call for collaborative schemes or alliances among participants. The competitive spirit will also remain strong; there will be room for large and small entrepreneurial-oriented organizations. Each situation will mean a new assessment on how to proceed. We expect, however, that a strong public-private-nonprofit interface will come into being.

CONCLUSION

This chapter has reviewed the manner of data collection (census vs. sampling), the presentation (the notion of graphic or information design), and the dissemination of the statistics (manner of delivery or distribution).

There is much progress, much flux in each area. The coming years will see even more diverse, distinct activities.

This chapter has also noted the relationship among users, producers, and disseminators of statistical information as they interact with rapidly changing technology for collection, analysis, and distribution of statistics. There is a growing public interest in statistical information, and the demands of decision makers are likely to become more sophisticated. These trends certainly support the view that the time is ripe for rebuilding the statistical structure for the future that in many ways is already here.

CHAPTER 4

SOCIAL STATISTICS, INCLUDING A CASE STUDY OF HEALTH CARE STATISTICS

INTRODUCTION

This book is focused on economic statistics. Yet, even that focus draws the authors to social statistics, since much of economic activity is based on population dynamics; on basic demographic information such as family composition and family income; and on individual characteristics such as health status, educational attainment, and labor force participation. Though each of these social measurements and indicators merits book-length treatment in its own right, this chapter takes a broad look at the subject.

First, the subject of health statistics is introduced to underscore the importance of developing a comprehensive approach to social measurement, especially now that public policy is seeking to achieve major reform in this area. During the political campaign of 1992, health care was moved to the center of the social policy agenda, and at the time this book is written, the policy debate is still evolving.

Second, we examine the foundation and periodic benchmark of most social statistics, the decennial census. The discussion in this chapter is an introduction to some of the critical issues that must be addressed in the second half of the 1990s as methodological preparations are made for the Year 2000 Census. There is extensive literature on this subject; our intent in this chapter is to frame some of the key decisions that lie ahead.

Finally, we examine education statistics. Education reform has been a major public concern for nearly two decades, yet much confusion remains, and a number of critical adjustments to education statistics must be made in the years ahead.

The next chapter deals with an intermediate area: statistics about energy and the environment. In that chapter, we consider the scientific measurements that are made, the economic and social dimensions of the field, and the need for a better statistical framework for international policy making.

HEALTH STATISTICS—A CASE STUDY IN STATISTICAL NEEDS FOR PUBLIC POLICY

Introduction

Health care statistics are an interesting example of the ways in which data can be and are used in the formulation of national policy for several reasons. First, the question of national health care reform has been much in the news since the 1992 presidential campaign. The Clinton administration began with First Lady Hillary Rodham Clinton heading a task force to tackle this complex set of issues. Second, the statistics that describe the nation's health, health care, and access to health care are intrinsically complex, especially when analysts are interested in generating numbers that show real causal connections. And third, recent revolutionary improvements in health technology, coupled with demographic shifts, have made the challenge of health measurement more daunting and complex than ever.

Overview: The Challenge

What is clear at the outset is that currently available health statistics do not answer the most important questions about the American health care system. They do help in posing those questions with an especially sharp focus. Readily available health care statistics show that American spending on health care has skyrocketed over recent decades, from about 6 percent of GDP 25 years ago to 12 percent at the beginning of the 1990s. In fact, total American spending on health care exceeded that of Canada by 40 percent and that of Germany by 91 percent.

Statistics make it equally clear that this high level of spending has not resulted in better health or better health care for the U.S. population. For example, the United States ranks 20th in infant mortality, 16th in female life expectancy, and 17th in male life expectancy.[1]

As the size of this health challenge has come more clearly into public view and debate, a number of speculations have been put forward to explain the discrepancy between the level of spending and the quality of health. Here are some of the most prominent:

- Third-party coverage obscures the true costs of health care from the consumers of health care.
- Ever-increasing sophistication of medical technologies has driven the general level of health care costs through the roof.
- Changing demographics have driven up health care costs.
- Lack of knowledge about the effectiveness of different health care interventions impedes greater cost-effectiveness and productivity.
- Rising expectations of consumers drive up the costs of business.

Given this list of suggested causes, it is no surprise that there has been a matching list of suggested cures put forward, including the following:

- Increasing use of Health Maintenance Organizations (HMOs).
- Changing Medicare from fee-for-service to diagnosis-related group prospective payment systems.
- Imposing cost controls.
- Shifting costs from third parties to patients.
- Increasing use of ambulatory care rather than in-patient care.
- Increasing use of "managed care" (HMOs and preferred provider options).
- More closely managing cases of high-risk patients.

Both the causes and the cures outlined above are all in the nature of "best estimates," or educated guesses. Clearly, a full-scale attempt to examine and reform health care in America, like the one headed by the first lady, requires more systematic and precise information than these

---

[1]Gooloo S. Wunderlich, ed., *Toward A National Health Care Survey: A Data System for the 21st Century.* Washington, DC: National Academy Press, 1992, pp. 20–21.

speculations. This chapter is designed to suggest some of the complexities encountered when a more systematic research effort is undertaken.

Some Complexities of Trying to Assess Health Care in America

The largest, and most complex, task is to establish linkages between the process of care and the outcomes of care. The former has traditionally been much easier to measure than the latter. As the data presented above make unmistakably clear, simply spending more money does not necessarily result in better national health.

Here are just a few of the data series that would be required to assess precisely the connection between causes and effects: better systems for classifying and coding information on a large number of variables, including sites and settings of care; data on the types of care, specifically procedures, drugs, diagnostic tests, and other technologies; and better data on the costs of care. All of those will require agreements on several issues, including the minimum number of data elements necessary to convey specific and aggregate cost and expenditures data adequately and to link the relevant populations, and operational definitions of these data elements.[2]

There are some daunting complexities in measuring health care, including defining the issue, changing demographics, and the changes wrought by more sophisticated medical technology.

Altogether, health status is a complex and multidimensional construct, which reflects significant aspects of an individual's and a population's life, including physical health, mental health, social functioning, role functions, and general health perceptions.[3]

Further complicating factors stem from the subtle change over time in the kinds of health problems Americans are experiencing, resulting both from the increased technological ability of medications such as vaccines to fight traditional diseases and from changing demographic patterns. The most significant demographic shift in the United States, from the point of view of health care, is "the graying of America." The fastest-growing segment of the population today is comprised of those over 85,

---

[2]Ibid., pp. 22–23.
[3]Ibid., p. 27.

and the number of Americans over 65 years old will increase from 12 percent to 21 percent over the next several years.[4]

All this has led to a shift of the major cause of death in America from infectious diseases to chronic diseases. That means changes in mortality rates are no longer proxies for changes in health status because people now live with chronic diseases in a way that they could not live with infectious diseases. Moreover, the chronic diseases of the 1990s are more complex than the infectious diseases they "replaced," and have much longer asymptomatic stages.[5]

Besides that, for today's chronic diseases, the physical and social environments are increasingly regarded as important risk or important protection factors and thus targets for intervention. These two factors of potential risk or protection are difficult to pin down statistically.

Here is a glimpse of the complexity of gauging health and health care in this new, more complicated American scene. The government initiative called Healthy People 2000 identifies 100 separate data sources, some of which have multiple parts. It is estimated that all of these will require more than 400 separate statistical series. Yet, for one-fourth of the health objectives contained in the Healthy People 2000 project, no baseline data exist.

At the level of the state and local governments, the task is even more difficult. As one report put it, "The main problems that state and local health departments face in developing their own objectives is the unavailability of the data that are needed."[6]

Two Lines of Inquiry

Assessing health care adequacy in America can be divided into overlapping lines of inquiry, each of them fed by separate data streams: (1) assessing the overall health of the American population; and (2) assessing the access Americans have to health care. Both lines of research are necessary, although they are not fully sufficient to assess the American health care system. The following sections look at both in greater detail after a couple of general observations about health care statistics.

---

[4]Ibid., p. 30.

[5]Michael A. Stoto, *Public Health Assessment in the 1990s.* Washington, DC: Institute of Medicine, 1992, p. 61.

[6]Ibid., p. 60.

In 1989, Michael A. Stoto of the National Academy of Sciences' Institute of Medicine formulated a series of criteria for the kinds of health objectives that should be formulated by the federal government:

> Objectives [for health care performance] should be presented in terms of a specific, absolute target, such as an infant mortality rate of 9 per thousand. Such a presentation removes all ambiguity, what the objective should be and where it has been met. . . . In turn, that presentation increases the requirement for clear documentation at every step of meeting the objective.

Stoto also argues that objectives should be stated in absolute terms rather than in terms of percentages or rates of change, because they are unambiguous, easier to track, and will have a bigger impact on policy makers. Rates, proportions, and averages should be disaggregated where possible into demography, ethnic, racial, and socioeconomic categories.[7]

Assessing American Health

In 1990, the Secretary of Heath and Human Services unveiled a national health project called Healthy People 2000: National Health Promotion and Disease Prevention Objectives for the Nation. It defines goals and objectives for improving the health of Americans by the end of this century. Out of that effort also came the Year 2000 Health Objectives Planning Act (P.L. 101-582), which requires that the Secretary of Health and Human Services implement health surveillance systems and fund states to monitor and improve the health status of their populations.

There are a number of different information bases for public health assessment. The World Health Organization published a report on the development of health indicators for its Health for All project. A decade ago, the U.S. Public Health Service published national goals in the original *Healthy People 1990*.

In 1987, the National Committee on Vital and Health Statistics reviewed the status of health promotion and disease prevention data. The Centers for Disease Control and Prevention and the American Public Health Association, in conjunction with other health associations, developed Model Standards for Community Health. The Public Health Foundation developed core data sets for reporting on state public health

---

[7]Michael A. Stoto, *Statistical Issues in Formulating Health Objectives for the Year 2000.* Washington, DC: Institute of Medicine, 1989.

activities. The National Health Official's APEX program also developed methods for assessing public health needs and resources.[8]

Out of that plethora of possible data, a committee was appointed, Committee 22.1, to adopt a group of desired characteristics and selection criteria for the indicators of public health. The committee agreed on the following as the criteria for a good set of health indicators:[9]

- There should be a relatively small number of them (10 to 20).
- They should allow for a broad measure of community health.
- They should include general measures of community health (such as morbidity, mortality, and quality of life).
- They should include specific measures of community health.
- They should contain a subset that is consistent at the federal, state, and local levels.
- They should be easily understandable, even self-evident.
- They should be measurable, using available or obtainable data.
- They should imply specific interventions, compelling action. They should be so closely linked to public health status that changes from past patterns signal the need for response.
- They should be outcome oriented.

Guided by those goals, the committee developed 18 indicators to help measure health status outcomes and the factors that put individuals at increased risk of disease or premature mortality. In the end, the range of topics in the Healthy People 2000 project is extensive: It includes personal behavior and risk factors, including physical fitness and activity, nutrition, and the use of tobacco and alcohol.

Here are the 18 indicators, each listed with the sources from which the data can be gathered to measure them:

1. Race- and ethnicity-specific infant mortality as measured by the rate (per 1,000 live births) of deaths among infants under one year old (Data source: National Vital Statistics System).
2. Motor vehicle crash deaths per 100,000 population (Data source: National Vital Statistics System).

---

[8]Michael A. Stoto, *Public Health Assessment in the 1990s*. Washington, DC: Institute of Medicine, 1992, p. 60.

[9]Mary Anne Freedman, "Health Status Indicators for the Year 2000," *Statistical Notes*. U.S. Dept. of Health and Human Services, Vol. 1, No. 1, 1991.

3. Work-related injury deaths per 100,000 population (Data source: National Vital Statistics System).

4. Suicides per 100,000 population (Data source: National Vital Statistics System).

5. Lung cancer deaths per 100,000 population (Data source: National Vital Statistics System).

6. Female breast cancer deaths per 100,000 population (Data source: National Vital Statistics System).

7. Cardiovascular disease deaths per 100,000 population (Data source: National Vital Statistics System).

8. Homicides per 100,000 population (Data source: National Vital Statistics System).

9. Total deaths per 100,000 population (Data source: National Vital Statistics System).

10. Reported incidence of acquired immunodeficiency syndrome per 100,000 population (Data source: CDC HIV/AIDS Surveillance System).

11. Reported incidence of measles per 100,000 population (Data source: National Notifiable Disease Surveillance System).

12. Reported incidence of tuberculosis per 100,000 population (Data source: National Notifiable Disease Surveillance System).

13. Reported incidence of primary and secondary syphilis per 100,000 population (Data source: National Notifiable Disease Surveillance System).

14. Prevalence of low birth weight as measured by the percentage of live infants born weighing under 2,500 grams at birth (Data source: National Vital Statistics System).

15. Births to adolescents (ages 10–17 years) as a percentage of total live births (Data source: National Vital Statistics System).

16. Prenatal care as measured by the percentage of mothers developing live infants who did not receive care during the first trimester of pregnancy (Data source: National Vital Statistics System).

17. Childhood poverty, as measured by the percentage of children under 15 years of age living in families at or below the poverty level (Data source: Census of Population, Detailed Population Characteristics, U.S. Department of Commerce, Bureau of the Census).

18. Proportion of persons living in counties exceeding U.S. Environmental Protection Agency standards for air quality during the previous year (Data source: National Air Quality and Emissions Trends Reports, Annual Reports from the Environmental Protection Agency).[10]

While carefully drawn up, this list has certain weaknesses, as commentators have pointed out. Michael Stoto, for example, has pointed out that different pictures can easily emerge, depending on which year is used as a baseline or standard for certain diseases: "The 1987 rate (of cancer deaths) is 50 percent higher when the 1990 population, rather than the 1940 population, is chosen as the standard. . . . Neither one of those standards is 'correct' in any absolute sense, but they give quite a different impression."[11]

Access to Health Care in America

Part of health care reform is measuring health in all its dimensions. Another part is measuring access to health care. The Institute of Medicine (part of the National Academy of Sciences) has concluded that

> The nation needs, but currently lacks, an entity to continuously monitor the numerous types of utilization and health status [problems arising from insurance inadequacies, cultural impediments, geographic barriers, or other factors and place those problems in the broader context of national health policies]. The fourteen-member IOM access monitoring committee was constituted in February 1990 as a first step toward this goal.[12]

Each of the data sources pertaining to health access has some built-in weaknesses. Beyond that, inferring what each of those data suggests about the question of health care access, as we will see, is inevitably complex and tricky. Here are some of the different data sources with their associated strengths and weaknesses.

Vital statistics. These are derived from birth statistics and from death statistics. The birth certificates are the primary source for infor-

---

[10]Ibid.

[11]Michael A. Stoto, *Public Health Assessment in the 1990s.* Washington, DC: Institute of Medicine, 1992, p. 65.

[12]Michael Millman, ed., *Access to Health Care in America.* Washington, DC: National Academy Press, 1993, p. 21.

mation about the use of prenatal care and about low birth weight. There can be problems determining the number of prenatal visits if, for example, a woman has no, or multiple, providers or when recall of service use is required after delivery. Death records provide mortality statistics. When they are linked to the birth record, they offer insight into the correlation of infant mortality connected to low birth weight. Questions have been raised about the accuracy of reported reasons for death since, in part, they depend on the judgment of the certifying physician. Moreover, as a measure of access for all age groups, the vital statistics system does not tell whether mortality is a result of a lack of insurance, low income, or some other reason.

Surveys. The National Health Interview Survey collects a wealth of information from households that allows analysts to relate the use of health services and self-reports to characteristics of individuals and families. Among its strengths is that it is conducted annually, that its items are well tested, and that it has a large and well-constructed sample of about 120,000 respondents. It is obvious that this method fails to reach some subpopulations with health-access problems, such as the homeless and migrant farm workers. Moreover, these surveys do not track the same family over time to discover how, say, changes in insurance coverage might change access to health care. The National Medical Expenditure Survey (NMES), undertaken by the Agency for Health Care Policy and Research in 1987, tried to overcome that weakness. The Census Bureau's Survey of Income and Program Participation also collects data on health insurance coverage.

Hospital discharge data. Computerized data of patient records organized into state databases are increasingly available. The lack of income data on a discharge abstract means that researchers have to use zip code data to appraise the effect of income on hospital use. That method of analysis misses the scattered poor, who do not live in a neighborhood of equally positioned families.

Tumor registries. Since many cancers can be defeated if detected early enough, data on deaths by those cancers allow for inferences about the access of those patients to health care. (For example, the inference is that if a person dies of a cancer treatable in its early stages, this person had problems with health access early on.) The major sources of this information are the state and local tumor registries, but they are not established in all states and localities and lack data on income and insurance.

Reportable diseases. Some of the health care indicators derive from the data gathered as a consequence of laws that require physicians to report certain communicable diseases. This data source suffers from the drawbacks of both underreporting and misreporting: Some physicians fail to understand the importance of constantly tracking these diseases and do not report on them as conscientiously as they should; other physicians might mis- or underreport due to concern for privacy rights, because of changing definitions and reporting guidelines, or because of the difficulties in recognizing diseases with relatively low incidences.

Claims data. Health insurance claims contain important and relevant information about utilization, health status, costs, and so on. But its major drawback is also its most obvious one: These data contain no information about those who are uninsured. Moreover, they are not uniform, which makes them difficult and expensive to analyze.[13]

These are some of the more obvious problems that attach to each separate source for information pertaining to the complex issue of health access. The issue is complex, which means that it cannot simply or easily be measured along any single or any small set of dimensions. It is a concept that must, in a sense, be inferred from a variety of different indices. And those inferences are never simple or straightforward.

The first part of the task of measuring health care access is formulating a good definition. The Committee on Monitoring Access to Personal Health Care Service (part of the Institute of Medicine) tried to formulate a definition that encompassed both the inputs to health and the successful health results. They defined health care access as "the timely use of personal health services to achieve the best possible health outcomes."[14]

Taking this more comprehensive definition, here are a few of the problems in making straightforward inferences from the various sources of data to conclusions about access. In the cases of some cancers that can be cured if detected early, deaths from those cancers would seem to be a clear indication of lack of access to health care. Not even this inference is entirely justified, because it infers *potentiality* from *actuality;* in other words, it assumes that if someone *did not* use health care it must have been because they *could not* use health care. That inference is not

---

[13]Ibid., pp. 25–28.
[14]Ibid., p. 33.

always valid. There might be a variety of barriers—based on psychology, culture, or lack of information—that would keep a person from using health care, even though it is available.

As the Committee's book puts it, "Some people are prone to overuse medical care, while others may underuse it having little to do with access barriers." Obviously, in the cases of cancers or other diseases that cannot be effectively countered in their early stages, no inference to mortality rates from those diseases can be made about health care access.

Another way to measure whether access to health care has been achieved is to look at the frequency of visits to health care facilities. Again, this dimension by itself will not support a valid inference about access. As the Committee writes, "A poor mother who brings her asthmatic child to a clinic but cannot afford to purchase the prescribed medication may have a visit recorded, but few would consider that she had adequate access. A poor pregnant woman with a drug addiction requires many more services than most middle-class women if she is to deliver a healthy baby. A physician may be reluctant to order an expensive diagnostic test for an uninsured patient while erring on the side of overutilization for someone with adequate insurance. Thus, the poor and uninsured may enter the medical system, but it is difficult to tell whether they receive the services they need."[15]

Employer Mandates

One of the major elements in the 1993–94 debate about health care centered on the topic of employer mandates. Yet the statistics concerning the number of businesses, the size of businesses, and the effect of "mandated health premiums" has been subject to considerable misunderstanding and conflicting statistics. For example, there is no accurate count of total businesses, and the discussion of entrepreneurship and new business startups and closings (including bankruptcy, voluntary discontinuance, and temporary suspension of activity) is subject to wide debate. Some of these issues are described in "The Misunderstood Role of Small Business."[16] In a discussion of "real firms" vs. informal business organizations, the problems are defined as follows.

---

[15]Ibid., p. 37.

[16]Joseph W. Duncan and Douglas P. Handler, "The Misunderstood Role of Small Business," *Business Economics,* July–August 1994, National Association of Business Economists, pp. 4–8.

The usual economic and tax-related statistics are no help in either identifying new businesses or isolating discontinuances on a timely basis. For example, often an incorporation is reported as a shell for a "potential new idea" or as a legal protection for a current activity or as a subdivision of a business to restrict liability (e.g., each *cul de sac* in a housing development is separately incorporated to limit risks such as foundation failures). Even more typical is the individual who declares a business based on casual activity conducted from the kitchen or study (e.g., an investment activity to manage modest investments or rental property) with the major intent to collect expenses as tax deductions. In between are sole proprietorships where a carpenter may sell some personal services on a part-time basis while being fully employed by a construction firm. Of course, there are also "off the record" business activities, such as bartered services, that are undertaken to avoid tax liability. Separating a genuinely new business from one that has metamorphosized in some manner (such as a transfer of ownership, change of name or relocation) is also exceedingly difficult.

When all of these casual or paper businesses are considered, the picture may be quite different because the start-up was not real, the effort was not sustained, or the idea was never workable. Thus, many of these "casual" businesses undoubtedly fail in the first three years of life, giving rise to the myth of high rates of failure, which is misunderstood as being representative of "real" small businesses.

Data from Dun & Bradstreet track "real" businesses: organizations that are active in business, often purchasing supplies, selling products, or otherwise meriting a review of their importance, reliability, and resources. In the most common case, these organizations are an "accounts receivable" to another organization that has provided commercial credit.

The gap between the number of "real" businesses and "casual" businesses is enormous. The IRS reported tax returns on approximately 20.4 million businesses in 1991 (Figure 19).[17]

In addition to the question of payment, another dimension of health care reform is the growth in "demand" that would result from universal coverage and/or expanded governmental programs. In an insightful publication entitled *Economic Effects of Health Reform*, Steurle points out

---

[17]This is the latest data available, with the data on corporations being for the year 1990. The magnitude is approximate, supporting the total cited.

FIGURE 19

Internal Revenue Service Data: Number of U.S. Business Tax Returns

	Limited Partnerships 1991	General Partnerships 1991	Sole Proprietorships 1991	Corporations 1991	Total
All industries	270,681	1,244,665	15,180,722	3,802,788	20,498,856
Agriculture, forestry, and fishing	9,780	117,293	431,594	129,886	688,553
Mining	16,295	22,728	149,548	39,199	227,770
Oil and gas extraction	15,149	19,031	139,052		173,232
Construction	1,406	55,789	1,735,980	416,987	2,210,162
Manufacturing	1,946	22,028	426,697	300,122	750,793
Transportation and public utilities	3,797	22,309	660,427	164,980	851,513
Wholesale and retail trade	13,640	157,342	2,677,709	1,043,534	3,892,225
Finance, insurance, and real estate	201,502	602,335	1,290,603	617,557	2,711,997
Real estate	162,890	506,077	760,131		1,429,098
Operators and lessors of buildings	134,481	410,722	10,169		555,372
Services	22,232	238,217	7,641,910	1,061,657	8,964,016

Source: *Statistics of Income Bulletin*, Vol. 14, No. 1, Summer 1994 (Corporations, 1991); Vol. 13, No. 2, Fall 1993 (Partnerships and Sole Proprietorships)

FIGURE 20
Number of U.S. Firms Under 500 Employees

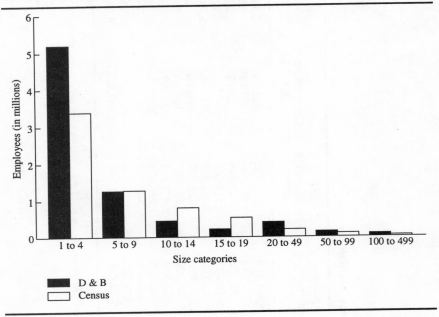

D & B
Census

that some models show that "uninsured individuals would increase their health spending by 60 percent under national health care reform . . . [and] demand also increases because of new benefits, such as drugs and long-term care under Medicaid."[18] Of course, such models represent only estimates, but the lack of definitive data makes policy making uncertain because there is limited understanding of the dynamics of public response under various health care policy alternatives.

Conclusion—Health Care Policy Statistics

Clearly, health care is one of the most pressing and most difficult social challenges to attempt to measure. It is multifaceted, constantly changing, and subject to differing results from different assumptions and different interpretations.

[18]C. Eugene Stuerle, *Economic Effects of Health Reform.* Washington, DC: American Enterprise Institute, 1994.

In the end, it can only be assessed by a process of constantly taking different sightings of the phenomenon from different statistical measurements along each of the separate dimensions, then constantly updating, revising, and reexamining them.

THE YEAR 2000 CENSUS

Introduction to the Year 2000 Census

Since the founding of our nation, the enumeration of the population has been a crucial basis for public policy. The census serves as the statistical basis for apportionment of the House of Representatives in the U.S. Congress, and over the years it has become the basic benchmark for economic and social surveys.

Over the years, the census has been a focal point for public debate and revision on issues such as (1) who should be counted (slaves were originally excluded); (2) what race and ethnic classifications should be used (the classifications have changed in three of the last four censuses); and (3) whether the "undercount" (and in some cases alleged overcount) distorts the distribution of representatives (and more recently the allocation of federal funds). Thus, the census is not simply a matter of counting individuals, but a portrait of the society that underlies much of the debate and analysis that forms social policy.

Each decade has witnessed a cycle where these and other issues are debated as the census is redesigned to meet the needs of public policy making. For the past several decades, the federal agencies that use census data in their program administration have debated, analyzed, and made final recommendations concerning both the content and the methodology of the census. This decade is no different.

A major review of the difficulties of the 1990 Census and the needs for the Year 2000 Census has been underway since 1991. This review has involved a major review both inside the Bureau of the Census and outside the Bureau, with the Committee on National Statistics of the National Academy of Sciences being an especially influential voice. However, the final form of the census will reflect the concerns of other outside groups, including the Census Bureau Advisory Committee and especially the congressional oversight committees. At the time we go to press, the debate is in midstream. A pretest for 1996 is being designed, and the final results of the pretest plus the decisions of the administration and the Congress will determine the final form of the census.

The decennial census has become the center for political and economic controversy for many individuals and community leaders as Congress has passed new legislation that bases the allocation of funds on demographic status of individuals and communities. In particular, many funds-allocation programs are based on population size and income distribution. Since the intent of many federal programs involves redistribution of income from affluent to less-affluent areas, the federal programs are designed to direct funds to those areas that have disproportionally high levels of poverty.

With the advent of federal funds allocations, individual communities have carefully scrutinized the census results to determine if the measurements are accurate. Unfortunately, it is difficult to find, enumerate, and verify certain segments of the population; particularly, illegal aliens who do not wish to be identified, homeless and transient persons, and others who feel no sense of social responsibility to include themselves among the "counted." According to the U.S. General Accounting Office, the undercount of the population in 1990 is estimated to be about 4.7 million persons, or approximately 1.8 percent of the population. This concern about the accuracy of the count has been further complicated by the fact that, with more two wage-earner households, it is increasingly difficult to find someone at home to report on family membership and status.

In constant 1990 dollars, it is generally estimated that the unit costs of counting an individual household have increased from approximately $10 in 1960, to $20 in 1980, and to $25 in 1990. This growing expense of the census has recently become a stimulus for reform, especially as pressures have grown to reduce the overheads of federal programs.

Shortly after the 1990 Census was completed, the U.S. Department of Commerce created a task force on the Year 2000 Census. One of the activities of the task force was to develop a contract with the Committee on National Statistics of the Commission on Behavioral and Social Sciences Education of the National Research Council. The panel, Evaluate Alternative Census Methods, issued an interim report in 1993. This report, *A Census That Mirrors America—Interim Report*, outlines several strategies for improving the census operation.[19]

---

[19]Committee on National Statistics, National Research Council, *A Census That Mirrors America—Interim Report*. Washington, DC: National Academy Press, 1993.

In planning for the Year 2000 Census, the Census Bureau initially developed a set of 14 design alternatives. Six of the 14 designs were based on the basic structure of the 1990 Census with provisions for:

1. Adding multiple techniques for respondents to provide census information.
2. Implementing varying degrees of sampling and statistical estimation as part of the census process.
3. Specific strategies for overcoming barriers to enumeration.

Other proposals addressed such areas as the use of administrative records, restricting the topics to be covered in the content of the census, and using techniques such as two-stage data collection or continuous measurement to provide needed information. Due to the complexity of developing a census operation, the Census Bureau staff and outside consultants quickly recognized the need to narrow the redesign alternatives in order to focus on the specific ideas that will be included in the 1995 pretest of the census. Thus the research into various choices will be limited to only a few key issues affecting the final design of the Year 2000 Census.

The current concept being explored is the creation of a "One Number Census." This approach involves a strategy of integrating statistical estimation into the census methodology rather than pursuing the separate post-enumeration tests of accuracy that have characterized the last three censuses. As noted in the interim report of the National Academy of Sciences:

> [A One Number Census] allows for the most cost effective design because it permits planning costs and quality improvements in the Census, particularly with regard to closing the differential coverage gap that coverage measurement makes possible. Second, decisions about whether to implement response improvement programs aimed at special populations can be made on the basis of improving accuracy rather than on the basis of which groups would be helped or hurt. If the decision to use estimation and the basic estimation strategy (although not necessarily all the details of the procedure) are specified at the beginning of the Census process, concerns that decisions have been influenced by desire to benefit certain geographic or demographic rules will be forestalled. Finally, a One Number Census that enjoys the support of the scientific community will have greater credibility with the American public.[20]

---

[20]Ibid., pp. 30–31.

During the 1990 Census, there was considerable debate about "statistical adjustment." With statistical adjustment, the proposal was to use results of the post-enumeration survey to evaluate coverage differentials and then to adjust statistically the enumeration results to account for the statistical variations that were uncovered in the post-enumeration analysis. Considerable debate ensued both prior to the census and after the census, with the Bush Administration ultimately determining that statistical adjustment would reduce public credibility. The decision was also influenced by the debate among statisticians about the acceptability and accuracy of certain techniques being considered. Thus, the current strategy of the "One Number Census" attempts to set aside the controversy of statistical adjustment and to incorporate some of the improved statistical methodology that could be made possible by coverage measurement programs that include sampling and statistical estimation while the enumeration is proceeding.

Methods of Coverage Measurement

To provide some background for the discussion of this issue, the Census Bureau has identified three basic methods for measuring the differential coverage:

1. A Post-Enumeration Survey (PES).
2. Census Plus—a sample of blocks based on the initial enumeration.
3. Super Census—a more intensive enumeration approach.

A Post-Enumeration Survey is a procedure similar to the 1990 methodology. An independent survey is conducted and then, on a case-by-case basis, respondents to the Post-Enumeration Survey are matched to the original enumeration results. A procedure for ratio estimation is then applied to correct for differences between the original enumeration and the results of the Post-Enumeration Survey.

In a Census Plus procedure, a sample of blocks is selected, and once the Census enumeration is complete, a special effort continues in the selective blocks to ensure that a complete count is achieved. The special effort involves techniques such as comparisons with administrative lists and the use of highly trained interviewers skilled in uncovering individuals not originally counted. Census Plus recognizes that such specific additional follow-up is too expensive to be used for the entire census, but the anticipation is that the results of the more intensive effort in a

series of blocks that is undertaken following the enumeration will lead
to more reliable information than could be obtained in the Post-Enumeration Survey.

The Super Census intensifies the effort that is associated with Census Plus. The proposal, however, is that for these selections of blocks
there would not be a regular census. Instead, the Super Census operations would begin at an earlier date than the census undertaken in other
blocks. However, the difference between the Census Plus and the Super
Census methods is in the amount of detail on difficult issues such as
shifts in place of residency, since the Super Census would include analysis over a longer period of time. In the case of Census Plus, it would be
necessary to determine which of the persons found in the survey several
months later were resident in the sample blocks on Census day. Because
Super Census would be carried out on a schedule other than Census Plus,
it could be easier to deal with the place of residency question.

All three of these procedures are subject to further research, study,
and evaluation.

The 1995 Pretest

Planning for the 1995 Census pretest makes it necessary to reduce the
range of alternatives that can be evaluated. It is widely recognized that
the Super Census approach is likely to be considerably more expensive
than the old approach, the Post-Enumeration Survey, or the Census Plus
approach. Thus, as the 1995 pretest evolves, it is likely to be more modest than this full range of proposals.

The key issue in many respects is improving the response rate. Several experiments are being considered, including the following:

Developing an option for respondents to call by telephone in order
to simplify the responding process.

There is concern that some of the respondents may not be following the questionnaire at the time of the telephone call and that com-
puter-aided interviewing may be necessary to make sure that all of
the variables are adequately considered.

The long form tends to create the most resistance. To explore motivation for the long form, a special experiment was conducted in
July 1993 entitled "Appeals and Long Form Experiment" (ALFE).

An alternative actual response by telephone would be to have telephone follow-up or reminder calls and nonresponse follow-up.

The census has typically had an advertising program along with a number of community-based efforts to encourage participation on Census day. Nevertheless, in preparing the 1995 pretest and the implementation of the Year 2000 Census, a number of special outreach and promotion programs are being considered, especially those that can reach the groups that have a differential undercount. Thus, the local area programs would probably be complemented by a national media campaign using the advertising council as had been accomplished in the past.

In addition to these broad questions of overall census methodology, etc., a number of specific technical issues are being reviewed at this time. They include the following:

1. Dealing with irregular and complex household arrangements. There seem to be a growing number of complex households containing unrelated individuals, and in some cases, multiple nuclear families.

2. Another source of measurement difficulty is irregular housing, including dwellings hidden from public view or illegal residences such as garages and basements.

3. The probability of certain areas having a large seasonal labor force, and thereby creating low-wage labor markets, will have large numbers of peripheral participants in the household, including illegal aliens who may move from house to house.

4. Immigrant populations typically have limited English proficiency, and special efforts are underway to explore special language questionnaires. For example, in the 1990 pretest, it was recently determined that in Oakland, California, with over 5 percent Chinese population and with Tagalog and Vietnamese populations cited over 1 percent, the 1995 test will include five languages: English, Spanish, Chinese, Tagalog, and Vietnamese. The cost implications of this for all regions will be part of the pretest evaluation.

5. There is a growing tendency for citizens to distrust government and to fear that census responses will affect their rights, benefits, or privileges in a negative way. The public outreach program must deal with this growing resistance if better results are to be obtained in the year 2000.

Thus, the issues facing the Year 2000 Census appear to be even more complex than those surrounding the controversy of the 1990 Census. It will be particularly difficult in a period of government austerity to implement high-cost procedures.

THE CONTINUOUS CENSUS

One strategy gaining interest is the elimination of the census long form, focusing during the Year 2000 Census on the critical short-term, short-form questions that determine basic population counts. This radical move would, of course, significantly reduce the burden of census reporting and the initial costs. However, the elimination of the long form is being introduced as part of a continuous measurement program that would extend collection of detail characteristics throughout the decade. Thus, rather than having data only once every 10 years, the continuance measurement could be used to:

1. Improve data quality by maintaining a permanent enumeration staff and improving surveys over time.
2. Increase availability of detailed characteristics throughout the decade to provide for continuous monitoring of social and demographic change.
3. Provide a vehicle for exploring emerging issues on a more timely basis.

In 1993, the Census Bureau issued design alternative recommendation Number 14 in which the Bureau stated:

> We are fully committed to designing a program which would produce data continuously throughout the decade. Collecting data with such a program would be a fundamental departure from collecting "long form" data from a sample as an integral part of the decennial Census. By definition, however, the 1995 Census test, which is a one time data collection activity, cannot explicitly address this option. The Census test will enable us to develop accurate and cost effective methods for the "zero year" portion of a continuous measurement system.[21]

The concept of continuous measurement has been suggested for a long time. It was central to the strategy proposed in *A Framework for*

---

[21]U.S. Bureau of the Census, *Design Alternative Recommendation Number 14*, Year 2000 Research and Development Staff, May 17, 1993.

Planning United States Federal Statistics for the 1980s.[22] It was defined in 1981 in a more detailed manner by Leslie Kish[23] and was further defined by Herriot and his colleagues.[24]

To those of us interested in the quality and coverage of economic and social data, the continuous census is particularly appealing. However, at this stage of the debate, *it would be risky to set aside the long form for the Year 2000 Census until there is a fully funded continuous survey program in place.* The risk is that the long form could be eliminated to save money and that nothing would be introduced to replace it. The net effect would be a dramatic decrease in the availability of social and statistical information.

Second, issues concerning the "One Number Census" still center on the nature of the statistical estimates that are made. The history of the census is that the "enumeration" results have been used for apportionment—the primary constitutional requirement for the census. While earlier legal actions have been focused on the allocation of benefits, it is possible that the apportionment issues could also bring legal questions if the allocation statistics are based on "statistical adjustments." While there are some who hold that statistical adjustment leads to quality improvements, there will inevitably be suspicion concerning any adjustments that appear to add individuals to the areas where they were not fully enumerated. If this addition results in congressional or legislative realignment, there will inevitably be some challenges.[25]

---

[22]Office of Federal Statistical Policy and Standards, *A Framework for Planning United States Federal Statistics for the 1980s.* Washington, DC: U.S. Government Printing Office, 1978.

[23]Leslie Kish, *Using Accumulated Rolling Samples.* Washington, DC: U.S. Government Printing Office, No. 80-52810, 1981.

[24]Roger Herriot, D. V. Bateman, and W. F. McCarthy, *The Decade Census Program—A New Approach for Meeting the Nation's Needs for Sub-national Data.* American Statistical Association, 1989.

[25]In a comprehensive front-page article in the *New York Times* on May 16, 1994, it was noted that "one change that is expected to be adopted," Census officials say, "is the use of sophisticated estimates based on surveys to supplement the actual counting—a volatile issue that was the center of a furious partisan battle in the last Census.

"The Bureau is also considering scrapping the long form survey that has been used once a decade to gather information as varied as household incomes or how many telephones a particular residence has. In its place the Bureau plans extensive monthly surveys conducted over an entire decade, providing more timely flow of this broad demographic data."

The issues posed by this strategy are enormous. They will undoubtedly be the source of great debate in the next several years. This section reviews some elements of the proposals and then highlights a couple of the key issues. See the *New York Times,* Monday, May 16, 1994, pp. 1 and C11.

EDUCATION STATISTICS

In the early chapters of this book, we noted the dramatic revolutions underway in the global economy. Central to these revolutions is the role of rapid technological change and the resulting restructuring of the labor force. These changes have brought enormous pressure on value structures, and different social and ethnic perspectives are brought into competition and into closer contact with each other. Global television images are introducing new values, new concepts, and new aspirations to all corners of the earth.

Political debate about the content, form, and even the purpose of education is now in the forefront of national economic and social policy. The World Bank study of economic growth and public policy in East Asia was summarized in a policy research report entitled *The East Asian Miracle; Economic Growth and Public Policy.* The study noted:

> Except for in Thailand, the quantity of basic education provided to boys and girls of school age has been consistently higher in the High Performing Asian Economies (HPAEs) than in economies with similar levels of income. After having achieved universal primary schooling, thereby eliminating the gap between boys and girls at the primary level a decade or more earlier than most, the HPAEs rapidly expanded secondary education and were particularly effective in reducing gender gaps at that level.
>
> What accounts for this extraordinary performance? We focus first on three enabling factors: high income growth, early demographic transitions, and more equal income distributions. Each of these greatly increased the resources available for education. We then shift focus to two policy variables: the overall budgetary commitment to education and the distribution of the education budget. We seek to show that the allocation of public resources to primary and secondary education was the major determining factor in East Asia's successful educational strategies.[26]

Thus, education policy is a central issue of national economic and social policy. This is reflected in the growth of the budget for the National Center for Education Statistics (NCES), the focal point for developing data at the national level concerning the status of education. Of course, the decennial census provides specific information on education attainment of the population by basic demographic characteristics, but the National Center for Education Statistics provides the basic information

---

[26]World Bank, *The East Asian Miracle; Economic Growth and Public Policy.* New York: Oxford University Press, 1993, pp. 192–193.

used for public policy analysis. As noted in their latest edition of *Programs and Plans*, education statistics are used for a number of purposes. Congress uses them to plan federal education programs, to apportion federal funds among the states, and to serve the needs of constituents.[27]

Federal agencies such as the Departments of Defense, Labor, and Commerce and the National Science Foundation are concerned with the supply of trained personnel coming out of our schools and colleges and also with the subjects being taught there. Education and local officials are concerned with the problems of staffing and financing public education. Educational organizations, such as the American Council on Education and the National Education Association, use data for planning and research. The news media, such as national television networks, national news magazines, and many of the nation's leading daily newspapers, frequently use NCES statistics to inform the public about matters such as school and college enrollment and expenditures per student. Business organizations use trend data on enrollment expenditures to forecast the demand for their products. The general public uses education statistics to become more informed and to make intelligent decisions concerning the educational issues of today.

The specific programs of the National Center for Education Statistics include a series of surveys on various levels of education. For example, for elementary and secondary education, there is a long-established program entitled "Common Core of Data" (CCD), which is the Center's primary database on elementary and secondary public education in the United States. The statistical information is collected annually from public elementary and secondary schools and is closely coordinated with the needs of state education departments. The Center also does surveys on staffing, and they have a private school survey to complement data on the public education system.

At the post-secondary education level, there is an integrated post-secondary education data system, a comprehensive system that encompasses all institutions whose primary purpose is education at the post-secondary level. This includes characteristics of enrollment and completions.

Perhaps the most widely known survey of the Center is the National Assessment of Educational Progress, which was mandated by Congress

---

[27]U.S. Department of Education, Office of Educational Research and Improvement, *Programs and Plans of the National Center for Education Statistics.* Washington, DC: Government Printing Office, May 1993.

as a statistical program to monitor the knowledge, skills, and performance of the nation's children and youth. Current legislation (which was amended in 1988) requires assessments in reading and mathematics at least every two years, in science and writing at least every four years, and in history or geography and other subjects selected by the National Assessment Governing Board at least every six years. Comparative achievement measures are controversial because of difficulties in comparison of education across and within different socioeconomic areas, but they have proved to be a fundamental underpinning of national education policy.

The National Center for Education Statistics also includes special studies of library statistics programs and their vocational education. Of particular interest have been the National Longitudinal Surveys, which are designed to follow students at various levels of education for the purpose of describing major transition phases in student lives. Longitudinal studies have made it possible to make long-term comparisons about what individuals expect and what actually occurs, thus serving as the basis for making educational processes more relevant and more complete in developing the abilities of the student populations.

EDUCATION STATISTICS—NEEDS FOR THE FUTURE

As noted throughout this book, the social, economic, political, and technological environment is in a period of rapid transition. This makes it necessary to develop social statistics—especially in education, which provides the intellectual capital for future developments—that will assure that the educational system is building the skills and the knowledge needed to cope with the rapidly changing circumstances of today's students. This means that statistical investigations must move from the descriptive counts of students in various grade levels and educational settings to more detailed investigations of educational achievement and its relationship to needed skills, including the ability to analyze new conditions, to adjust to rapidly changing workplace conditions, and to build value foundations that will develop better citizenship and responsibility.

These challenges are clearly beyond the scope of this volume. Our goal in this discussion is to open up the challenge of needed reform of education statistics to serve as a better foundation for evaluation of current conditions and to aid in the development of future educational policy.

CHAPTER 5

STATISTICS ABOUT ENERGY SUPPLY AND DEMAND

INTRODUCTION

Data requirements concerning the supply and demand for energy is a complex topic. Our intent here is simply to provide an overview in order to underscore the range of statistical improvement that is needed if we are to address future policy development. As has already been noted, because the lead time required for the generation of accurate and useful statistical information is long, it is important to begin programs for meeting future needs as soon as possible.

The good news on the energy front is that there is currently no crisis; no major shortage of fuel looms immediately ahead. We appear to be doing a good job on conservation and improving efficiency. However, there are serious concerns and controversies ranging from safety to environmental issues, from research to distribution. The good news on the energy statistics front is that there is no shortage of data; indeed, in some instances we have long and in-depth time series (e.g., coal).

There is a lack of data on certain aspects (e.g., wood as a fuel in developing nations). However, we are doing a better job collecting, analyzing, and disseminating data. This section focuses on both the energy situation and energy statistics, since one must understand the dimensions of the former before tackling the latter.

First we review the energy supply and demand situation by major categories from a global and a United States perspective. Then, selected issues are dealt with briefly, including energy intensity (efficiency, conservation, etc.), safety, and environmental impact. Finally, the discussion moves on to data handling: definitions, classification, sources of information, analysis, and dissemination.

A SUPPLY-DEMAND OVERVIEW

A schematic view of the energy situation is shown in Figure 21. As seen in this traditional classification scheme, both supply and demand can be categorized into various subdivisions. Energy supply can be fossil and non-fossil. The current scheme is to speak of primary energy production and

FIGURE 21
Overview of Energy Supply and Demand

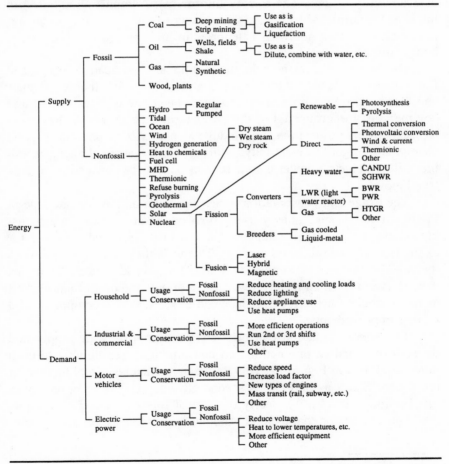

Source: A.C. Gross and W.W. Ware, "Energy Prospects to 1990," *Business Horizons,* vol. xviii, no.3, June 1975, p.7.

to have four major categories. Three are fossil fuels, namely coal, crude oil (petroleum), and natural gas (dry and liquid). Wood and plants, often used in developing nations, are not recognized due to lack of available data.

The fourth category is nonhydrocarbons, or nonfossil fuels. As seen in the diagram, there are several subcategories, many of which admittedly play a small role and are considered advanced or esoteric possibilities. The international and national energy data collection agencies recognize only two distinct primary sources of nonhydrocarbon fuels: hydroelectric power and nuclear electric power. Again, this is a matter of availability of data. The Energy Information Administration (EIA) in the U.S. Department of Energy is promising to start collecting more statistics on the other nonfossil categories in and outside the U.S., if its budget allows.[1]

On the energy demand side, the traditional classification recognized four categories: households, industrial and commercial, motor vehicles, and electric power. This scheme has now been altered. Residential and commercial are grouped together; the term *motor vehicle* has been replaced by *transportation*; and industrial use is separate. The biggest change is in regard to electricity; although some statistical agencies still break it out, electric power is now seen as part of the conversion process (see below).

The usage and conservation issues as shown on the demand side in Figure 21 do remain. Energy users, both public and private, are focusing on the kind of fuel being used, often installing dual systems; for example, coal and oil, or oil and gas. This way, they can switch between the two for cost or other considerations. The other key facet, of course, is conservation, which means lower usage of any one or all fuels as well as more efficient use through redesigned processes, new equipment, and related improvements.

The energy situation can be viewed differently, with supply and demand (now called production and consumption) tied directly to each other, as shown in Figure 22. This flow diagram shows actual figures for the United States as of 1992. A second advantage of viewing energy in this fashion is to identify clearly the role of foreign trade, for example, crude oil imports or coal exports. Another impressive aspect seen in Fig-

---

[1]Based on phone conversations with selected officials at the Energy Information Administration, U.S. Department of Energy, May 1994.

Total U.S. Energy Flow, 1992 (Quadrillion BTU)

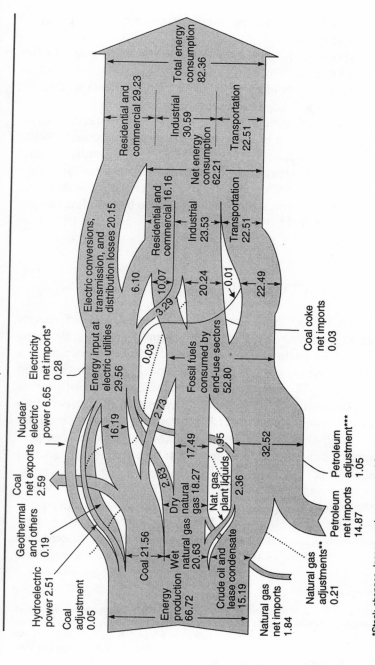

*Stock changes, losses, and unaccounted for.

**Supplemental gaseous fuels, net storage withdrawals, and balancing item.

***Other liquids, net stock change, refinery processing gain, and unaccounted for.

Notes: Data are preliminary. Sum of components may not be equal totals due to independent rounding; the use of preliminary conversion factors; and the exclusion of changes in stocks, miscellaneous supply and disposition, and unaccounted for quantities.

Sources: Table 1.2 and *Monthly Energy Review*, March 1993, Tables 1.5 and 2.1.

Source: Energy Information Administration, *International Energy Outlook 1992*. Washington, DC: USDOE/EIA, 1992, p. 3.

117

ure 22 is the large amount of losses sustained in electricity conversion, transmission, and distribution.

In Figure 23, we see a detailed view of the electricity flow (for the United States), which reveals that by far the vast majority of losses occur at the process of conversion in electric power plants. This is said to be inevitable, but the fact remains that almost all homes, offices, factories, stores, and so on are wired for electricity. Thus, we are beholden to large capacity power plants and to existing transmission/distribution systems in the developed nations. Electric power utilities, long regarded as natural monopolies, are now coming under competitive pressure from other utilities, cogeneration, buyback schemes, and the regulatory authorities. Over the long run, it is conceivable that small will be beautiful in energy, just as in the computer field, where mainframes are giving way to networked personal computers.

A GLOBAL PERSPECTIVE: THE PAST

Throughout much of the 20th century, the world supply of energy exceeded demand. Defining surplus as the amount of energy allocated for inventories and for fueling ships on a worldwide basis, surplus was at about 4 percent total demand in both 1961 and 1972. Then came the energy crisis of 1973–74 when the OPEC nations asserted themselves vis-à-vis the multinational oil companies. In retrospect, the crisis can be viewed as an opportunity long overdue for energy conservation by nations, firms, and households. Users in the past 20 years did not gain a dominant upper hand, but did force producers to alter their production and pricing strategies.[2]

How this happened is seen in the data of Figures 24 and 25 which show the global world energy supply and demand situation during the 1972–85 period. To put it bluntly, the forecasters and doomsayers were wrong and thus humbled. In retrospect, we now know that citizens and organizations were resilient as they made the adjustments. The response

---

[2]The treatment of electric power has changed; it is no longer seen as an energy end-use sector. Nuclear, hydro, and other renewable sources of electric power appear on the supply side along with fossil fuels. Electricity generation is viewed as converting the primary energy sources for use by the consuming (demand) sectors. For further details, see Electric Edison Institute reports and journals, such as *Electric World* and *Public Utilities Fortnightly*.

U.S. Electricity Flow, 1992 (Quadrillion BTU)

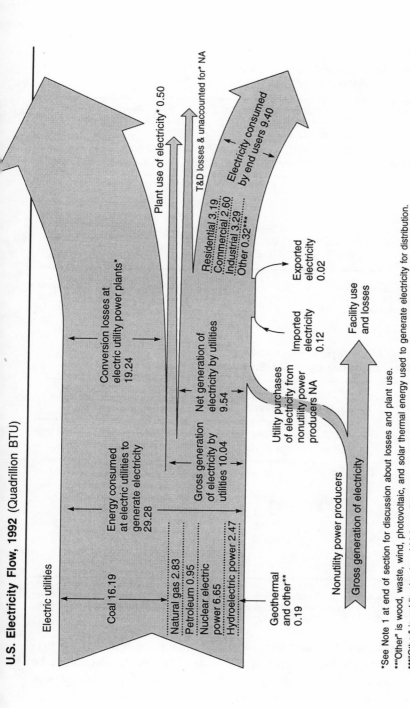

Electric utilities

Coal 16.19

Natural gas 2.83
Petroleum 0.95
Nuclear electric power 6.65
Hydroelectric power 2.47

Geothermal and other** 0.19

Nonutility power producers

Gross generation of electricity

Energy consumed at electric utilities to generate electricity 29.28

Gross generation of electricity by utilities 10.04

Utility purchases of electricity from nonutility power producers NA

Conversion losses at electric utility power plants* 19.24

Net generation of electricity by utilities 9.54

Imported electricity 0.12

Exported electricity 0.02

Facility use and losses

Plant use of electricity* 0.50

T&D losses & unaccounted for* NA

Electricity consumed by end users 9.40

Residential 3.19
Commercial 2.60
Industrial 3.29
Other 0.32***

*See Note 1 at end of section for discussion about losses and plant use.

**"Other" is wood, waste, wind, photovoltaic, and solar thermal energy used to generate electricity for distribution.

****"Other" is public street and highway lighting, other sales to public authorities, sales to railroads and railways, and interdepartmental sales.

NA = Not available.

Notes: Data are preliminary. Sum of components may not equal totals due to independent rounding.

Sources: Tables 8.1, 8.2, 8.4, 8.5, 8.12, 10.8, and A7.

Source: Energy Information Administration, *International Energy Outlook 1992.* Washington, DC: USDOE/EIA, 1992, p. 213.

FIGURE 24
World Energy in Historical Perspective:
Supply (Production) by Major Fuel

Type of Fuel	Absolute Numbers (quadrillion BTU)			Annual Growth (percent)	
	1972 Actual	1985 Forecast Made in 1973	1985 Actual	1985/1972 Forecast	1985/1972 Actual
Coal	76.3	111.6	84.2	3.0	0.8
Crude oil	105.3	200.1	112.2	5.1	0.5
Natural gas (dry & liquid)	50.8	105.1	79.7	5.7	3.5
Nonhydrocarbons	14.9	62.7	34.2	11.7	6.6
Total	247.3	479.5	302.1	5.2	1.6

Sources: W. Ware and A. Gross, "World Energy: Demand and Supply," *Columbia Journal of World Business,* Fall 1974, p. 13; and Energy Information Administration, *International Energy Annual 1992.* Washington, DC: USDOE/EIA, 1994, pp. 110 ff.

FIGURE 25
World Energy in Historical Perspective:
Demand (Consumption) by Major End Use

End Use	Absolute Numbers (quadrillion BTU)			Annual Growth (percent)	
	1972 Actual	1985 Forecast Made in 1973	1985 Actual	1985/1972 Forecast	1985/1972 Actual
Transportation	25.7	44.3	42.0[e]	4.3	3.8
Residential & commercial	33.2	41.2	40.0[e]	1.7	1.4
Electric power	57.7	145.1	80.0[e]	7.4	2.6
Industry	121.1	221.6	143.0[e]	4.8	1.3
Total	237.7	452.2	304.7	5.1	1.9

[e] = estimated

Sources: W. Ware and A. Gross, "World Energy: Demand and Supply," *Columbia Journal of World Business,* Fall 1974, p. 11; and Energy Information Administration, *International Energy Annual 1992.* Washington, DC: USDOE/EIA, 1994, pp. 118 ff.

to higher prices was lowered demand. The annual growth rate of 5.2 percent for all fuel production turned out to be 1.6 percent. As might be expected, natural gas and nonhydrocarbons showed far better growth than did crude oil or sulfur-laden coal.

In the mid-1970s, OPEC oil production as a percentage of world oil consumption hovered around the 50 percent mark. By 1985, this figure plummeted to about 30 percent. The price of crude oil rose from around $10 per barrel in 1970 to $30 in the mid-1970s, to over $50 in 1980, only to decline to the $20 mark by the mid- to late 1980s. The OPEC cartel did not fade away, but it had to make some drastic adjustments.

On the demand or consumption side, all of the major end-use sectors undertook an effective program of conservation and redesign. The original forecast of 5.1 percent growth turned out to be much too high. The actual annual growth during 1972–85 came in at 1.9 percent. Industry and the electric power sectors made the biggest adjustments, with actual growth rates turning out to be one-third of the forecasted ones. Transportation was the least resilient sector, as cars and trucks were wedded to running on refined petroleum.

A GLOBAL PERSPECTIVE: THE PRESENT AND THE FUTURE

World primary energy consumption rose rather slowly in the 1980s, reaching the 350 quadrillion BTU or 7,800 million tons oil equivalent mark in 1990. Oil accounted for 39 percent, natural gas for 21 percent, coal for 27 percent, and other sources for 13 percent of this total that year. These shares will not change much in coming decades, according to current forecasts. The corresponding figures in 2010 will be oil at 36 percent, natural gas at 23 percent, coal at 26 percent, and others for 15 percent of the total. The share going to market economies will remain stable at 70 percent between 1990 and 2010, with the other 30 percent going to former or current centrally planned economies. The details are shown in Figure 26, which also reveals that the annual growth rates are forecast to be in the modest range of 1.2 percent to 2.1 percent.[3]

In terms of country data, the United States will still be the largest user, but Europe and Japan combined will match the U.S. consumption

---

[3]W. W. Ware and A. C. Gross, "World Energy: Demand and Supply," *Columbia Journal of World Business*, Fall 1974, pp. 7–17 and especially p. 7. Many others also predicted high energy supply and demand growth rates at the time.

FIGURE 26
World Total Energy Consumption by Type of Fuel

Energy Source	1990	Reference Mid-Range Projections (quadrillion BTU)		Actual Growth 2010/1990 (percent)
		2000	2010	
Market economies	242.7	290	331	1.6
Centrally planned economies[a]	105.9	120	144	1.6
World total				
Oil	135.1	154	173	1.2
Gas	73.7	90	111	2.1
Coal	92.3	108	122	1.4
Nuclear	20.4	24	29	1.8
Other	26.3	34	41	2.3
Total	348.6	410	475	1.6

[a]Includes former, evolving, and current Centrally Planned Economies.

Source: Energy Information Administration, *International Energy Outlook 1992*, Washington, DC: USDOE/EIA, 1992, p. 27.

figures in 2000 and 2010, just as they did in 1990. The growth rate for these developed nations will be in the range of 1.1 percent to 1.8 percent, as seen in Figure 27. The fastest growth rate will be exhibited by China, with annual consumption of primary energy rising at 3.1 percent during the 1990 to 2010 time period. Consumption in both the OPEC nations and developing countries will rise at about 2.5 percent.

With respect to primary energy production, crude oil will be the key, and the Middle East will continue to be the dominant region. Oil production is forecasted to rise modestly, in line with consumption. Detailed data by key regions are given for 2000 and 2010 in Figure 28. The forecasts by various agencies depend on assumptions about world oil prices. More recent comparative forecasts of world oil prices can be found in Figure 29. Just a few of the "high price scenarios" of Figures 28 and 29 forecast a $30 to $35 price for a barrel of oil—and not by 2000, but only by 2010. Clearly, competition from other fuels, conservation by end users, and more fuel-efficient devices have an impact on crude oil production.

The fundamental question is not whether, but how world economic growth is dependent on energy and energy prices. The answer is rather

FIGURE 27
World Total Energy Consumption by Region

Energy Source	1990	Reference Mid-Range Projections (quadrillion BTU)		Actual Growth 2010/1990 (percent)
		2000	2010	
Market Economies	242.7	290	331	1.6
OECD				
United States[a]	85.0	95.6	106.1	1.1
Canada	10.8	13.0	15.1	1.7
Japan	18.2	22.6	26.0	1.8
Europe	61.9	71.9	78.0	1.2
Other OECD	5.2	5.9	6.4	1.0
Total	181.0	209.0	231.5	1.3
OPEC	16.1	20.5	25.7	2.4
Other developing countries	45.7	60.3	74.1	2.5
Total market economies	242.7	289.8	331.4	1.6
Centrally Planned Economies[b]				
China	28.8	42.8	52.9	3.1
Former Soviet Union	57.1	55.4	65.0	0.8
Other CPE	19.9	22.2	26.0	1.3
Total	105.9	120.3	144.0	1.6
World total	348.6	410.1	475.3	1.6

[a]Includes the 50 states and the District of Columbia. U.S. Territories are included in "Other OECD." Includes biofuels.
[b]Includes former, evolving, and current Centrally Planned Economies.
OECD = Organization for Economic Cooperation and Development
OPEC = Organization of Petroleum Exporting Countries

Source: Energy Information Administration, *International Energy Outlook 1992,* Washington, DC: USDOE/EIA, 1992, p. 28.

complex, but in its recent outlook report, the USDOE/EIA assumes that world energy consumption is growing and will continue to grow about half as fast as world gross domestic product (GDP). This is the reverse of what occurred during the 1950–80 period. Technology, energy-saving activities, and international cooperation all played a role in this reversal. A graphic illustration of the economy-energy relationship for OECD countries during the 1980s can be seen in Figure 30. GDP rises far faster

FIGURE 28
Comparison of World Oil Projections (Million Barrels per Day)

Projections	Oil Consumption				Oil Production				World Oil Price[a]
	World	OECD	Former USSR/ China	Other	World	OECD	Former USSR/ China	Other	
Year 2000									
IEO92	75.0	41.6	10.6	22.8	74.7	30.9	12.6	31.2	$26.4(
IEO91	73.2	41.9	10.9	20.4	72.8	32.3	13.0	27.5	26.4(
Canada[b]	72.8	41.9	10.0	20.9	72.8	33.4	13.3	26.1	23.2(
DRI	72.9	40.9	10.8	21.2	73.2	33.4	13.2	26.6	27.2(
County NatWest[c]	75.4	42.3	10.6	22.5	75.7	32.9	12.8	30.0	20.0(
World Bank	72.6	37.8	12.5	22.3	72.6	31.0	14.7	26.9	22.9(
Year 2010									
IEO92	84.3	43.6	12.6	28.1	84.0	41.9	14.7	27.4	33.4(
IEO91	78.7	43.8	13.0	21.9	78.3	39.8	13.9	24.6	33.4(
Canada	78.5	44.4	9.1	25.0	78.4	42.7	10.7	25.0	27.0(
DRI	80.6	43.6	11.4	25.6	80.8	40.6	13.3	26.9	35.7(

[a]1990 dollars per barrel.
[b]Estimates from Canada include only net exports from the former Centrally Planned Economies, an not consumption/production estimates. For purposes of comparability, the consumption/production est mates underlying the net export projections (derived from the *International Energy Outlook 1989*) ar added to the Canadian estimates.
[c]West Texas Intermediate oil price. The U.S. refiner acquisition cost of imported crude oil used as th world oil price for the IEO92 and other projections listed here runs about $2 to $3 per barrel less tha West Texas Intermediate.
OECD = Organization for Economic Cooperation and Development
IEO = International Energy Outlook (USDOE/EIA)
DRI = Data Resources, Inc./McGraw Hill

Source: Energy Information Administration, *International Energy Outlook 1992*, Washington, DC: USDOE/EIA, 199? p.15.

than TPES (total primary energy supply) and TFC (total final consumption). Note the steep decline of real energy prices; yet consumption of energy is rising slowly.[4]

---

[4]The data shown in Figures 26 and 27 are based on Energy Information Administration, *International Energy Outlook 1992* (IEO92), Washington, DC: USDOE/EIA.

FIGURE 29
Comparative Forecasts of World Oil Prices

| | 1992 Dollars per Barrel | |
Forecast	2000	2010
AEO94 Reference Case	20.72	28.16
AEO94 Low Price Case	15.44	20.15
AEO94 High Price Case	24.16	34.11
DRI	22.66	29.95
WEFA	20.34	24.94
IEA	26.70	29.30
GRI	21.01	27.02

AEO = Annual Energy Outlook 1994
DRI = Data Resources, Inc./McGraw Hill
WEFA = WEFA Group (formerly Wharton Econometric Forecasting Associates)
IEA = International Energy Agency
GRI = Gas Research Institute

Source: Energy Information Administration, *Annual Energy Outlook 1994*, Washington, DC: USDOE/EIA, 1994, p. 6.

Energy intensity is a ratio that relates these two measures to the gross domestic product. Between 1973 and 1991, OECD member nations reduced their energy intensity 23 percent as measured by TPES/GDP, or about 1.5 percent per year; the TFC/GDP ratio declined 30 percent during this time, or about 2 percent per year. Trends in intensity vary by fuel, as seen in Figure 31. The decline was about 38 percent for oil and 21 percent for gas. Such declines in energy intensity are due to improvements in energy efficiency and to structural changes in the OECD countries. In a similar way, the 9 percent rise in electricity intensity is due to restructuring and to more electrification—with its attendant losses—in these same countries.

By far, North America still uses more energy per capita than the rest of the world. Indeed, its per capita use has been more than twice as high as that of OECD Europe and more than six times higher than that of developing nations. The details are shown in Figure 33 for the 1968–93 period. What is encouraging is that the United States is taking additional energy conservation steps, which are clearly needed.

On the supply side, OPEC nations and other producers know they cannot control both price and usage, but they certainly are trying to reassert their power. There is general agreement that OPEC will continue to play a key role in regard to primary energy production. Several experts

FIGURE 30
GDP, TFC, TPES, and Energy Prices, OECD, 1980–1991

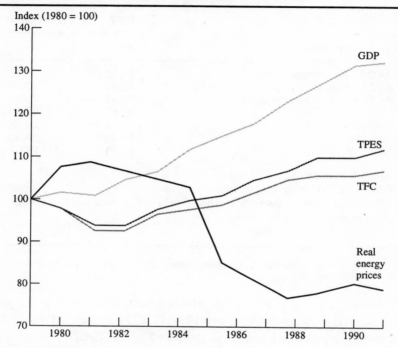

TPES = Total primary energy supply
TFC = Total final consumption of energy
Note: GDP figures do not include eastern Germany prior to 1991.
Source: IEA, *Energy Balances of OECD Countries* (Paris: OECD).

Source: International Energy Agency, *Energy Policies of IEA Countries: 1992 Review.* OECD/IEA: 1993, p. 15.

expect it to recapture its former glory and to supply half of all the oil consumed in the world of 2010. The vulnerability of the United States and other market economies to energy supply disruptions is a complex issue. A weighted vulnerability index has been developed; it stood at around 60 during 1975–80; dropped practically to 0 in 1985; rose to 60 in 1990; and is now around 45 to 50.[5]

[5]See the chapter devoted to discussion of energy efficiency and intensity in International Energy Agency, *Energy Policies of IEA Countries—1992 Review* (EP-IEA92). Paris: IEA/OECD, pp. 15–27.

FIGURE 31

Energy Intensity, OECD, 1973–1991 (TFC in Mtoe per US$ 1 000 of GDP at 1985 prices and exchange rates)

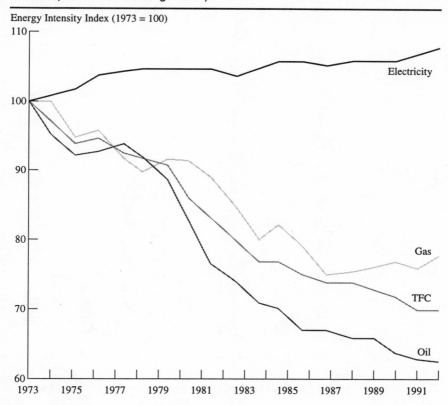

Energy Intensity Index (1973 = 100)

TFC = Total final consumption of energy
Mtoe = Millions of metric tons equivalent
Note: GDP figures do not include eastern Germany prior to 1991.
Source: IEA, *Energy Balances of OECD Countries* (Paris: OECD).

Source: International Energy Agency, *Energy Policies of IEA Countries: 1992 Review*. OECD/IEA: 1993, p. 6.

One of the crucial considerations is the extent of reserves and the ratio between reserves and output levels. Here, again, we find major differences among fuels. At current levels of proven reserves and production, global coal reserves will last twice as long as the combined reserves of crude oil and natural gas. The coal is expected to last for nearly 225 years, whereas gas comes in at under 75 years and oil at under 50 years. The

FIGURE 32
World Fossil Fuel Reserve to Production Ratios at End of 1993

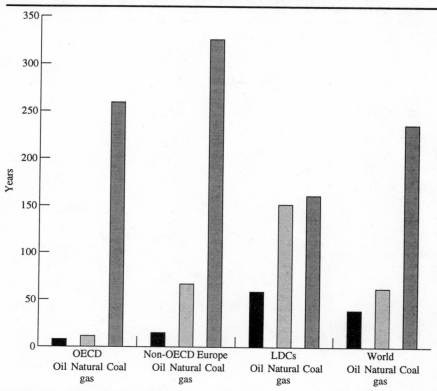

At current levels of proven reserves and production, global coal reserves will last twice as long as the combined reserves of oil and gas.

Source: *BP Statistical Review of World Energy.* London: BP, 1994, p. 36.

details, including differences among the three major regions of the world, are shown in Figure 32. Clearly, the OECD countries must continue with their conservation policies and encourage fuel-efficient processes.

THE U.S. PERSPECTIVE: THE PAST

As seen in Figure 33, during the postwar period, North America stood in stark contrast to Western Europe; its per capita usage of energy was more than twice as high. Can the United States (and Canada) emulate

FIGURE 33
World Energy Consumption per Capita by Regions

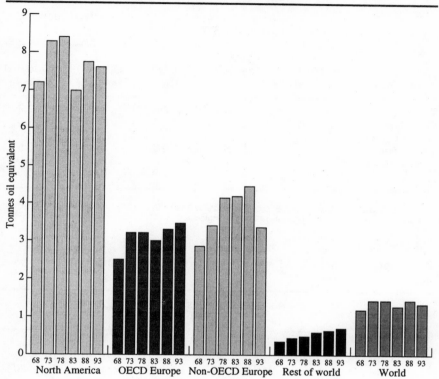

World energy demand has grown in line with popuation. North America's energy consumption per capita remains far higher than that of any other region.

Source: *BP Statistical Review of World Energy*. London: BP, 1994, p. 36.

the trends noted in European nations? There is evidence that this is happening already.

The historical track record of the United States during the 1970–90 period is illustrated in the data of Figures 34 and 35. As was the case for the global forecasts, the U.S. projections—on both the supply and demand side—proved to be far off the mark. What happened, of course, is that customers in households, on the roads, and in industry reacted to the sharp OPEC oil price rises. Conservation and fuel-efficient processes were embraced—up to a point. The United States still depends heavily on imported crude oil.

FIGURE 34

U.S. Energy in Historical Perspective: Supply (Production) by Major Fuel

Type of Fuel	Absolute Numbers (quadrillion BTU)			Annual Growth (percent)	
	1970 Actual	1990 Forecast Made in 1973	1990 Actual	1990/1970 Forecast	1990/1970 Actual
Coal	14.6	26.9	22.5	3.1	2.2
Crude oil	20.4	33.7	15.6	2.5	−1.3
Natural gas (dry & liquid)	24.2	29.5	20.5	1.0	−0.8
Nonhydrocarbons	2.9	31.7	9.3	12.6	6.0
Total	62.1	121.8	67.9	3.4	0.5

Source: A. Gross and W. Ware, "Energy Prospects to 1990," *Business Horizons,* June 1975, p. 11; and update in *Annual Energy Review 1992.* Washington, DC: USDOE/EIA, 1993, pp. 7–9.

FIGURE 35

U.S. Energy in Historical Perspective: Demand (Consumption) by Major End Use

End Use	Absolute Numbers (quadrillion BTU)			Annual Growth (percent)	
	1970 Actual	1990 Forecast Made in 1973	1990 Actual	1990/1970 Forecast	1990/1970 Actual
Transportation	16.1	20.4	22.5	1.2	1.7
Residential & commercial	12.1	11.0	9.6	−0.5	−1.1
Electric power	16.3	57.0	29.6	6.5	3.0
Industry	21.9	50.8	19.6	4.3	−0.5
Total	66.4	139.2	81.3	3.8	1.0

Note: Electric power and electric power losses not included in Transportation, Residential & Commercial, and Industry.

Source: A. Gross and W. Ware, "Energy Prospects to 1990," *Business Horizons,* June 1975, p. 9; and update in *Annual Energy Review 1992.* Washington, DC: USDOE/EIA, 1993, pp. 13 ff.

On the supply side, as shown in Figure 34, coal and nonhydrocarbons enjoyed a resurgence at the expense of crude oil and natural gas. The former recorded positive growth rates, but even coal grew at no more than 2.2 percent per year. Meanwhile, oil and gas have shrunk in market share and recorded negative growth rates. Overall, instead of the forecasted 3.4 percent growth during 1970–90, the supply rose at 0.5 percent. The absolute numbers and percentages refer, of course, to domestic production. Not shown is the fact that imports of crude oil rose from 2.8 quadrillion BTU in 1970 to 12.8 quadrillion BTU in 1990, representing a 7.9 percent annual growth in two decades.

On the demand side, as noted in Figure 35, all major end-use sectors used far less than forecasted. The overall consumption did grow at 1.0 percent per year during 1970–90, with transportation and electric power exhibiting higher rates while industry, commerce, and residences recorded negative growth. In effect, therefore, the conservation measures made inroads in these sectors. Transportation, wedded to the use of refined petroleum, has not been able to switch to coal or natural gas. Electric power has tried some shifting, with some success (to oil, gas, nuclear, hydro), but such switching involves considerable lead time, money, and institutional change.

THE U.S. PERSPECTIVE: PRESENT AND FUTURE

In the mid-1990s, the United States is enjoying slow but steady economic growth, with inflation and unemployment at relatively low levels. On the political scene, the cold war has ended and peace has been largely restored, despite continuing small regional conflicts. Once again, forecasters are rather optimistic, but projections are tempered with caution. On the energy front, it is now a given that growth in energy usage should be below rather than above the growth of the overall economy.

The range of economic growth forecasts for three key indicators is shown in Figure 36. None of the forecasts—even the high-scenario ones—for gross domestic product, labor force, and productivity exceed the 3.0 percent annual mark for the period 1990–2010. The so-called reference, or base, cases look most realistic to us at this juncture.[6]

---

[6]A. C. Gross and W. W. Ware, "Energy Prospects to 1990," *Business Horizons,* June 1975, pp. 5–18, based on A. C. Gross, *Nuclear and Advanced Energy Sources,* Report #89. Cleveland: Predicasts, 1974. As was the case for world energy, high growth rates were predicted for nuclear, geothermal, and solar sources, which did not materialize.

FIGURE 36
U.S. Comparative Forecasts of Economic Growth, 1990–2010

Forecast	Average Annual Percentage Growth		
	Real GDP	Labor Force	Productivity
AEO94			
Low	1.8	1.0	0.8
Reference	2.1	1.1	1.0
High	2.4	1.3	1.1
DRI			
Low	1.7	1.0	0.7
Base	2.1	1.1	1.0
High	2.5	1.3	1.2
WEFA			
Low	2.1	1.2	1.0
Base	2.5	1.3	1.2
High	2.9	1.5	1.4
Council of Economic Advisors	2.1	n/a	n/a

n/a = not available
AEO = Annual Energy Outlook 1994
DRI = Data Resources Inc./McGraw Hill
WEFA = WEFA Group (formerly Wharton Econometric Forecasting Associates)

Source: Energy Information Administration, *Annual Energy Outlook 1994*, Washington, DC: USDOE/EIA, 1994, p. 5.

The U.S. energy situation from now until 2010 is portrayed in the data displayed in Figures 37 and 38. The data in Figure 37 reveal that in regard to supply, the nation will continue to rely on imported crude oil and other petroleum products that show the highest growth rate. The price of crude oil globally in this scenario is shown rising at only 1.0 percent per year. The data of Figure 38 show an overall energy growth rate at 1.1 percent per year.

According to the *Annual Energy Outlook 1994* by the U.S. Energy Information Administration, "The price of oil in international markets drives U.S. petroleum markets and has powerful spillover effects on the markets for other fuels. International market conditions, particularly

FIGURE 37
U.S. Energy Supply and Demand: "Reference Case" Projections, 1990–2010

	Reference Mid-Range (quadrillion BTU)			Actual Growth 2010/1990 (percent)
	1990	2000	2010	
Production	71.1	71.1	76.1	0.3
Imports	18.5	30.3	35.2	3.3
Exports	4.6	5.7	6.2	1.5
Discrepancy	−0.7	0.1	0.1	n/a
Consumption	84.3	95.7	105.2	1.1
Net imports—petroleum	14.4	23.5	27.3	3.3
Prices (1992$/unit)				
World oil price ($/barrel)	23.22	20.72	28.16	1.0
Gas wellhead price ($/mcf)	1.83	2.42	3.47	3.3
Coal minemouth price ($/ton)	23.22	25.29	30.87	1.4

Source: Energy Information Administration, *Annual Energy Outlook 1994,* Washington, DC: USDOE/EIA, 1994, p. 55.

FIGURE 38
U.S. Energy Consumption by End-Use Sectors: "Reference Case" Projections, 1990–2010

End-Use Sector	Reference Mid-Range (quadrillion BTU)			Actual Growth 2010/1990 (percent)
	1990	2000	2010	
Residential	9.61	10.41	10.60	0.5
Commercial	6.57	7.22	7.55	0.7
Industrial	24.78	28.27	31.68	1.2
Transportation	22.50	26.16	29.50	1.4
Electric utilities	30.07	34.30	37.74	1.1
Total	93.53	106.36	117.07	1.1
Less electricity consumption (all sectors)	9.25	10.62	11.84	1.2
Primary energy consumption	84.29	95.73	105.23	1.1

Note: The 1990 figures differ from those in Figure 35 due to differing definitions and methods.

Source: Energy Information Administration, *Annual Energy Outlook 1994,* Washington, DC: USDOE/EIA, 1994, p. 56.

crude oil supply by OPEC, are major determinants of the world oil price, but U.S. demand and production also affect it. An innovation in the *Annual Energy Outlook 94* forecast is the incorporation of a dependence of the world oil price on U.S. oil demand and production."[7] Another consideration is the role of China and Eastern Europe; the EIA sees slow growth for both supply and demand in the former USSR. The EIA thinks that its National Energy Modeling System is more realistic and more on target than previous models and scenarios.

KEY ISSUES

Intensity/Efficiency/Conservation—"Had the consumption energy patterns of the 1970s continued through the 1990s, total U.S. energy use would be 50 percent higher in 2000 than is projected in this year's Annual Energy Outlook," stated J. E. Hakes, Administration, EIA, in January 1994.[8] Thus, clearly, the nation with the highest energy use has made progress, as it responded to the oil embargo and oil price shocks of the 1970s. The progress is documented in the accompanying Figures 36, 37, and 38. Clearly, much work remains to be done, for—as noted already—North America is still recording a per-capita energy use that is twice as high as the OECD countries (essentially, Western Europe and Japan).

Conservation is occurring on all fronts in the United States. In transportation, more fuel-efficient vehicles (cars, trucks, airplanes) continue to make their appearance. Taking 1973=100 for fuel consumption of passenger cars, the index stood at 65 at the start of the 1990s, a major improvement. In the household sector, appliances carry energy-saving labels. For example, "If we assume that purchasers of appliances through 2010 select the most energy-efficient technology available in 1991, residential energy demand in the U.S. would be about 25 percent less than it would have been if the average technology had been adopted."[9] Com-

---

[7]See Energy Information Administration, *Annual Energy Outlook, 1994* (AEO94), Washington, DC: USDOE/EIA, 1994, p. 5. The growth rate in the AEO94 reference is close to those of DRI and the Council of Economic Advisers. The WEFA projections differ from the others in their labor force participation rates: WEFA forecasts that 70 percent of the population age 16 and over will be in the labor force in 2010, compared with 66 percent in the DRI forecast.

[8]Ibid.

[9]Ibid., p. vii.

mercial properties feature windows and materials that contribute to lower cooling bills in summer and lower heating bills in winter. Energy consumption per building improved from 1,630 million BTU in 1979 to 1,278 million BTU in 1989. The industry also made giant strides in redesigning processes and in adopting fuel-efficient machinery.

Clearly, much remains to be done in both North America and the other OECD countries. Meanwhile, in the developing nations, energy-saving measures must also be taken as these countries embark on full-scale industrialization. Measures advocated range from restricting urban traffic to evaluating capital projects in regard to energy use.[10]

Renewable Energy/Reserves—After the "oil crisis" of the 1970s, much thought was given to using advanced, esoteric, or renewable energy resources. Before and especially after, there were concerns about stability of domestic supply, reliance on foreign sources, and environmental impact. Oil from shale, solar cells, wind energy, geothermal heat, and nuclear power were cited as possible replacements. A return to the use of wood would be yet another option. Some of these would serve to generate electricity; others would generate power on-site, avoiding building new large-capacity plants.[11]

In 1970, nuclear, hydro, and all renewable energy sources accounted for a tiny 0.6 percent of primary energy production; their share rose to 1.5 percent by 1992. The three traditional fossil fuels of crude oil, natural gas, and coal will continue to carry the overwhelming load for the foreseeable future. Nuclear electricity generation rose sharply in the past 20 years in the United States (from 2.5 percent to 22 percent of total electric power), but the number of reactors is now stabilized at 109 with no units on order and no construction permits pending. Safety, economic, and environmental concerns have all played a role in this. Solar, wind, geothermal, and ocean thermal energy may yet make a significant contribution to supply, but only in the 21st century.

---

[10]Ibid.

[11]Many energy policy and energy conservation books were published in the late 1970s and throughout the 1980s; several focused on regaining the power from OPEC via domestic exploration, etc. See M. H. Ross and R. H. Williams, *Our Energy: Regaining Control*. New York: McGraw-Hill, 1981; and W. A. Rosenbaum, *Energy, Politics, and Public Policy*. Washington, DC: CQ Press, 1987. For a good overview and regional data for the U.S., see D. J. Cuff and W. J. Young, eds., *The U.S. Energy Atlas*. New York: MacMillan, 1986. Currently (1994), there are about 300 titles in print on energy conservation and just about the same number on energy policy (see *Books in Print, Subject Guide*, 1993–94).

Energy vs. Environment—As oilfields are explored, coal is mined, and nuclear electricity is generated, numerous environmental concerns have arisen. The most serious problem at this time seems to be emissions of carbon dioxide and other air pollutants from coal-fired power plants. A sign of progress, however, is that emissions of carbon dioxide (about 10 billion metric tons in 1990), sulfur dioxide, and nitrogen oxide are falling or rising less rapidly than gross domestic product in the industrialized countries. Economic recession, installing air pollution control equipment, and switching to low-sulfur coal or to natural gas account for this.

According to the International Energy Agency, "A distinct lack of movement to replace conditional and interim targets with more concrete ones reflects the difficulty most OECD countries are having in defining programs that will allow them to meet targets with certainty."[12] There is evidence that environmental concerns have come to the forefront and influenced both energy production and consumption. Government and private-sector initiatives now include various incentives; the "compensation" or "joint implementation" scheme even calls for cooperation across national borders. At the same time, environmental impact analysis can halt progress: Building cogeneration plants, or renewable-based projects such as a wind-turbine plant in the United Kingdom, has been held up due to lengthy reviews.[13]

Safety—Energy exploration has its dangers, as seen in major tanker spills that threaten wildlife and vegetation. Nuclear power has raised special concerns, with incidents in the United States and former Soviet Union contributing to a halt in construction of new facilities. Governments and the public have become more concerned with various aspects: high costs, possible theft of nuclear fuel or bomb making, breakdown of security in plants, and, especially, location of sites for long-term disposal of nuclear waste. These issues simply will not go away; as a result, nuclear power leveled off at 24 percent of electricity generation in OECD countries as of 1991. Only Japan and France have plans to continue developing nuclear power at this time.[14]

---

[12]Energy Information Administration, *Annual Energy Review 1992* (AER92), Washington, DC: USDOE/EIA, 1993, Chapter 10, pp. 245–261, with a discussion on wood as fuel for primary and secondary space heating, pp. 248–251. The *BP Statistical Review of World Energy 1993* (BP93), London: BP, 1993 recognizes that wood is used widely in many countries, but the review deals only with commercially traded fuels.

[13]EP-IEA92, p. 28.

[14]Ibid., p. 59.

ENERGY STATISTICS: SOURCES AND GOALS

At the global level, the International Energy Agency (affiliated with OECD), the United Nations, and the Economic Commission for Europe are regular collectors of energy data, relying on national statistics provided for them. They also do their own monitoring and analysis. The Energy Information Administration in the U.S. Department of Energy is the primary collector of energy data in the United States. In most countries, the central statistical bureaus are given mandates to collect energy data. State and local governments play a relatively small role, though there are exceptions. The Province of Quebec, for example, is involved because of its development and ownership of hydro power.

The mandate of the International Energy Agency (IEA) is to maintain an energy statistics system in order to support the following activities: (1) preparedness for (oil) emergencies; (2) monitoring of energy, especially oil markets; (3) promotion of energy efficiency; (4) review of OECD national energy policies; (5) pursuit of energy research and development; (6) study of fiscal/financial aspects; and (7) identification of issues related to energy matters.[15] The Energy Information Administration has a similar mission, with emphasis on U.S. data, but since the United States continues to rely heavily on imports of crude oil, EIA also prepares international energy assessments and outlook reports.

In addition to public sources, nonprofit organizations and private-sector firms play a key role in energy data gathering and dissemination. Among the former in the United States are the American Gas Association, the American Petroleum Institute, the Edison Electric Institute, and the Gas Research Institute. In the latter group, we find the major coal, gas, and oil companies. Internationally, British Petroleum prepares its *BP Statistical Review of World Energy*, while Royal Dutch Shell is known for its scenario building. Major journals also play a key role; for example, the *Oil & Gas Journal*, *Platt's Oilgram*, *Petroleum Intelligence Weekly*, and *World Oil*.

Think tanks, commercial business research agencies, foundations, some university bureaus, and individual experts are also involved in gathering and analyzing energy statistics. Thus, in the United States, the models and forecasts made by Data Resources Inc./McGraw-Hill and

---

[15]Ibid., p. 45. See also: IEA92, p. 22; AEO94, p. 26; AER92, pp. 237–244 and pp. 300–309. The United Nations volumes, *World Energy Supplies*, are also useful in this regard.

Wharton Economic Forecasting Associates are often quoted, even by federal authorities. For many years, the Twentieth Century Fund focused on natural resources. Carl Pforzheimer & Company is cited for its work on comparative oil company statements, and John Waring is cited for his work on prime movers, such as turbines.[16] In the United Kingdom, the University of Sussex conducted some major energy studies. Atomic energy agencies in Canada, France, and Sweden have much information on nuclear power.

ENERGY STATISTICS: METHODOLOGY (WHAT COUNTS IS COUNTED)

The most authoritative source on global energy statistics is the IEA, which has built up a database on all the OECD countries and over 85 individual non-OECD countries (which account for 98 percent of non-OECD energy requirements). In building up its database, IEA has given priority to data from government ministries and agencies; it then supplemented these data with data from the U.N. and the ECE. By its own admission, "Data thus obtained have occasionally been adjusted or estimated after consultations with industry—especially with international oil and energy companies. Their comments allow us to reconcile, refine, and expand our data sources."[17]

    Since the lifting of the Iron Curtain and the fall of the Berlin Wall, the IEA has undertaken a thorough review of energy statistics in Central and Eastern Europe. It found some information gaps in the region in regard to both supply and demand. For example, on the supply side, statistics were not highly reliable in regard to external trade in fuels. Little information below total energy requirements was available on the supply side. The IEA proposed the use of common reporting form and a common classification scheme, but its work is hampered greatly by the black market and the underground economy, prevalent especially in Russia.

---

[16]U.S. Department of Commerce, *Statistical Abstract of the U.S.,* 1993. Washington: USDC, 1993, Tables 910 and 936.

[17]D. Blades, ed., *Statistics for a Market Economy.* Paris: OECD, 1991, has a special section on energy statistics, pp. 185–189.

Energy production and consumption data in the developed countries can be considered complete. Reliable historical time series have been built up on coal, crude oil, and natural gas. In a similar fashion, information about electric power capacity, generation, and usage is considered excellent. However, some series are relatively new, so government agencies must make estimates, rely on indirect data, and hope for additional budgets to undertake data collection. In developing nations, energy data are collected to the extent to which its supply and demand play a role in the economy.

One example of estimation is the case of renewable resources. Because it is difficult to measure solar energy consumption directly, producer shipments of solar collectors are used as an indirect measure. An old renewable fossil fuel, wood, has enjoyed resurging popularity recently in the United States. Thus, EIA now keeps count of households using wood as a primary or a secondary heating fuel. At the same time, EIA admits that, due to budgetary restraints, it has not collected data on the use of wood in developing nations, large as the use of wood may appear for some of these countries.[18]

ENERGY STATISTICS: SELECTED ISSUES

Efficiency Analysis—According to the IEA and others, a key factor hindering the measurement and evaluation of energy efficiency policies is the paucity of technical and economic end-use data. This applies to both developed and developing countries. National governments are just starting to implement programs to bring about energy efficiency through a mixture of incentives and regulations. Some electric and gas utilities have practiced for years what has been called demand-side management. An example is to provide users of electricity and gas with lower rates in off-peak hours. Similar data from other providers and users of energy would be useful in the formulation of energy policies. A related issue has to do with emission controls and other environmental measures: What is their impact on energy efficiency? The evidence is just starting to come in.

---

[18]Ibid., p. 185. The volumes of the IEA, including EP-IEA92 and *World Energy Outlook,* Paris: OECD/IEA, 1993 say little on methodology, data collection, etc. The volume by Blades focuses on Eastern Europe and its lack of data on energy. For the U.N. view, see *Energy Statistics Yearbook,* New York: United Nations, 1991.

Classification—As noted earlier, a few decades ago it was customary to classify energy supply and energy demand into four groups each: (coal, oil, gas, nonhydrocarbons) and demand (households, industry, electric power, motor vehicles). This scheme had some shortcomings; for example, wood on the supply side and commercial users on the demand side were not distinctly identified. There was also debate as to the proper grouping of electricity, because in one sense it is on the supply side (nuclear, hydro, solar, etc.) and in another it is on the demand side (power plants burning oil or coal). It is now common to list hydrocarbons and nonfossils (i.e., renewable fuels) on the supply side, and industry, residential-commercial, and transport users on the demand side. Electricity shows up as a conversion step, with only nuclear, hydro, etc. (primary energy) shown on the supply side.

In the United States, the EIA's National Energy Modeling System is a unified model that tries to overcome ambiguities and to integrate both domestic and foreign macroeconomic activities. It also supports analysis of emerging issues, such as efficiency and environmental considerations. The model has three major categories: (1) supply, consisting of oil, gas, coal, uranium, and such renewables as nuclear, hydro, wood, and so on; (2) conversion, encompassing electricity, petroleum refining, and synthetics; and (3) demand, from residential, commercial, transportation, and industrial uses.[19] Like its predecessors, this model incorporates a market-based approach to energy analysis by balancing supply and demand for each fuel and consuming sector and taking into account the economic competition among energy sources. Items included in the model are alternative fuels for vehicles, emission control regulations, different types of the same fuel, transport capacities (e.g., pipelines), regional differences in energy markets, and scenarios for disruptions or crises. Other public and private organizations have their own models, but the current EIA design is seen as one of the most comprehensive and integrated systems.

Classification and related issues persist in the energy field. This is often due to differing definitions, underlying assumptions, and the specific traditions/missions of the agencies involved. For example, in their current assessments and projections for electricity, DRI/McGraw-Hill and

---

[19]Based on phone conversations with selected officials at the Energy Information Administration, U.S. Department of Energy, May 1994.

WEFA, as well as the trade association EEI, report cogeneration capability together with nonutility capability. Also, DRI and the Gas Research Institute use nameplate capability (power plant capacity in gigawatts) rather than net summer capability; the former is 5 percent to 10 percent greater than the latter. These practices are opposite to those of EIA. Similar minor differences exist for other fuels and end-use sectors; in total, they "add up," and so analysts must always look at the fine print.[20]

Proved reserves—Reserves are estimates of fossil fuels that are left untapped in the ground and under the sea; some of it can be obtained, other portions are difficult to extract. According to the EIA, (1) there is no international standard for defining or estimating reserves, (2) each country and company has its own definitions, and (3) most countries have several categories of reserve estimates, reflecting the likelihood of actual extraction and circumstances in the field. The most important reserve category is "proved reserves," which reflect a high or reasonable certainty of actual production. Proved reserves are economically and technically feasible to produce, given the current infrastructure. But what is high or reasonable certainty, or economic feasibility? Again, countries differ on their definition of the term; some do not even report their proved reserves.

> In addition to problems of inconsistent definitions and standards, analysts work with data that are incomplete, imprecise, and often of questionable quality. They must decide what information will be used and how and what data will be discounted based on their own experience and judgment. They may also call on their own expertise when estimating some parameters and in choosing an estimation procedure. Therefore, equally competent engineers may arrive at significantly different reserve estimates for a given field. In addition, there is always the potential of a country or individual company reporting misleading or conflicting data for a particular field to gain financial or political advantages. In many instances, gas reserves data are held in strict confidence by countries and independent verification is not possible.[21]

The above quote, from the EIA *International Energy Annual 1992*, is itself subject to controversy at least on one count. The 1993 *BP Statistical Review of World Energy* claims that the increase in proved reserves of natural gas continues unabated, with the growth in 1992 coming mainly from the former Soviet Union and the Middle East.

---

[20]AEO94, p. 8.

[21]AEO94, p. 22; see also sources mentioned in footnote 2 above; see also AER92, Chapter 8.

The two key sources for proved reserve estimates of crude oil and natural gas are two U.S.-based publications, *Oil & Gas Journal* and *World Oil*. Both are highly respected by government and private sectors alike; both produce authoritative issues. *Oil & Gas Journal* publishes year-end issues on proved reserves and on production. Yet they do differ on their estimates. For example, between 1991 and 1992, *Oil & Gas Journal* reported an increase of less than 1 percent in world crude oil reserves to 996 billion barrels, while *World Oil* reported an increase of 13 percent to 1,092 billion barrels. For natural gas, the higher estimate is by *Oil & Gas Journal*, which showed an increase of 12 percent to 4,883 trillion cubic feet versus *World Oil* with only a 3 percent rise to 4,817 trillion cubic feet. Differences can be attributed to varying definitions of reserves data. The variances come from both developed and developing nations: Australia, China, Egypt, Germany, Indonesia, Norway, Pakistan, Yemen, et al.[22]

The EIA relies on two other organizations for estimates of world coal reserves: British Petroleum (BP) and the World Energy Council. There are no significant differences, as both put global coal reserves at about 1,145 billion short tons. This makes coal the most plentiful of the fossil fuel reserves, with over 200 years at 1992 consumption levels.

Dissemination—Energy statistics are disseminated broadly now due to at least three factors: (1) the important role of energy in economic growth, which continues despite—or possibly because of—the increased emphasis on energy conservation; (2) the strong link between energy and environmental issues; and (3) the recognition that putting more useful statistics in the hands of users assists them as well as the data-collection agencies. A host of journal articles, monographs, reports, and books have come forth in the past 20 years, particularly after 1973.

We shall not demonstrate the increased flow of information in detail, but note that two key agencies cited in the discussion above have established clearinghouse centers. Thus, the U.S. Department of Energy established not only the Energy Information Administration, but also the

---

[22]See IEA92, p. 102 and AER92, p. 310. The World Energy Council defines proved recoverable reserves as the tonnage of proved amount in place that can be recovered (extracted from the earth in raw form) under present and expected local economic conditions with existing technology. British Petroleum in BP93 defines proved reserves as those quantities that geological and engineering information indicate with reasonable certainty can be recovered in the future from known reservoirs under existing economic and operating conditions.

National Energy Information Center at its Washington headquarters. The EIA also has chosen to proceed with a series of publications on two fronts, one global and the other U.S.-oriented. The International Energy Agency is now fully affiliated with OECD, the Organization for Economic Cooperation and Development in Paris. Having the OECD, now primarily a statistical agency, behind it has helped the IEA in getting its database to users via both massive volumes and occasional articles in the *OECD Observer*.[23]

Data dissemination does not happen only via publications, but also via personal contacts. The EIA publicizes its list of experts in each publication and provides the reader with their direct phone numbers. The National Energy Information Center has its own line where the first-time user can be directed to other departments. Like other federal government agencies, the EIA recognizes the importance of public-private cooperation. A good example of this is the extent to which the EIA elaborates on the differing proved reserve statistics of *Oil & Gas Journal* and *World Oil*. EIA also refers to the work of various industry and technical associations, citing their publications within EIA reports. Finally, each EIA report now offers a long list of references to the academic and popular literature.[24]

CONCLUSION

This portion of the chapter examined the energy supply and demand situation in a global and U.S. setting for the period 1970 to 2010. We found that current projections seem far more realistic than earlier ones. Using data primarily from the U.S. Energy Information Administration and the Paris-based International Energy Agency, we examined the major producing and end-using sectors. In addition, we focused on such selected issues as energy intensity and the interaction of energy and the environ-

---

[23]IEA92, pp. 102–103.

Some key energy journals are: *Applied Energy; Biomass & Bioenergy; Energy; Energy and Fuels; Energy Economics; Energy Engineering; Energy Journal; Energy Policy; Energy Sources; International Journal of Energy; Environment Economics; Journal of Energy and Development; Renewable Energy; Resource & Energy Economics; Resources Policy.* See also the specialized journals cited in text and above, e.g., *Electrical World, Oil & Gas Journal, World Oil*, etc.

[24]For example, see the references in the previous footnote .

ment. Then emphasis shifted to energy statistics, specifically to data sources, classification schemes, methodology, proved reserves, forecasting, and data dissemination.

As stated at the start, there is no real danger of an energy crisis and no immediate major problems are seen in regard to supplies of primary fuels. Global and national economic growth will proceed, while energy conservation and other fuel-saving measures continue. As for energy statistics, there is no major problem on that front either. Gaps in the data are relatively few, and disagreement on "proved reserves" still allows a relatively narrow range of useful estimates. There is no question, however, that reserve estimates constitute one of the "soft spots" in our energy knowledge. Overall, reliable time series are available that give insights on energy production and consumption. More sophisticated modeling techniques permit the formulation of realistic forecasting scenarios. The present process of data dissemination keeps users informed about trends.

CHAPTER 6

DATA FOR
ENVIRONMENTAL ANALYSIS

INTRODUCTION

A simplistic view of the degradation of the physical environment is that factories emit dirty water and visible smoke; that these cause minor health, material, and aesthetic damage; that industrialists choose to ignore such problems; and that the solution lies in stricter regulation and penalties. A crisis view sees just about everyone, including farmers, miners, car and truck drivers, manufacturers, office workers, and, of course, consumers, as major contributors to such damage. The truth, as Pogo said, is that "We have met the enemy and it's us." But an analytical assessment is in order.

Just as the causes of pollution are many and varied, the impact or effects of such environmental degradation are diverse, and the solutions are complex and multifaceted. Most human activities—economic, social, or otherwise—cause physical degradation, accelerating natural causes. The intertwining of such forces is anything but simple, and their effects are not easily measured. Tracing specific damage to a source is especially difficult. Solutions lie not only in legal, economic, and technical advances, but in changing underlying cultural values and social conditions. Passing laws and issuing rules do not mean they will be either observed or enforced.[1]

---

[1]A.C. Gross and N.H. Scott, "Comparative Environmental Legislation and Actions," *International & Comparative Law Quarterly,* Fall 1980, pp. 619–663; and A.C. Gross, "Water Quality Management Worldwide," *Environmental Management,* Vol. 10, No. 1, January 1986, pp. 25–40. On business opportunities: A. C. Gross, "Global Competition for Environmental Markets," *European Journal of Marketing,* Spring 1986, pp. 22–34.

Figure 39 shows a classification of the causes of environmental damage. As can be seen, degradation occurs in the absence of human activities, though the latter are responsible for most of the problems. Evidence indicates that concentration is clearly a major concern; if population, production, and consumption could be dispersed evenly over the land, up to 90 percent of the pollution could be eliminated, as nature is largely self-healing. While some attempts are being made at such dispersion, it is unlikely to be achieved, given current patterns of economic development and growth. Additionally, noneconomic factors, such as lack of trained personnel, resistance from vested interests, and bureaucratic bungling, are also significant contributors to environmental dam-

FIGURE 39
Key Facets of Environmental Pollution: Causes/Classification Schemes

I. Natural vs. Human-made Occurrences
  A. Natural
    1. Volcanic eruptions
    2. Soil erosion, topsoil removal
    3. Nutrient runoff from land
  B. Human-made
    1. General
      a. Growth of populations
      b. Industrialization
      c. Urbanization
      d. Acquisitive lifestyle
    2. Specific
      a. Factory and auto emissions
      b. Plant and household waterwaste
      c. Oil tanker spillage
      d. Nuclear waste
      e. New chemicals
II. Economic vs. Noneconomic Failures
  A. Economic
    1. Consideration of air and water as free goods
    2. Reluctance to spend on "nonproductive goods"
    3. Lack of financing, tax base
    4. Lack of subsidies, incentives
  B. Noneconomic
    1. Lack of professional and technical personnel
    2. Poorly designed legislation, enforcement, jurisdiction
    3. Resistance from vested interests

(continued)

FIGURE 39 *(continued)*

III. Point vs. Nonpoint Sources
    A. Point: Specific factories, cars, households
    B. Nonpoint: Untraceable emission/effluent
IV. All Other Classification Schemes
    A. On basis of degradability
    B. By type of medium emitted to air, water, etc.
    C. On basis of toxicity

(concluded)

Source: A.C. Gross, "Water Quality Management Worldwide," *Environmental Management,* Vol. 10, No.1, January 1986, pp. 25–39.

age. Finally, there are many untraceable factors, such as nonpoint sources (e.g., fertilizer runoffs from hundreds of farms), that are major sources of pollution. These are difficult to monitor or eliminate. The detective work on pinpointing such sources and then controlling them has just started.

The impact of pollution may be short-run or long-run, or both. The effects can be visible or undetectable, but the assessment of the damage is a complex undertaking. Figure 40 shows three major categories: (1) worsening public health, (2) economic damage, and (3) noneconomic degradation. Quantifying the exact damage is extremely difficult. Scientists have spent years tracing the adverse impact of many chemicals—whether originating from air, land, or water—on human food consumption, but the results are controversial (there is a joke that the press offers a "pollutant or hazard of the week"). That dirty air from power plants creates acid rain and causes heavy pollution in lakes and forests hundreds of miles away has been demonstrated in North America or Europe—or has it? The debate continues, but cleanup has started. Better measurement, the theme of this chapter, will also help.

Remedies for environmental damage lie at three levels, as shown in Figure 41: cultural and social change; scientific and technical advances (some call these "fixes"); and alteration of legal, political, and economic policies. Solutions can be general or specific, long- or short-run. Changing attitudes, values, and lifestyles is clearly a long-run proposition. Offering incentives and passing regulations are viewed as short- to medium-term remedies. There is increased impetus for levying discharge fees in contrast to regulation or subsidizing. There is also a move toward

FIGURE 40
Key Facets of Environmental Pollution: Impact/Effect

I. Public Health Attacks
   A. Respiratory ailments
   B. Digestive ailments
   C. Communicable diseases, etc.
II. Economic Damages
   A. Damage to human productivity
   B. Damage to animal health and productivity
   C. Damage to vegetation, plant life
   D. Damage to materials: corrosion, etc.
   E. Damage to recreational facilities, etc.
III. Noneconomic Impact
   A. Aesthetic and psychological impact
   B. Social and cultural values
   C. Disruption to lifestyle(s)

Source: A.C. Gross, "Water Quality Management Worldwide," *Environmental Management,* Vol. 10, No. 1, January 1986, pp. 25–39.

ad hoc, regional bodies (e.g., river basin management) as opposed to creating new federal and state regulating bodies. A consensus is emerging that overly strict regulation is unfair and inefficient (such as the wasteful Superfund for toxic sites). Pragmatic solutions lie in looking at many alternatives, allowing choices to polluters, and avoiding detailed point-by-point rulings. But there is recognition that pollutant transfer is not a desirable remedy.

APPROACHES TO POLLUTION CONTROL

Common law has always been concerned with the relationship between an individual's or an organization's use of property and the impact of such use on neighbors near and far. The central theme governing this situation is: "Use your property so as not to injure your neighbor's property." This rule is now a principle of national law and can apply to international agreements as well. The nature of modern society, complex industrial processes, and a bent toward political/legal solutions take us from common sense and precedents to statutory law, administrative machinery, and overlapping jurisdiction. Even defining pollution can be a daunting task, as seen in Figure 42. After pollution criteria are established there are many administrative approaches to the policy actions to

FIGURE 41
Key Facets of Environmental Pollution: Remedies/Solutions

I. Cultural and Social Change
   A. Change lifestyle, consumption patterns
   B. Change social/cultural values
   C. Change underlying attitudes
II. Scientific, Technical, and Industrial Changes
   A. Change pollution from one medium to another
   B. Change assimilative capacity of the environment
   C. Neutralize or offset reactions
   D. Utilize of effluent/waste
   E. Switch to new materials and processes
   F. Limit production of new/untested chemicals
III. Legal, Political, and Economic Changes
   A. Regulation by the government
      1. Outright ban
      2. Across the board or point-by-point regulation
      3. Environmental impact statements filing
   B. Economic subsidies
      1. Public spending on treatment facilities
      2. Subsidy to individuals, groups
   C. Economic and other incentives
      1. Levy fee on discharges—issue "permits to pollute"
      2. License dischargers
   D. Adjustment of administrative machinery
      1. Retain existing boundaries
      2. Establish basin or regional authority
      3. Establish new ministries or coordinating bodies or "pollution management agencies"
      4. Allow suits by individuals and groups

Source: A.C. Gross, "Water Quality Management Worldwide," *Environmental Management,* Vol. 10, No. 1, January 1986, pp. 25–39.

be taken. In Figure 43 we present a listing of selected legislative and administrative approaches that have been taken by different countries. The differences in administrative machinery for handling these issues are shown in Figure 44. Finally, Figure 45 shows an overview of how individuals can take action.

As noted for many other fields, ranging from poverty to test scores, how you classify and administer a problem will influence greatly the process of data collection as well as the proposed solutions. Thus, as was presented in Figure 42, it can make a difference in the gathering of statistics whether we view environmental degradation as damage to other

FIGURE 42
**Legal and Administrative Aspects of Environmental Pollution: Definition/
Determination of Pollution**

I. Traditional Definitions and Views
  A. Alteration of the existing environment
  B. Right of the territorial sovereign (no extraterritorial effects recognized)
  C. Damage to humans, property, environment
  D. Interference with others' rights to use the environment
  E. Exceeding the assimilative capacity of the environment
II. Nontraditional Definitions or Views
  A. "Label substitution" or specification of harmful substances emitted or discharged
  B. Combination of approaches, i.e., any two or more of the above

Source: A.C. Gross, "Water Quality Management Worldwide," *Environmental Management,* Vol. 10, No. 1, January 1986, pp. 25–39.

parties or as exceeding the capacity of the river, land, or air to absorb human-made pollutants. Experts now call for identifying and setting limits to specific pollutants, agreeing on threshold standards and negotiating consequences.

The legal and administrative approaches taken by various nations to protect the physical environment, including the United States, are quite varied (see Figure 43). There is now a strong tendency toward broad statutory steps at the federal level; this means overall environmental laws. An alternate trend is toward "mixed systems," having concurrent laws for air, water, and land pollution control. Either approach means deemphasizing protection of just one medium or resource. Recognition is growing that "all parts are linked," so transferring pollution from one place to another is a localized and temporary remedy that will not be tolerated for long.

There are different administrative machineries for pollution control that can be put in place (Figure 44). At the international level, we find bilateral agreements and regional accords. Even if an environmental equivalent to WHO, the World Health Organization, emerges, it is unlikely to be a data-gathering or rule-making agency acceptable to all industrialized and developing countries. The latter resent being accused of "denuding the environment." At the national level and below, there is a dichotomy. Some prefer the creation of new structures, while others use existing bodies. A compromise solution lies in the use of coordinating agencies as in Western Europe, which also pioneered the use of dis-

FIGURE 43

Legal and Administrative Aspects of Environmental Pollution: Primary Legislative and Administrative Approaches

I. Comprehensive Environmental Policy and Laws, e.g.:

Australia	Ireland	Sweden
Colombia	Japan	United Kingdom
France	Malaysia	United States
Greece	Portugal	

II. Specific Environmental (Medium) Policy and Laws, e.g.:

Austria	Germany	Spain
Canada	Italy	Switzerland
Finland	Norway	Turkey

III. Combination Environmental Policy and Laws ("Mixed Systems"), e.g.:

Belgium	Mexico	New Zealand
Selected provinces in Canada		

IV. Natural Resource Legislation, e.g.:

Algeria	Libya
Cyprus	Peru
Czechoslovakia	Poland
Israel	USSR

V. Other Systems

   A. Protection of certain living or natural organisms, e.g., Syria

   B. Specific discharge or emission prohibitions, e.g., Egypt

Note: Comprehensive laws coexist with specific medium (air, water) laws in many countries; i.e., these are not exclusive categories, but indicate main approaches.

Source: A.C. Gross, "Water Quality Management Worldwide," *Environmental Management,* Vol. 10, No. 1, January 1986, pp. 25–39.

charge permits. Others, including the United States, frowned on this until now, because it looked politically negative to issue licenses to pollute. This view is changing.

Citizens, individually or in groups, can and do take action against pollution when their interests are affected (Figure 45). This can influence legislation, enforcement, expenditures, and data collection. Some view the extension of individual rights beyond remedy for direct injuries as distasteful; but others advocate the extension, believing that government commissions or task forces may be too sympathetic to industrial or other interests.[2]

---

[2]A.C. Gross and N. H. Scott, "Comparative Environmental Legislation and Actions," *International & Comparative Law Quarterly,* Fall 1980, pp. 619–663.

FIGURE 44

Legal and Administrative Aspects of Environmental Pollution: Levels of Legislation and/or Administrative Structure

---

I. Supranational and International Organizations and Agreements

  A. Global, e.g.:

UN	WHO	WMO
UNEP	FAO	IGOC
UNESCO	MCO	Earthwatch
UNCTAD	WCJ	

  B. Regional, e.g.:

OECD	CMEA
EU	Rhine Catchment Basin Danube Countries

  C. Bilateral, e.g.:
      Canada/U.S.
      Mexico/U.S.
      Two-country tribunals

II. National Level Government

  A. 1. New department or ministry, e.g.:

Canada	E. Germany	Norway
Denmark	Japan	United Kingdom

    2. Old department or ministry with extended jurisdiction, e.g., Netherlands, Nigeria

  B. Coordinating body, e.g.:

Algeria	Israel	Spain
Chile	Germany	Syria
France	Morocco	

III. State or Provincial Government/Organization

  A. 1. New department or agency
    2. Existing political boundaries and bodies

  B. Coordinating committee for local government

Source: A.C. Gross, "Water Quality Management Worldwide," *Environmental Management,* Vol. 10, No. 1, January 1986, pp. 25–39.

FRAMEWORK FOR ENVIRONMENTAL INFORMATION (AND INDICATORS)

The U.N. and the OECD have a very broad view of what constitutes the physical environment. The U.N. list ranges from the atmosphere to inland waters, from energy to emissions, from natural disasters to public perception and spending on pollution control. The OECD list ranges from housing amenities to serve accessibility. The U.N. enumeration, however, can be summed up in three groups of indicators: fixed or slowly

FIGURE 45
Legal and Administrative Aspects of Environmental Pollution: Facets of Individual Rights and Action

I. Judicial Proceedings (hearing of lawsuits brought against the activity complained of)
    A. Where the acts complained of have threatened the plaintiff
    B. Where the plantiff has sustained no "direct" injury
II. Administrative Proceedings
    A. Extent to which a public hearing is required before administrative rule making
    B. Individuals' right to participate in hearings concerning the environment
    C. Challenging administrative action concerning the environment
    D. Needed improvements

Source: A.C. Gross, "Water Quality Management Worldwide," *Environmental Management,* Vol. 10, No. 1, January 1986, pp. 25–39.

changing features, such as mountains and coastlines; recurring phenomena, such as rainfall or energy use; and parameters of major concern, such as climatic change or soil degradation. Measures are usually in terms of physical units.[3]

For the past 15 years, the OECD has published reports on the state of the environment. In the 1991 volume on the topic, the key headings included global atmospheric issues, air, inland waters, marine environment, land, forest, wildlife, solid waste, and noise. In addition, the report also dealt with the economic context (agriculture, industry, transport, energy, sociodemographic changes) and responses.[4] A companion OECD volume parallels this by listing 18 environmental indicators: 4 on air (CO_2, SO, NO, and greenhouse gas emissions); 3 on water (water resource, river quality, wastewater treatment), 5 on land (land use, protected areas, forests, tropical wood trade, fertilizer use), 2 on wildlife (threatened species, fish), 2 on solid waste, and 2 other (industrial accidents, opinion polls). There are also 7 indicators of economic activity (2 on energy, transport trends, production, consumption, growth, population).[5]

In addition to the many U.N. and OECD volumes, the *World Development Report 1992* by the World Bank focused on economic develop-

[3]United Nations, Statistical Office, *Framework for Environmental Statistics Prelim. M/75, M/78.* New York: United Nations, 1983.

[4]OECD Staff, *The State of the Environment 1991.* Paris: OECD, 1991.

[5]OECD Staff, *Environmental Indicators—A Preliminary Set.* Paris: OECD, 1991.

ment and the environment. In addition to discussing priorities and policies, the book offers a framework of its own (see Figure 21) and argues that the current problem is not running out of scarce resources, but rather "the unmarketed side effects associated with their extraction and consumption" (i.e., the externality question). The report extols the virtue of the U.N. system of satellite national accounts, which explicitly incorporates the links between economic activity and the use of resources. Mexico and Papua New Guinea are currently doing this in collaboration with the U.N. and the World Bank. The 1992 World Bank report, like the two OECD volumes, offers both cross-sectional diagrams for many countries and longitudinal data that permit comparisons over time. There is detailed discussion of air, water, and land problems as well as many mini-case studies.[6]

In regard to gathering information, especially for developing nations, collecting basic data can be expensive, but the rewards are usually high. Efforts are underway to help countries with environmental monitoring and to compile even more internationally comparable data. While nations differ in their needs, data should be gathered on drinking water, sanitation, ambient air pollutants, hazardous wastes, fecal coliform and heavy metals in rivers, soil quality, groundwater quality, forest area, fish harvest, wildlife depletion, and damage to coastal and wetland resources. In a recent book, R. V. Horn suggests a shift in environmental indicators from the physical science viewpoint toward those with socioeconomic implications. The major question, he claims, has become the assessment of the economic cost of externalities in the form of resource use and pollution. Since resources are scarce, not just for individuals and organizations, but overall, the emphasis must be on limits to growth. The debate shifted, he claims, from manageable externalities to the greater issue of global effects.[7]

Horn mentions that major attempts are still being made to measure pollution—or resource depletion—by a single or combined index but concludes that there is a problem in finding a common value standard. He contends that comprehensive pollution control measurement requires a translation of physical damages into a monetary sum regardless of what

---

[6]World Bank Staff, *World Development Report 1992: Economic Development and the Environment.* New York: Oxford University Press for the World Bank, 1992.

[7]R.V. Horn, *Statistical Indicators for the Economic and Social Sciences.* New York: Cambridge University Press, 1993, pp. 171–177.

methodology or theory is utilized. He ends with a partial endorsement of the idea of national resource accounting; that is, integrating resource use estimates (pollution control costs and benefits) into the gross national product. This will be discussed shortly in more detail.

A conceptual framework and a unified approach to environmental statistics were proposed earlier by T. Friend of Statistics Canada. After reviewing the history of growing enthusiasm for environmental data, he suggests integrating socioeconomic and biophysical statistics. Friend then proposes two routes, a material-energy balance and a stress-response system, which are not substitutes for each other but different facets of a more total framework, adaptable for developing nations.[8]

In the former, the key is the concept of mass balance (laws of conservation and energy) and related physical transformation processes. The structure is analogous to an input-output system, with emphasis on two stock accounts (natural and human-made) and three flows (energy conversion, production, consumption). The practical statistical work involves compiling a set of stock-flow accounts. This taxonomy parallels the Standard Industrial Classification (SIC) system (an industrial process yielding an output), but there is a substantial modification for material-energy accounting and for integrating production with consumption.

In the second approach, the critical parameters are statistical measures of environmental stress resulting from human activity, with further measures on their interaction with nature, and complementary measures of response derived from monitored observations of changes. Figure 46 depicts the essential components or modules. Three categories of collective and individual response are proposed: preventive, curative, and conservation steps.

At a 1991 conference dealing with global environment information, several attempts were made to integrate conceptual frameworks with the need for specific indicators.[9] Participants endorsed the idea of sustainable development (defined as taking care of present and future generations). Pearce and Freeman, in a fashion similar to Friend's work, suggest a model that incorporates the idea of pressure (i.e., stress) and response

---

[8]T. Friend, "Conceptual Frameworks and a Unified Approach to Environmental Statistics," working paper, Statistics Canada, 1980, p. *xii,* reprinted in *Bulletin of the International Statistical Institute,* Vol. 48.

[9]Jean-Paul Gourdeau, ed., *Proceedings—Environmental Information Forum.* Ottawa: Environment Canada, 1992.

FIGURE 46
Structural Framework for the Stress-Responses Environmental Statistical System (STRESS)

Activity Category	Activity Statistics	Stress Indicators	Response Indicators	Collective and Individual Response	Inventory of Stock
I Generation of waste residuals	Production and consumption of economic commodities	Pollution loadings in environmental media	Pollution levels	Actions to reduce pollution loadings	Pollution abatement and recycling capacity
II Permanent environmental restructuring	Construction activity and land use change	Location of construction activity and land use change	Ecosystem transformation	Acts to protect and conserve environmental assets	Accumulated stock of human-made structures. Area of protected environments
III Harvesting activity	Production from renewable resources	Exploitation and technological stresses	Sustainable yields. Quality of renewable resources	Actions to control technology and establish harvest quotas	Stock of renewable resource
IV Extraction of nonrenewable resource	Rates of depletion	Rate of substitution. Exploration activity	Environmental impact of substitutes and explotations	Conservation measures of nonrenewable resources	Stock of nonrenewable resources

V Environmental contamination	Production, disposition, and disposal of Potentially Hazardous Substances	Leakage of P.H.S. in environment. Application of P.H.S.	Level of contaminants in the environmental media and biota	Action to control the P.H.S.	Stock of P.H.S.
VI Energy	Production, use, and distribution	Thermal loadings, noise (acoustic energy). Energy infrastructure	Impact of energy thermal pollution	Energy conservation	Energy infrastructure and networks
VII Natural activity	Climate, geophysical events	Floods, droughts, earthquakes, tidal waves	Change in harvest productivity, loss of productive lands	Expenditure incurred to protect against extreme "natural events"	Mapping of climates and biophysical regions
VIII Population	Population change on temporal and spatial plane	Population in relation to carrying capacity	Disease and diminution of quality of life	Control of population growth and habitat	Census of populations

Source: T. Friend, "Conceptual Frameworks and a Unified Approach to Environmental Statistics," working paper, Statistics Canada, 1980, p. *xii*, published in *Bulletin of the International Statistical Institute*, Vol. 48, as quoted in D. Pearce and S. Freeman, "Informational Requirements of Policy Decision-Makers," in *Environmental Information Forum, Proceedings of a 1991 International Conference in Montreal*. Ottawa: Environment Canada, 1992, p. 76.

(see Figure 47). They explore how to set priorities for environmental information in general and for indicators in particular.[10] Nishioka and Moriguchi make a valuable contribution by relating environmental data production to stages of policy process plus show a possible institutional arrangement (see Figures 48 to 52).[11]

FIGURE 47
A Basic Model of Environmental Indicators

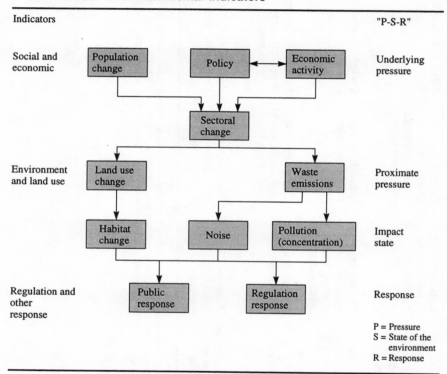

Source: D.W. Pearce, R.K. Turner, et al., "The Development of Environmental Indicators," Report to the U.K. Department of the Environment, University College London, February 1991.

[10]D. Pearce and S. Freeman, "Informational Requirements of Policy Decision-Makers," in *Proceedings—Environmental Information Forum,* Jean-Paul Gourdeau, ed. Ottawa: Environment Canada, 1992, pp. 56–101.

[11]S. Nishioka and U. Moriguchi, "Institutional Arrangements and Environmental Information Needs," in *Proceedings—Environmental Information Forum,* Jean-Paul Gourdeau, ed. Ottawa: Environment Canada, 1992, pp. 145–166.

FIGURE 48

Institutional Arrangements for Environmental Information

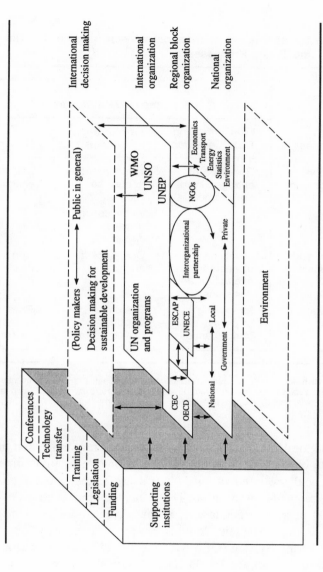

Source: F. Nishioka and Y. Moriguchi, "Institutional Arrangements and Environmental Information Needs," in *Environmental Information Forum, Proceedings of a 1991 International Conference in Montreal.* Ottawa: Environment Canada, 1992, p. 149.

FIGURE 49

Function of Environmental Information at Each Stage of the Data Production and Policy Processes

Stages of Policy Process	Stages of Data Production		
	Monitoring and Data Collection	Processing and Analysis	Dissemination
Identification and recognition of issues	Detection of changes in the environment	Transformation to concise information Identification of cause and effect	Education/ enlightenment
Evaluation and decision making	Provision of basis for evaluation and decisions	Cost-benefit analysis	Consensus building
Implementation	Monitoring of policy performance	Evaluation of policy performance	Promotion of public awareness

Source: F. Nishioka and Y. Moriguchi, "Institutional Arrangements and Environmental Information Needs," in *Environmental Information Forum, Proceedings of a 1991 International Conference in Montreal.* Ottawa: Environment Canada, 1992, p.153.

While the United Nations Environmental Programme and the OECD Directorate on the Environment play a major role in environmental data collection and are cited often as key sources, many other groups also gather the requisite information. These include other sections of the U.N. and OECD at their headquarters; affiliated, quasi-independent agencies, for example, the Economic Commission for Europe, the Global Environment Monitoring System (GEMS),[12] the World Health Organization, and so on; and, of course, the World Bank. National governments often assist

---

[12]For a good summary of GEMS/Water, see M.K. Tolma, *The State of the World Environment.* Nairobi, Kenya: United Nations Environmental Programme, 1991, especially pp. 14–16 and pp. 27–34.

FIGURE 50

Criteria for Evaluating Environmental Information at Each of the Data Production and Policy Processes

Stages of Policy Process	Stages of Data Production		
	Monitoring and Data Collection	Processing and Analysis	Dissemination
Identification and recognition of issues	Accuracy/ coverage of issues	Understandability of presentation	Quickness
	Historical and geographical coverage	Understandability of indicator	Periodicity
Evaluation and decision making	Comparability/ consistency	Integration with other information	Appropriateness for target user
Implementation	Established methodology	Simplicity/ measurability	Accessibility to the public

Source: F. Nishioka and Y. Moriguchi, "Institutional Arrangements and Environmental Information Needs," in *Environmental Information Forum, Proceedings of a 1991 International Conference in Montreal.* Ottawa: Environment Canada, 1992, p.153.

international agencies; for example, the Canada Centre for Inland Waters is host to the GEMS water monitoring project.[13]

There are numerous nonprofit environmental organizations that collect data on their own and/or analyze those gathered by others. These include organizations such as the World Resources Institute, Worldwatch Institute, and the World Wildlife Fund plus some major botanical and

[13]There is no shortage of volumes dealing with the environment, even on a global scale. Many authors rely on the UN or OECD statistics, but a few collect their own data, and many offer analysis. Here is a sample of titles: L.R. Brown et al., eds., *State of the World, 1993.* Washington, DC: Worldwatch Institute, 1993; A.L. Hammond, ed., *World Resources, 1990–91.* New York: Oxford University Press for WRI, 1990; A.L. Hammond, ed., *1993 Information Please Environmental Almanac.* Boston: Houghton Mifflin, 1993; M. Kidron and S. Segal, *The New State of the World Atlas.* New York: Simon & Schuster, 1987; G. Lean et al., *World Wildlife Fund Atlas of the Environment.* New York: Prentice-Hall, 1990. New editions come out often.

FIGURE 51
Areas of Responsibility and Operations of Existing Institutions at Each of the Data Production and Policy Processes

Stages of Policy Process	Stages of Data Production		
	Monitoring and Data Collection	Processing and Analysis	Dissemination
Identification and recognition of issues	BAPMoN GEMS/GRID	Environmental indicator OECD	Statistical compendium SOE reporting
Evaluation and decision making	EMEP	Natural resources accounting	NGO's (WRI, WWI)
Implementation	GOsOS Alert system	Green GNP	

Source: F. Nishioka and Y. Moriguchi, "Institutional Arrangements and Environmental Information Needs," in *Environmental Information Forum, Proceedings of a 1991 International Conference in Montreal*. Ottawa: Environment Canada, 1992, p.154.

zoological associations. Universities and academies play a role; for example, the Institute of Geography, National Academy of Sciences of the USSR has been recognized as a major force in collecting data on river runoff, groundwater, and soil moisture. The list of such groups when combined with the U.N. and OECD agencies runs in the hundreds.

Private-sector firms as well as many individuals, affiliated or not, have contributed to the wealth of data now available on the environment. Trade, industry, and technical associations also play a role by design or by default. For example, major oil spills are reported by the International Tanker Owners Pollution Federation.[14] In the United States, the Water

---

[14]Quoted in M. Kidron and S. Segal, *The New State of the World Atlas*. New York: Simon & Schuster, 1987, Figure 45.

FIGURE 52

Functions That Need to Be Strengthened in Order to Respond to Emerging Issues

Stages of Policy Process	Stages of Data Production		
	Monitoring and Data Collection	Processing and Analysis	Dissemination
Identification and recognition of issues	Global monitoring and quick reporting	International comparisons	Right to know
			Privacy
	Assessment of scientific research results	Integration with other policies	Intellectual property rights
Evaluation and decision making		Consideration of cost-effectiveness	International consensus building
Implementation		Measuring the progress towards sustainable development	

Source: F. Nishioka and Y. Moriguchi, "Institutional Arrangements and Environmental Information Needs," in *Environmental Information Forum, Proceedings of a 1991 International Conference in Montreal.* Ottawa: Environment Canada, 1992, p.154.

and Wastewater Equipment Manufacturers Association coordinates some of its data gathering with public agencies and environmental groups. While some of the information gathered is indeed conflicting, we are at the early stages. But progress is being made; for example, the GEMS/Water project launched in 1977 has compiled an impressive set of longitudinal as well as cross-sectional data. The first assessment, made in 1989, reported data from 344 stations in 59 countries on about 50 different parameters of water quality. Gaps remain, especially for Eastern Europe, Africa, and China.[15]

---

[15]Quoted in M.K. Tolma, *The State of the World Environment.* Nairobi, Kenya: United Nations Environmental Programme, 1991, p. 15.

ENVIRONMENTAL STEWARDSHIP AND NATIONAL INCOME ACCOUNTS

For a long time, various groups advocated that we must go beyond simple impact statements and that such measures as gross domestic product, productivity, discount rates, public expenditures, product prices, and so on, should reflect the idea of environmental stewardship. A corollary along these lines is that rules, treaties, and policies (e.g., antitrust laws, trade agreements, project cost-benefit estimates, etc.) should also reflect the notion of "proper" or sustainable development. Others contend that such assignments cannot be carried out or that the marketplace will ultimately reflect people's and organizations' preference for a cleaner environment. Critics of environmentalists also claim that an ecocrisis simply does not exist and that proenvironmental rules result in specific harm to humanity.[16]

There is no question, however, that the environmental movement did and does affect public statistics and policy. In the 1970s, the governments of France and Norway established systems of natural resource accounting and budgeting, while the Japanese government introduced the concept of net national welfare, adjusting national income for environmental and other factors. As this book goes to press, Gary Rutledge is heading a project at the Bureau of Economic Analysis in the U.S. Department of Commerce to adjust the national income accounting system to reflect environmental variables; progress reports are available in the *Survey of Current Business*.[17] At the World Bank, Ernst Lutz edited a volume in 1993, focusing on improved accounting for the environment.[18] For further details on how the situation is being resolved in the United States, see chapter 7 on national accounts in this book.

There is significant evidence that the private sector is eager to clarify the relationship between environmental and economic data. One key

---

[16]See J.G. Edwards, "The Lies of Rachel Carson," *21st Century Science and Technology,* Summer, 1992, pp. 41–51. Many books appeared recently attacking environmentalists and calling their stance fraudulent.

[17]See "Accounting for Mineral Resources: Issues and BEA's Initial Estimates," and "Integrated Economic and Environmental Satellite Accounts," *Survey of Current Business,* April 1994.

[18]E. Lutz, ed., *Toward Improved Accounting for the Environment.* Washington, DC: World Bank, 1993.

publication along these lines is the recent work of S. Schmidheiny with the Business Council for Sustainable Development. This group, which included corporate leaders from around the globe, brought out a major volume, providing a business perspective on reconciling growth and the environment.[19] In this book, there is a call for governments to introduce regulations gradually, to let industry choose the best way to respond to rules, to have a level playing field, and so on, but the group also appears to favor the internalization of environmental costs by altering the system of national accounts (SNA) to reflect environmental damage and the depreciation of natural resources.

> Bureaucratic socialism collapsed because it did not allow prices to tell the economic truth. Market economy may ruin the environment and ultimately itself if prices are not allowed to tell the ecological truth.[20]

So how can markets work for the environment? The SNA should reflect the ecological truth. The gross domestic product should be reduced and become net national product by subtracting the cost for repairing environmental damage, cost of any residual degradation, and an allowance for depletion of such natural resources as forests. While some of these may be difficult to quantify, especially residual degradation (e.g., eroded soil that is not replaced), SNAs incorporating the above yield more realistic insights. While Japanese gross national product rose by 8.5 percent per annum between 1955 and 1985, net national welfare rose only at the rate of 5.8 percent.[21]

Changing the SNA is just one step. In addition, some advocate the following steps: (1) prices of natural resources should reflect their extraction costs plus environmental costs plus user costs; (2) the "polluter pays" principle should be observed; and (3) development projects should include environmental values. The World Bank volume cited earlier states that environmental damage costs should be estimated and compared with the costs of preventing the damage. "Measurement is essential, since tradeoffs are inescapable." There are four possible

---

[19]S. Schmidheiny, *Changing Course: A Global Business Perspective on Development and the Environment.* Cambridge: MIT Press, 1992.

[20]E.U. von Weizsacker quoted in Schmidheiny, ibid., p. 14.

[21]See Schmidheiny, ibid., p. 31; discussed in detail in D. Pearce, *Blueprint for a Green Economy.* London: Earthscan, 1990.

approaches: market prices, costs of replacement, surrogate markets, and surveys.[22]

Vice President Al Gore in *Earth in the Balance* endorses the idea of sustainable development; that is, giving full recognition to the trade-offs between immediate benefits versus the potential costs or risks that may occur in the long term. This is, in effect, an issue of balancing the benefits and costs to current and future generations—a concept of inter-generational equity. He thinks that the failure to keep track of environmental damages (residual sludge, useless by-products, noxious emissions, etc.) and defining them as external to the process is intellectual dishonesty.[23] He and others call for national income and productivity measures to reflect the "real situation." Though he has been criticized for several other ideas in the book, especially for exaggerating the environmental crisis, he is in the mainstream in calling for "internalizing the externalities."[24]

The task of bringing ecology and national accounting together is not a simple process; collecting the basic indicators, as noted earlier, can also be cumbersome and costly. Drawing operational policy guidelines based on the above is difficult. Some observers think, however, that the most vexing problem is convincing the private sector to consider the idea of internalization. This also means establishing a dialogue between the private and public sectors.

To assist with this task, there are some mini-case studies in the World Bank volume and several OECD publications (see also articles in the *OECD Observer*). In the volume by the Business Council for Sustainable Development, there are nearly 40 case studies illustrating what the private sector is doing and how environmental issues can be resolved. Firms cited include ABB, Alcoa, Ciba-Geigy, Con-Agra, DuPont, ENI, Electrolux, GE, Henkel, Mitsubishi, Northern Telecom, and Volkswagen. Topics include developing cleaner products and cleaner production processes, managing sustainable resource use, and creating internal environmental audits and stakeholder partnerships.[25]

---

[22] *World Development Report,* 1993, p. 71.

[23] Al Gore, *Earth in the Balance.* Boston: Houghton Mifflin, 1992.

[24] For a strong, well-argued dissent, see R.L. Gordon, "Energy, Exhaustion, Environmentalism, and Etatism," *The Energy Journal,* Vol. 15, No. 1, 1994, pp. 1–16.

[25] S. Schmidheiny, *Changing Course: A Global Business Perspective on Development and the Environment.* Cambridge: MIT Press, 1992, pp. 181–333.

DATA ON WATER AND WASTEWATER (GLOBAL AND UNITED STATES)

Statistics regarding water, wastewater, and related topics have been available for many years from national governments as well as multinational agencies, regional bodies, nonprofit groups, and research institutes. Certain time series can be traced back decades or even centuries. The task of measuring water quality and commenting on its management on a global basis remains elusive, but progress has been made and reported in several journal articles, including some by one of the authors of this book.

While the data on global and U.S. demand for and supply of water are now readily available, there are still some information gaps. The U.N., the OECD, the GEMS/Water project, and the World Bank are key sources; private authors such as Ambroggi, Biswas, El-Hinnawi, Gross, Lvovich, and Sivard also made contributions. Water withdrawal as a percent of annual water availability is one key indicator; statistical time series are now available for all developed nations and many developing nations. The other side of the coin is sanitation—wastewater treatment facilities. These data, including the population served by primary, secondary, and tertiary treatments, are now readily available for major countries, though there is disagreement at times about the accuracy of such information.

The extent of water pollution—that is, the quality of water supply and wastewater effluent—must be judged in various ways, because there is no single measure that would suffice. As noted above, the GEMS/Water project keeps tabs on about 50 parameters of water quality. The most crucial variable is BOD, or biological oxygen demand, which is the amount of oxygen required for attacking organic matter by bacterial action. Other key measures involved dissolved oxygen, dissolved metals, fecal coliform count, and nitrate concentration. Figure 53 shows key river water quality measures over time and across nations from two sources. Heavy pollution by oxygen consuming substances declined in many nations due to wastewater treatment for households and industries. However, pollution by nutrients rose due to fertilizer use and agricultural runoff. Overall, this can be considered progress in view of growing population, urbanization, and industrialization.

Evaluating the sources of information and the accuracy of the data on global water quality is difficult because the collecting agencies do not

FIGURE 53

Selected Water Quality Indicators for Various Rivers (Part A: Gems/Water Data)

Country	River, City	Dissolved Oxygen — Annual Mean Concentration (milligrams per liter) 1979–82	1983–86	1987–90	Average Annual Growth Rate for Series (percent)	Fecal Coliform — Annual Mean Concentration (number per 100 milliliter sample) 1979–82	1983–86	1987–90	Average Annual Growth Rate for Series (percent)
		Low income							
Bangladesh	Karnaphuli	5.7	6.1	—	-1.1 (5)	—	—	—	— (3)
Bangladesh	Meghna	6.5	7.0	—	2.6 (5)	3,133	700	—	-35.1 (5)
China	Pearl, Hong Kong	7.6	7.8	7.8	0.4 (11)	519	563	174	-14.4 (10)
China	Yangtze, Shanghai	8.3	8.3	8.2	-0.1 (11)	316	464	731	10.6 (11)
China	Yellow, Beijing	9.8	9.7	9.8	-0.1 (11)	711	1,337	1,539	9.8 (11)
India	Cauveri, d/s from KRS	7.2	7.6	7.3	0.8 (9)	51	681	445	63.8 (9)
		Middle income							
Argentina	de la Plata, Buenos Aires	7.6	7.5	—	0.0 (8)	828	230	—	-23.1 (8)
Argentina	Parana Corrientes	8.1	8.0	8.1	0.1 (10)	185	146	111	-6.6 (10)
Brazil	Guandu, Tomada d' Agua	8.1	7.8	7.7	-0.7 (11)	1,202	2,452	6	-47.0 (8)
Brazil	Paraiba, Aparecida	6.0	6.1	6.0	-0.4 (7)	13,950	9,800	6,075	-11.5 (7)
Brazil	Paraiba, Barra Mansa	7.4	7.6	7.8	0.4 (11)	8,003	8,100	8	-33.4 (7)
Chile	Maipo, el Manzano	12.9	13.2	10.8	-1.4 (10)	871	705	775	5.3 (8)
Chile	Mapocho, Los Almendros	11.8	12.1	10.0	-1.7 (10)	2	2	5	8.0 (8)
		High Income							
Australia	Murray, Mannum	10.0	9.4	9.1	1.0 (6)	—	—	—	— (0)
Australia	Murray	7.1	8.2	8.6	2.4 (8)	33	103	80	15.8 (8)
Belgium	Escaut, Bleharies	5.7	6.2	5.9	1.1 (11)	76	579	867	40.8 (11)
Belgium	Meuse, Heer/Agimont	10.5	10.8	11.3	0.8 (11)	30	1,391	1,700	69.7 (11)
Belgium	Meuse, Lanaye Ternaaien	9.2	8.4	8.9	-0.7 (11)	147	5,233	7,100	78.2 (11)
Japan	Kiso, Asahi	10.0	10.6	11.7	1.7 (11)	300	400	216	-4.1 (11)

(Part B: OECD Data)

Country	Rivers	Dissolved Oxygen (mg/l)						Nitrate Concentration (mgN/l)					
		1970	1975	1980	1985	Late 1980s	Average Last 3 yrs.	1970	1975	1980	1985	Late 1980s	Average Last 3 yrs.
Canada	St. Laurent	8.1	10.0	—	9.7	11.0	10.4	0.19	0.23	0.16	0.16	0.29	0.25
	Saskatchewan	—	10.0	10.8	10.6	10.3	10.4	0.05	0.30	0.06	0.10	0.10	0.09
USA	Delaware	9.6	10.8	11.9	10.8	10.5	11.3	—	0.88	1.08	1.20	1.20	1.12
	Mississippi	8.4	8.5	8.3	8.6	9.1	9.1	—	0.98	1.26	1.23	0.96	1.02
Japan	Ishikari	8.9	10.7	10.0	10.0	11.0	10.7	0.36	—	0.53	—	—	—
	Yodo	8.2	8.9	9.1	8.7	8.8	8.4	—	0.80	0.76	—	—	—
Belgium	Meuse	7.7	8.9	9.5	8.1	8.0	8.7	3.90	2.12	2.52	2.79	2.63	2.96
Denmark	Gudenaa	—	12.5	9.6	11.0	9.9	10.0	—	1.25	1.70	1.37	1.25	1.39
Finland	Kokemiewoki	8.2	8.8	9.5	10.1	11.4	11.5	—	0.39	0.35	0.42	0.52	0.55
France	Loire	10.7	11.1	11.8	12.1	11.7	11.5	1.58	1.44	1.99	2.21	2.53	2.56
Germany	Rhone	7.5	7.7	8.7	8.6	9.6	9.0	0.88	0.90	1.24	1.60	1.38	1.82
	Rhein	5.6	6.8	9.0	9.3	10.1	9.9	1.82	3.02	3.59	4.20	3.70	3.77
	Donau	10.5	10.3	10.6	10.5	10.7	10.7	0.20	0.30	0.50	0.60	0.50	1.53
Italy	Po	8.3	—	7.7	8.6	6.1	7.5	0.95	1.35	1.63	2.44	1.68	2.34
Netherlands	Meuse	8.6	9.4	10.0	9.7	10.2	10.0	3.07	3.69	3.77	4.28	3.86	4.08
Portugal	Tejo	—	—	9.2	7.8	8.2	8.3	0.52	—	1.26	1.12	0.67	0.97
Spain	Ebro	—	—	9.8	9.4	9.4	9.5	—	2.63	2.21	3.29	3.47	3.34
Switzerland	Rhin	11.6	11.2	10.3	10.5	10.2	10.7	—	1.32	1.42	1.75	2.05	2.02
UK	Thames	—	10.8	9.9	10.0	9.9	10.2	—	6.50	6.89	7.51	7.67	7.08
	Mersey	—	5.1	6.1	6.2	7.1	7.5	—	1.84	2.29	3.12	2.86	2.82

Sources: Part A: Gems/Water Project of the U.N. quoted in *World Development Report 1992.* New York: Oxford University Press for World Bank, 1992, p.198. Part B: *Environmental Indicators—A Preliminary Set.* Paris: OECD, 1991, p. 27.

Note: For Nitrate Concentration, the rivers column lists Rivers separately: St. Laurent, Fraser, Delaware, Mississippi, Ishikari, Yodo, Meuse, Gudenaa, Kokemiewoki, Loire, Rhone, Rhein, Donau, Po, Meuse, Tejo, Guadalquivir, Aare, Thames, Mersey.

reveal many details. It appears, however, that the time series in this case, unlike for some others, such as gross fixed capital, are more detailed (possibly more reliable) for the U.N. and its affiliated agencies, especially the GEMS/Water project, than for the OECD. The technical appendices reveal more for the former than for the latter.

Water resource and withdrawal data originate from national or state governments. Two outstanding sources, according to the World Bank, are the Departement Hydrogeologie in Orleans, France, and the Institute of Geography at the National Academy of Sciences in Moscow. Both compile data from various published works and make estimates where necessary, using models. The World Research Institute is also active on this front. The two key series are internal renewable water resources and water withdrawal as a share of such resources, both on an annual basis (plus per capita and by sector for the second series).

The river water quality indicators shown in the table feature OECD data on dissolved oxygen and nitrate concentration at selected river sites during the 1970 to late 1980s period, but no details are available. The GEMS/Water reporting has grown from 344 stations in 59 countries in the late 1980s to 488 reporting stations in 64 nations in the early 1990s. Water quality data are available since 1979 to the present on 50 indicators, two of which are covered here: dissolved oxygen and fecal coliform. Not all stations collect all data, and the frequency and physical accuracy of measurement vary among stations. Four-year periods are used to minimize seasonal variability and to emphasize general trends.

When we try to compare the OECD and the GEMS/Water data, we cannot readily do so. Consider the Meuse River in Belgium in the mid-1980s. The specific station is not stated in the OECD volume, but the reading for dissolved oxygen was 8.1 milligrams per liter as of 1985. In the GEMS/Water project, two stations on the Meuse are specified. The reading was 10.8 mg/l at the Heer-Agimont, but only 8.4 mg/l at Lanaye Ternaainen, both for the 1983–86 period. The important point, however, is that both the OECD and the GEMS/Water project are consistent internally. Comparisons within each system are possible over time and across countries. Also, as just shown, the two measuring systems can be contrasted and possibly act as a check on each other. Whether a grand scheme will be attempted to merge these two (and possibly other) sources remains to be seen. The GEMS/Water project seems more encompassing, but the OECD goes back to 1970 rather than to 1979.

In moving from the global arena to the United States, only two key questions will be considered, both focusing on water resources and quality:

- Who collects, stores, and disseminates the data?
- What would a "proper" national water information look like?

These topics are tackled briefly, but incisively, in *America's Water,* a recent text by P. Rogers, a professor of environmental engineering at Harvard.[26] (His book ranges further afield, with a fine discussion on technical, political, and economic imperatives regarding this key resource, but the focus in our discussion is only on data and their use.)

There are about 1,100 water-related information sources in the United States, with no apparent major gaps. However, we are often in the dark as to which data are available, from whom, and where. This sorry state of distribution or dissemination can be traced back to different mandates given to various commissions, some focused on just creating databases, others on the application of the data, and still others on management of the statistics. Two national assessments between 1965 and 1980 failed to produce good results. Low appropriations, delays, and lack of commitment to integrated data management followed. In the 1980s, the U.S. Geological Survey (USGS) was told to coordinate efforts, yet omitted contributions from several key agencies, including the National Oceanic and Atmospheric Administration (NOAA), the Soil Conservation Service, and the Environmental Protection Agency (EPA). In short, a referral center was never established.

At present, there are three major players in water information: USGS, EPA, and NOAA. The USGS has several databases. Assessment is via fixed station monitoring, ad hoc measurements during major storms or floods, and intensive cause and effect studies. There is a repository for streamflow and groundwater data and results of chemical analyses. Finally, USGS maintains an exchange facility to aid access to various databases. The EPA has developed a water storage and retrieval system on surface and groundwater information received from other federal agencies and from over 40 states plus some data from USGS. It claims information on up to 750,000 sites around the nation. The NOAA chose to collect climatological data useful for flood warning. No direct

---

[26]Peter Rogers, *America's Water.* Cambridge: MIT Press, 1993.

linkages exist between USGS and NOAA or between EPA and NOAA, but some switching of data is now underway between USGS and EPA.[27]

In making a strong call for a national water information program, Rogers makes his preferences known in no uncertain terms. This call at the end of the book is all the more impressive because he has studied intensely the institutional arrangements of the past. Since Rogers states his suggestions in a forthright manner, it is worthwhile to quote his four paragraphs verbatim. Note that his endorsement of a USGS mandate comes from the fact that this agency has been awarded major responsibilities by the Office of Management and Budget (OMB). This parallels our ideas and recommendations in other parts of this book.

> Employing the influence and capacities of the new federal and regional councils, there should be a fully coordinated, national water information program to gather pertinent and useful data about water at scales that are meaningful and in systems that are compatible with each other and user-friendly. A federal agency other than the council—preferably one like the USGS with limited responsibilities or mission biases—should be designated as the lead institution. Where possible, the information program should be a cooperative venture with the states and regions, and should be designed to facilitate use by state and local cooperators. It should provide for data management as well as collection. The database should reflect jurisdictional as well as hydrologic realities so that it can accommodate other important data sets (e.g., census tract information, soil and water conservation needs and inventories, and geographical information systems). Some degree of standardization in the collection of both storage and retrieval of data—federal and state—would be both prudent and cost-effective. Data common to or needed by all water programs would be centralized; specialized data would remain the province of line agencies. However, as the National Water Commission recommended in 1973, the new President's Water Council should create and operate a modest national water data referral center simply to facilitate data retrieval and use across all water-related agencies.
>
> The present dual system of national water summaries issued periodically by USGS and national water quality inventories prepared by EPA seems duplicative and confusing. At a minimum, the repetition should be eliminated, and at best a single integrated report should be issued at intervals of no more than five years assessing the nation's water quantity and quality. At intervals of possibly 10 years comprehensive regional water resources assessments should be undertaken. In all cases, the goals of the assessments should be stated clearly and kept in mind throughout the process; the complexity of data collected and analyzed should be appropriate to those goals; the information should come in on time and within budget; and the assessing agency should have enough independence

---

[27]Ibid., pp. 183–185.

to assure unbiased analyses of federal water policies and programs. Agencies accountable to Congress and the American public should not serve as their own expert witnesses.

This leads to the fundamental issue of data reform, namely the question of where in the federal establishment the water data responsibilities should be lodged. The recommendation here is for the USGS to become the primary federal water data collection agency. This agency already has substantial capabilities and activities of its own. It has been awarded major coordination responsibilities by OMB. Its cooperative program with the states is well regarded and well accepted. Further, the USGS seems to be on the threshold of an expansion of its services to the water quality field and into the expanding area of groundwater monitoring and analysis. Before redundant and competitive independent systems become firmly established, a three-sided arrangement should be hammered out between USGS, EPA, and the states. To the extent possible, all of the federal missions agencies should be encouraged to contract with and utilize the USGS's capabilities as an alternative to supplying their own data needs.

But any agency, no matter how professional, tends to reflect its own institutional priorities and biases. Thus it is important to distinguish between the data gathering and analysis assigned to the USGS and the independent assessments needed to ensure comprehensive and coordinated federal and national water resources policies. These should become the responsibility of the recommended President's Water Council.[28]

CONCLUSION

Our physical environment has many facets, but given that it is a finite Earth, we have to manage it well for now and future generations to come. Pollution is of concern to both public and private interests. Our task is to manage it with care. But while there is often agreement about broad, long-range goals, there can be and is disagreement about tactics and means. In this section, we touched briefly on several facets, and specifically on water resources.

Since the environment is complex, data about it cannot be summed up in one set of time series or index numbers. Much depends on how we define and describe both the physical environment and the extent of degradation. The classifications we make, the cleanup solutions we desire, and the rules, policies, enforcement, and institutional machinery we adopt will also determine what set of statistics will be collected.

---

[28]Ibid., pp. 209–210.

In this section, we probed the state of the environment briefly and the state of statistics about our physical environs. We conclude that while the Earth is a polluted place, progress is being achieved on several fronts, including cleanup efforts and attempts to prevent pollution. In a similar fashion, we are learning more about data collection, processing, analysis, and dissemination. Attention is also being focused on areas of responsibility, the functions, and institutional arrangements that need strengthening. The U.N., the OECD, other public organizations, and numerous nonprofit organizations are engaged in comprehensive data collection and analysis. The work also goes on at national and local levels.

It is clear that there is overlap and duplication in gathering statistics about the physical environment, just as there is in most other fields. This is not necessarily wasteful; indeed, this situation can serve as a system of checks and balances. At the same time, as noted in regard to water resources in the United States, it is highly desirable to have coordinated information programs and databases that are both user-friendly and compatible with each other. Specific suggestions are being investigated in this regard. Finally, it should be noted that major attempts are underway to adjust general economic indicators in light of environmental data, thereby gaining a more realistic picture of the quality of our life, both globally and locally.

CHAPTER 7

FUNDAMENTALS—NATIONAL INCOME ACCOUNTING

It is important to understand why change in statistical systems is slow, as well as how demands arise from user groups both inside and outside of government. It is also critical to understand how agencies that produce statistics work and how such emerging issues as health care and the changing nature of information systems impact the collection, production, and dissemination of statistics.

This chapter sets forth some of the issues that must be addressed in a comprehensive program of rebuilding economic statistics. An intermediate approach with specific recommendations is presented in Chapter 9. Chapter 9 covers developing a national income accounting program for meeting the challenges of the 21st century, and pulls together suggestions from a variety of sources in order to reflect today's conditions. The 1993 revision of the System of National Accounts by all participating international agencies provides a clear opportunity to incorporate many of these proposals into a broad international effort to improve national income accounting methodology and practice.

In the discussion that follows, we will review some fundamental work needed to update economic theory, with particular attention to the System of National Accounts.

CHANGES IN THE NATIONAL ECONOMY

The economy of the 21st century will be fundamentally different from the economy that underlay development of classical economic theory. Productivity gains in the classical view flowed from improved production per hour in agriculture to create the investment for developing the manufacturing sector. An immediate impact on agriculture was to reduce

175

the need for labor on the farm and to free labor for work in manufacturing. Today tertiary industries (transportation, public utilities, government, health, and education) dominate the employment structure and as productivity gains result in those sectors as the result of better use of computers, of reengineering and management gains, the employment base will shift to quaternary economic activities such as information services, highly specialized personal services (entertainment, live-in health care, tutorial education, etc). Activities in both the tertiary and quaternary sectors are not adequately measured and, as a result, the understanding of productivity in such activities is not at a high standard today.

Fundamental work is needed on the theory of economic development in the years ahead, as countries try to leapfrog the traditional "stages of growth" development theory that proceeds from supply of natural resources to the supply of relatively "low-cost labor." In the 1990s, these issues are complicated by the transition of some major economies from socialistic "command" or "planned" economies to market-oriented economies. "Such a transition involves simultaneous attention to several major factors, including prices, currency convertability, productivity, the legal framework, and public attitudes."[1] To illustrate one of the challenges to theorists, consider the complexity of developing a transition theory (let alone a politically acceptable policy) for dealing with all of the following in a simultaneous system!

TRANSITION OF A COMMAND ECONOMY TO A MARKET ECONOMY

The republics of the former Soviet Union and the former planned economies in Central and Eastern Europe must address the following interdependent issues. Because the solutions must be approached as a total system, the challenge is daunting.

Prices

The planned economies of the former Soviet Bloc had price levels that were established by state planners, not by markets. Hence, any Western company seeking to build a business in these countries is faced with arti-

---

[1]This quote and following explanation are from Joseph W. Duncan, "What Does Eastern Bloc Upheaval Mean for U.S. Business?" *D&B Reports,* January/February 1990, pp. 8, 63.

ficial costs for the internal goods and services needed to serve consumers in formerly planned economies. Further, while Western products may be superior to locally produced products, the artificial prices of the local products tended to create competitive conditions that are difficult to over-come in attempting to achieve significant market penetration.

This illustrates that planned economies face great difficulties in stimulating internal economic growth when artificial prices cause misal-location of resources or when they stimulate plant managers to produce only those products that make the greatest contribution to local produc-tion goals. For example, the price of bread remained unchanged in the former Soviet Union between 1955 and 1988. For some farmers, it was cheaper to feed cattle with this subsidized bread than to feed other grains.

Currency Convertibility

The ability of consumers in the countries of the former Soviet Bloc to purchase imports from the West is still severely limited by the avail-ability of hard currency. As a result, Western business managers operat-ing in the former Soviet Bloc are restricted in their ability to repatriate profits from these countries. While many barter deals have been arranged, a very limited set of exportable items is suitable for such arrangements. The problems are not limited to East-West trade, but extend to trade between the Russian Republics and the Eastern European countries.

The debate about official vs. black-market exchange rates is a direct reflection of the difficulties of moving in the direction of full convert-ibility. Immediate convertibility with artificial (centrally planned) prices in the background clearly leads to economic shortages in some areas and pronounced surpluses in others. The combination of planned prices and the inconvertibility of the currency is at the heart of the economic stress that is challenging economists and policy makers as they seek to plan effective approaches to make the transition from command to market economic sytems.

Productivity

At the center of planned societies is the concept that the state will pro-vide the basic needs of each household. Thus, state-owned apartments are made available to the workers; rent is a percentage of wages; and there is no possibility of changing apartments except by direct trade. This reduces incentives to maintain or improve properties, and shabby living conditions result.

The lack of private ownership also has a direct impact on the factory floor. Since there is no incentive for workers to increase productivity, output is usually evaluated only on such gross measures as number of units produced relative to plan requirements. No adjustments are made to improve the quality of the output. Losses due to pilferage, damage, or other weaknesses in the distribution stream are rarely taken into account.

In order for Western firms to build and manage effective production facilities in the former Soviet Bloc countries, it will be necessary to train a new generation of workers and to instill incentives and production measurements that are in sharp contrast to those prevailing. Increased productivity is essential if the poorly performing economy is to be revived.

Legal Framework

A byproduct of current political reform in the republics of the former Soviet Union is the rewriting of many basic laws. Much experimentation is under way. Changes are being introduced every month, and only a few individuals understand the new laws. This has resulted in an atmosphere of uncertainty for firms that wish to create joint ventures or open new distribution systems.

The old pattern of the Communist party overruling current laws when it was expedient to do so is being replaced with new laws and regulations, but the learning curve is steep, and clearly many revisions in the legal framework will be necessary for orderly economic transactions to work smoothly. A reliable legal system is a prerequisite to the free movement of labor and capital and the building of trade relationships.

Attitudes

The introduction of market-related prices, revalued currency, new production goals, and rewritten laws is producing a high level of conflict in public attitudes. For example, in the Russian Republic, cooperatives are being challenged for generating excessive profits, even though profits are necessary to create the incentives to undertake ventures outside the planned system.

Workers in the planned economy are demanding wages equal to those earned in the new market-driven firms, yet their productivity does not merit higher pay. Inflationary pressures are resulting. As the role of Western and market-oriented enterprises grows, the tension between market-driven activities and planned or state-controlled activities is likely to increase.

Risks and Rewards

The integration of world markets is indeed the promise of the 1990s. Success will mean rising standards of living and a more peaceful world, but the integration will not be easy. Political and social stress are already evident even in the most advanced areas, such as the unified market countries of Western Europe. In Central and Eastern Europe, the changes will be even more dramatic and challenging.

U.S. firms cannot afford to adopt a wait-and-see attitude. By the time the opportunities are clear and the rules firm, others will be there, and entry will be very difficult. Building on the opportunities in these new markets created by the transition to market economies will require a long-term view, policy and strategy flexibility, and an astute reading of rapidly changing internal conditions. The risks are great, but the potential rewards look well worth the effort.

These points summarize some of the challenges being faced by the former planned economies as they seek to transform to market economies. The evolution will be difficult. The reality is that the process is moving forward, and the result will be a demand for more market-oriented data. As noted in a number of presentations made in the countries of the former Soviet Union, "Information is the lubricant of the market economy."[2]

REQUIREMENTS FOR NATIONAL INCOME ACCOUNTING

The first step in developing a statistical system that can meet future needs is to update economic theory so that it reflects the emerging relationships both within developed economies and among economies at various stages of economic development. Such a system must also account for transitions from planned to market economies.

The pressure for such a reexamination of economic theory is most evident in Europe, where long-standing concepts of market development are now under strain. European political and economic integration have

---

[2]Presentations by one of the authors, Joseph W. Duncan, during the period 1988–91.

faltered due to stagnant domestic employment growth and the sudden availability of relatively low-cost labor from the Central and Eastern European countries. These conditions have been exacerbated by economic distortions flowing from the failure of massive subsidies of specific companies and industries (such as Airbus and agriculture) and from the pressures of massive refugee flows. The countries of the former Soviet Union and the countries in Central and Eastern Europe now face the difficulties of determining a strategy for the transition to market economies.

The development of a new theory of economic development for these transition countries, as well as the function of their official statistical agencies in developing market-oriented data, is beyond the scope of this report. It is important, however, to recognize the need for a concerted effort to pull together the best efforts of academic thinking to address these issues.

The second step is more achievable and, in fact, significant progress has been made in recent years. This area is the development of common statistical definitions, classifications, and standards. To assure that international comparisons are meaningful, it is essential that similar statistical concepts be employed. This is obviously difficult since each country has its own policies of taxation, social services, and legal organization. For example:

1. *The Harmonized Trade Classification*—As discussed in chapter 1, the Harmonized Commodity Description and Coding System has been approved by members of the United Nations. This provides a common system for classifying commodities at borders and in international transport. These classifications will be important in the development of trade data.

2. *U.S. Standard Industrial Classification*—Work under the leadership of the Bureau of Economic Analysis and the Office of Management and Budget is focused on developing an improved system of economic classification to use in analysis of industries and various segments of the economy.

3. *United Nations System of National Accounts*—This chapter will provide an overview of developments in this area.[3]

---

[3]Commission of the European Communities, International Monetary Fund, Organization for Economic Cooperation and Development, United Nations, and World Bank, *System of National Accounts—1993*, Brussels/Luxembourg, New York, Paris, Washington, D.C., 1993.

4. *Accounting guidelines for nations*—The U.S. Financial Accounting Standards Board and other professional accounting organizations have stepped up efforts to gain more international comparability in basic accounting rules and regulations. While limited by national laws, in the long term these efforts are likely to make more comparability in financial data a reality.

UNITED NATIONS SYSTEM OF NATIONAL ACCOUNTS

For economists and for business decision makers evaluating the economic context for their decisions, the United Nations System of National Accounts (SNA) is important, even though it is not well known. A brief description of the 1993 SNA revision is presented in this chapter to provide background for some of the recommendations for improving measurement of the national economy. The U.S. Government has already agreed to implement the revised SNA in the coming years.

Concepts for Measuring National Income

The development of the U.S. National Income and Product Accounts (NIPA) and the SNA have represented a significant effort over several decades to provide a fundamental accounting system for understanding economic development.

The development of the National Income Accounts was accelerated as part of the effort to measure economic activity during World War II. The seminal concepts were developed by a number of individuals in the U.S. Department of Commerce, including significant contributions by Simon Kuznets, Robert Nathan, Milton Gilbert, George Jaszi, Charles Schwartz, Edward Dennison, and Daniel Creamer, and many others.[4]

---

[4]The concept of national income goes back even further, of course. For example, Sir William Petty apparently prepared "guesstimates" of the income of a nation in 1665. The *Wealth of Nations* published in 1776 by Adam Smith presented a concept of national income similar to measures used today, except that he apparently excluded many services. For a detailed discussion of the historical evolution of U.S. national income and product accounts, see Chapter 3 of *Revolution in United States Government Statistics, 1926–1976*, Joseph W. Duncan and William C. Shelton, October 1978, published by the U.S. Department of Commerce. The text of the 1993 System of National Accounts describes the historical evolution of that system.

The Employment Act of 1946 was a major stimulus to the development of economic policy, including the establishment of the Council of Economic Advisers in the Executive Office of the President, and the establishment of the Joint Economic Committee of the U.S. Congress, which has expressed a great interest in improving economic statistics in the years since it was established. For example, as early as 1948, the Joint Economic Committee published a report entitled *Statistical Gaps,* which was instrumental in stimulating many improvements in economic statistics.

The post-war reorganization of the Department of Commerce created an Office of Business Economics (OBE), the precursor of the Bureau of Economic Analysis (BEA), which now has responsibility for constructing the National Income and Product Accounts. NIPA obtained a relatively independent status from the SNA recommended by the United Nations. During the past decade, under the leadership of Carol Carson, currently the Director of the BEA, the United States played a major role in leading the U.N. working group responsible for improving the SNA. Further, as noted earlier, the Bureau of Economic Analysis is now committed to moving the U.S. income accounts toward the newly revised SNA.

The United Nations Statistical Commission adopted the revised SNA at its meeting in New York, February 22 to March 3, 1993. The Commission's resolution "recommends that member states consider using the 1993 System of National Accounts as the international standard for the compilation of their national accounts and statistics, to promote the integration of economic and related statistics, and as an analytical tool."[5] These actions of the Statistical Commission were approved by the U.N. Economic and Social Council at its regular meeting in July 1993.

The move toward the SNA was described in the June 1990 issue of the *Survey of Current Business.*[6] The two main goals of the System of National Accounts are:

---

[5]See United Nations, Economic and Social Council, Official Records, 1993, Supplement No. 6, *Report of the Twenty-Seventh Session of the United Nations Statistical Commission,* E/CN.3/1993/27.

[6]Carol S. Carson and Jeanette Honsa, "The United Nations System of National Accounts: An Introduction," *Survey of Current Business,* Vol. 70, No. 6, June 1990, pp. 20–30.

1. "to facilitate international comparisons;" and
2. "to serve as a guide to countries as they develop their own economic accounting systems."

The article further noted that most countries with market economies currently use the SNA as a guide in the design of their statistical systems. The goal is to record the nature of stocks and flows that are part of the economic system. The framework is designed to group transactions and transactors in an accounting system that is meaningful for economic analysis, forecasting, and policy.[7]

Since the SNA is different from the NIPA, which is so widely known among U.S. economists and statisticians, and since the SNA provides an important framework for elaboration and improvement of international economic statistics, this chapter presents a brief overview of the SNA and the related accounts that are planned to augment and extend the accounting to sectors such as environmental impact. Business economists and other users who rely upon economic statistics should, of course, read the more detailed working papers that are being prepared by the BEA, as well as the text published by the United Nations, since a major objective of the SNA is to develop international comparisons in economic statistics. Much of this chapter is taken from draft materials which, while subject to some change, are not expected to fundamentally change the concepts presented.[8]

If the reader wants immediate background materials on many of the important methodological issues, information can be gained by reviewing the fundamental methodology papers that document the conceptual framework of the NIPA. Unfortunately, many users and analysts of economic statistics are unfamiliar with the details of these papers and, as a consequence, the richness of the current system is not fully appreciated. For more details on the system, see the methodology papers in Figure 54.

---

[7]For a discussion of the principles of economic accounting in the United States, see "An Introduction to National Economic Accounting," Allan Young and Helen Stone, in the March 1985 *Survey of Current Business.*

[8]Documents used in the preparation of the balance of this section on the System of National Accounts include the draft guidelines reviewed by the U.N. Statistical Commission and internal working papers prepared by BEA. We are grateful to Carol Carson and her staff for making it possible for us to present this lay version.

FIGURE 54
Methodology Papers

See Bureau of Economic Analysis, "Users Guide to BEA Information," *Survey of Current Business,* January 1993, pp. 47–71. The methodology papers currently available include:

An Introduction to National Economic Accounting (NIPA Methodology Paper No. 1). An introduction to the concepts of the U.S. NIPAs that places these accounts within the larger framework of national economic accounting. This paper shows the step-by-step derivation of a general national economic accounting system from the conventional accounting statements used by business income and product accounts, the capital-finance accounts, and the input-output accounts—the major branches of national economic accounting in the United States today. Also appeared in the March 1985 *Survey of Current Business* (1985). Available from the National Technical Information Service (NTIS): Accession No. PB 85-247567, price $12.50 (paper copy), $9.00 (microfiche).

Corporate Profits: Profits Before Tax, Profits Tax Liability, and Dividends (NIPA Methodology Paper No. 2). A description of the concepts, sources, and methods of the corporate profits components of the NIPAs. (1985) Available from NTIS: Accession No. PB 85-245397, price $19.50 (paper copy), $9.00 (microfiche).

Foreign Transactions (NIPA Methodology Paper No. 3). A description of the preparation of estimates in the NIPAs of net exports (both current- and constant-dollar), transfer payments to foreigners, capital grants received by the United States, interest paid by government to foreigners, and net foreign estimates in the NIPAs and those in the balance of payments accounts. (1987) Available from NTIS: Accession No. PB 88-100649, price $19.50 (paper copy), $9.00 (microfiche).

GNP: An Overview of Source Data and Estimating Methods (NIPA Methodology Paper No. 4). Basic information about GNP, including the conceptual basis for the account that presents GNP, definitions of each of the components on the income and product sides of that account, and a summary, presented in tabular form, of the source data and methods used in preparing estimates of current- and constant-dollar GNP. Also provides an annotated bibliography, with a directory of more than 50 items over the last decade that provided methodological information about GNP. Appeared in the July 1987 *Survey of Current Business.* (1987) Available from NTIS: Accession No. PB 88-134838, price $17.50 (paper copy), $9.00 (microfiche). The summary of source data and methods was updated in the July 1992 issue of the *Survey* (Tables 7 and 8, pages 25 through 41).

Government Transactions (NIPA Methodology Paper No. 5). Presents the conceptual basis and framework of government transactions in the national income and product accounts, describes the presentation of the estimates, and details the sources and methods used to prepare estimates of federal transactions and of state and local transactions. (1988) Available from NTIS: Accession No. PB 90-118480, price $27.00 (paper copy), $9.00 (microfiche).

Personal Consumption Expenditures (NIPA Methodology Paper No. 6). Presents the conceptual basis and framework for personal consumption expenditures (PCE) in the NIPAs, describes the presentation of the estimates, and details the sources and methods used to prepare annual, quarterly, and monthly estimates of PCE. Includes a bibliography, definitions, and convenient summaries of estimating procedures. (1990) Available from U.S. Government Printing Office: Stock No. 003-010-00200-0, price $4.50.

(continued)

FIGURE 54 *(continued)*

The Underground Economy: An Introduction (reprint). A discussion of the coverage, measurement methods, and implications of the underground economy. Part of the discussion features the relation between the NIPAs and the underground economy: Illegal activities in the context of NIPAs, three sets of NIPA estimates sometimes misunderstood as being measures of the underground economy, and the effect on NIPA estimates of possible misreporting in source data due to the underground economy. Articles appeared in the May 1984 and July 1984 issues of the *Survey of Current Business.* (1984) Available from BEA: Accession No. 53-84-10-001, price $5.00.

(concluded)

Overall Concepts of the United Nations System of National Accounts

The United Nations System of National Accounts (SNA) is designed, as noted earlier, to record all of the stocks and flows of transactions that are part of the economy. Initially adopted in 1953, the SNA was substantially extended in 1968 to include input-output accounts, flow of funds accounts, and balance sheets. Consequently, the SNA framework includes measures of production, income, saving and investment, and wealth. It incorporates both domestic and foreign activities, and financial and nonfinancial transactions, and it attempts to provide for both current- and constant-dollar measures.

The 1993 revision begins with the foundation of the 1968 SNA. A notable improvement is the objective for providing more attention to the role of services in the economy. For example, the revised SNA "describes the production of storage services and recognizes that services, as well as goods, may be produced over more than one accounting period.[9] Further, the revised SNA establishes criteria for delineation of the financial corporate sector and for the treatment of financial instruments in light of the many innovations in this field."[10] The 1993 SNA revision has been designed to define many of the rules of economic accounting, such as the principles of valuation, time of recording, and grouping by aggregation, netting, and grossing as a method for reducing the complexity of this comprehensive accounting system. The revised SNA also has been harmonized with the *Balance of Payments Manual* of the International Monetary Fund (IMF), bringing to fruition a goal that was set forth by

[9]U.S. Department of Commerce, Bureau of Economic Analysis, in an article entitled "New International Guidelines in Economic Accounting," pp. 44–45.

[10]Ibid., p. 43.

the U.N. Statistical Commission in the early 1970s. There have been attempts to reconcile the U.N. and IMF definitions over the years, but it is just finally being realized with the adoption of the new SNA guidelines. Harmonization with the IMF data should, in future years, eliminate much of the confusion in international accounting statistics (a topic discussed later in this book).

Of particular significance is the fact that the revised SNA now incorporates "satellite accounts" to provide additional flexibility. The satellite accounts provide a framework for testing new extensions of economic accounting, in particular, environmental accounting.

The revised SNA includes an extraordinary amount of the detail needed to provide sufficient guidelines to national statistical offices. As an introduction to the SNA, the following descriptive material has been prepared, based on "A Reader's Guide to the Draft Revised United Nations System of National Accounts," which was developed as an aid to BEA staff. The following sections are organized in order of the proposed outline for the forthcoming manual.

Basic Definitions within the SNA

The fundamental elements of the SNA are incorporated into an accounting structure. Figure 55 illustrates some of the basic relationships between flow accounts and the balance sheets. In order to make this an integrated system, *the SNA strives to apply the same concepts, definitions, and classifications to all accounts and subaccounts.* For example, all dwellings are treated as assets used to produce goods and services. Thus, all housing services, whether sold or consumed by the owners, are included within production, and all of the corresponding income originating from the production of housing appears in the accounts using the same definitions and classifications.

The objective of national accounting is to record economic flows between two dates and the resulting stocks. Flow means that the situation has changed between the transactors (buyer or seller). In the analysis of the SNA, the fundamental question of economic links tries to respond to the question "**Who** does **what**, by **what** means, for **what** purpose, with **whom**, in exchange for **what**, with **what** changes in *stocks?*"[11] The classifications that structure the system involve the following:

---

[11]This formulation was developed by the UN Working Party and is presented in the introduction to the Overview—Chapter 2 in the draft Manual.

FIGURE 55
A Simplified Sequence of Flow Accounts and Balance Sheets*

Opening Balance Sheet		**Balance Sheet**
	Net Worth	
Production Account		
Value added/GDP		
Generation of Income Account		
Operating surplus		
Allocation of Primary Income Account		
Balance of primary incomes		**Current Accounts**
Secondary Distribution of Income Account		
Disposable income		
Redistribution of Income in Kind Account		
Adjusted disposable income		
Use of Disposable Income Account		
Saving, net		
Use of Adjusted Disposable Income Account		
Saving, net		
Capital Account		
Net lending (+)/ Net borrowing (−)	Changes in net worth due to saving and net capital transfers	
Financial Account		
	Net lending(+)/ Net Borrowing(−)	**Accumulation Accounts**
Other Changes in Volume of Assets Account		
	Changes in net worth due to other changes in volume of assets	
Revaluation Account		
	Changes in net worth due to nominal holding gains/losses	
Closing Balance Sheet		**Balance Sheet**
	Net worth	

*Prepared by the Bureau of Economic Analysis as an aid to this discussion.

- institutional units and sectors (**who?**);
- transactions and other flows (**what?**);
- assets and liabilities (**what stocks?**);
- activities, establishments, products (other aspects of **who** and **what?**); and
- purposes (**what for?**).

The elaboration of the system quickly generates considerable detail. For example, on the question of institutional units and sectors—the who—there are a variety of players including the following:

1. Nonfinancial corporations: institutional units principally engaged in the production of market goods and nonfinancial services.
2. Financial corporations: institutional units principally engaged in financial intermediation or in auxiliary financial activities.
3. General government: institutional units, which, in addition to fulfilling their political responsibilities and their role in economic regulation, produce principally nonmarket services (possibly goods) for individual or collective consumption and redistribute income and wealth.
4. Households: all physical persons in the economy, the institutional unit in the household sector consisting of one individual or a group of individuals. The household of the owner of an unincorporated enterprise is not considered an institutional unit (except under certain conditions). The principal functions of households are the supply of labor, final consumption, and, as entrepreneurs, the production of market goods in nonfinancial (possibly financial) services.
5. Nonprofit institutions (NPIs) serving households: legal entities that are principally engaged in the production of nonmarket services for households and whose main resources are voluntary contributions by households.

This listing illustrates how the system builds fundamental concepts, which are then subdivided into conceptual definitions that are further refined to define the overall tests of activities in the economic system.

The second classification of importance is the consideration of stocks. In essence, assets and liabilities are components of the balance sheet of the total economy and its constituent institutional sectors. In contrast to economic flows, the balance sheet shows the stocks of assets and liabilities held at a point in time. Clearly, stocks are connected with flows, and the essence of the accounting system is to provide a definition of those interrelationships.

In market economies, accounting rules focus on double-entry bookkeeping. The SNA strives to follow that procedure but, in fact, since most transactions involve two economic agents/institutional units, transactions are recorded twice by the two transactors involved, leading to a principle of *quadruple entry*. For example, a social benefit in cash paid by a government unit to a household is recorded in the accounts of government as all of the following:

1. A use under the relevant type of transfer.
2. A negative acquisition of assets under currency and deposits in the accounts of the household sector.
3. A resource under transfers.
4. An acquisition of assets under currency and deposits.

Complexity of the system is quickly recognized when it is necessary to collect information from diverse sources with differing definitions and make statistical decisions concerning such things as the timing of transactions, the valuation of transactions, appropriate consolidation of transactions, and evaluation of the consistency between volume measures and real measures. Thus, one of the merits of the SNA is to standardize measurement concepts.

Transactions in the SNA

The SNA, in looking at transactions, considers four types that are cross-classified by sector, industry and product, or purpose. The four types of transaction are :

1. Transactions, goods and services, which show the origin and use of goods and services.
2. Distributed transactions, which show how the value added generated by production is distributed into labor, capital, and government, as well as the redistribution of income and wealth through taxes and transfers (current and capital transfers are distinguished).

3. Transactions and financial assets, which show the net acquisition of financial assets or the net incurrence of liabilities for each type of financial instrument.

4. Other accumulation entries, which cover transactions and other economic flows not taken into account elsewhere that change the quantity or value of assets and liabilities.

Balance Sheets in the SNA

Balance sheets are a familiar business tool. They can also be applied to national income accounting. Up to this point, the discussion of the SNA looked at the current accounts and the accumulation accounts, which record transactions and other flows that occur over time. Balance sheets, on the other hand, are a stock concept: They are a snapshop of assets and liabilities at a given point in time.

Stocks are connected with flows: They result from the accumulation of prior transactions and other flows, and they are changed by transactions and other flows in the current period. Stocks result from a continuum of entries and withdrawals (accounting for some changes in volume or in value) occurring during the time a given asset or liability is held. In the SNA, there is an Opening Balance Sheet, which for all practical purposes is the Closing Balance Sheet from the previous accounting period; a Balance Sheet of Changes, which recapitulate the accumulation accounts via their balancing items (i.e., changes in net worth); and a Closing Balance Sheet, which is derived from these two accounts.

Net worth, which is the balancing item for the Balance Sheet, is defined as the value of all the nonfinancial and financial assets owned by an institutional unit or sector, less the value of all its outstanding liabilities. Although this definition places emphasis on assets and liabilities, and the Changes in Balance Sheet Account draws further attention to the accumulation accounts by recapitulating the "changes in net worth due to . . ." balancing items, most changes in the accumulation accounts only rearrange assets and liabilities if current account activity (i.e., saving) is excluded.

Transactions Accounts in the SNA

Transactions accounts show the flows associated with a given kind of transaction or group of transactions for each sector or industry involved. These accounts specify the kinds of transactions and show the resources and uses for each sector; that is, they show "from whom" for the total flows for each sector (and the total economy). They do not show the specific "from whom/to whom" information of the transactions. Because they do not show "from whom/to whom," they are classified as dummy, or screen, accounts. Transactions accounts balance resources and uses without the use of balancing items.

The Goods and Services Account is a transactions account that shows, for the economy as a whole (or for groups of products), the total resources and total uses of goods and services. Taxes and subsidies on products are included on the resources side of the account. This reflects the recommendation that output be valued at basic prices and uses be valued at purchasers' prices. The account is balanced globally—for all resources and uses—but not for each kind of transaction. When the Goods and Services Accounts shows type(s) of product, output is shown by industry of origin and intermediate consumption is shown by industry of use. To facilitate analysis for accounts where all sectors may have resources and uses, it is useful also to have accounts that detail the "from whom/to whom" flows.

The Assets and Liabilities Accounts
The assets and liabilities accounts detail stocks of assets and liabilities at the beginning and end of an accounting period and record the transactions and other flows that explain the changes between the balance sheets.

The transactions and other flows detailed are:

1. Transactions recorded in the Capital Account, by type of transaction.
2. Transactions recorded in the Financial Account, by type of transaction.
3. Other flows recorded in the Other Changes in the Volume of Assets Account, by type of change.
4. Holding gains/losses recorded in the Revaluation Account, by type.

These accounts are presented for each type of asset or liability, at a greater level of detail than in the sequence of accounts for institutional units or sectors.

The Rest of the World Account
The Rest of the World Account shows transactions between resident and nonresident institutional units and the related stocks of assets and liabilities. The rest of the world plays a role in the accounts similar to a sec-

tor and, therefore, the account is established from the point of view of the rest of the world. That is, a resource for the rest of the world is a use for the total economy, and a use for the rest of the world is a resource for the economy. Positive balancing items are a surplus for the rest of the world.

Current transactions are recorded in only two accounts:

1. The External Account of Goods and Services shows imports of goods and services as resources and exports as uses. Its balancing item is the external balance of goods and services.

2. The External Account of Primary Income and Current Transfers shows income flows between the total economy and the rest of the world. Its balancing item is the current external balance.

Accumulation accounts are also relevant for the rest of the world, although only for a limited set of transactions—primarily financial transactions. The External Assets and Liabilities Account is equivalent to the financial assets and liabilities of the total economy's Balance Sheet, with reversed signs. National resident institutional units are created to register the ownership of most other domestic (nonfinancial) assets owned by foreigners.

The Rest of the World Account, unlike the balance of payments, is drawn up from the perspective of the rest of the world. In this way, it can be treated as if it were a sector in the SNA. It is not drawn up from the perspective of the total economy—that is, measuring the total economy's claims on the rest of the world—because, by defining balancing items on the left as claims on the total economy by the rest of the world, the overall balance of the SNA is maintained.

The Aggregates

The aggregates are totals for sectors of either balancing items or particular transactions that measure the result of economic activity considered from a particular point of view. Some prominent ones include the following:

Gross domestic product (GDP) is the sum of the gross value added of all producer units plus any taxes, less subsidies, on products that have not been included in the valuation of output. GDP is also the sum of the final uses of goods and services, measured in purchasers' prices, less imports of goods and (nonfactor) services. GDP is also the sum of primary incomes distributed by resident producer units.

Net domestic product is equal to GDP less consumption of fixed capital. Neither it, nor gross product, is a measure of welfare or sustainable income.

Gross national income (a concept of primary income, not value added) is equal to GDP plus net primary (factor) income flows to and from the rest of the world. It is the sum of gross primary incomes distributed to resident institutional units.

Gross national disposable income is equal to gross national income plus net current transfers received from the rest of the world.

No aggregate measure of welfare is provided by the SNA.

The Integrated Economic Accounts

The Integrated Economic Accounts (IEA) array the full sequence of accounts of the total economy, including balance sheets, in a presentation that shows the principal economic relations and the main aggregates. The presentation shows the general accounting structure of the SNA and presents a set of data for the institutional sectors, the economy as a whole, and the relations with the rest of the world. The objective is to be flexible so that different dimensions of economic transactions can be portrayed. The IEA is highly aggregated in order to be manageable. In principle, however, specific subsectors can be shown in additional columns, or further detail on the various line items can be shown in additional rows to provide information on topics of interest.

The detailed analysis of production by industries and flows of goods and services by kinds of products is an integral part of the integrated central framework. The detailed analysis of production activities and goods and services balances is made in the input-output tables. The central input-output table of the SNA presents:

- The resources and uses of goods and services for each type of product.
- The production and generation of income accounts for each industry according to kind of economic activity.

Other Tables

In addition to the input-output tables, the SNA provides for a number of tables outside of the IEA to allow greater detail to be presented. One set—of financial transactions and financial assets and liabilities—provides greater detail on financial transactions. Another set—of integrated balance sheets and assets and liabilities accounts—shows, for each type of asset, the value of the asset on the opening and closing balance sheets as well as the various sources of their change in value. A third set is detailed breakdowns of various categories of expenditure by function, such as outlays of government by function.

The Integrated Central Framework and Flexibility

The SNA does not seek to imply any order of priority or frequency for implementing national accounts. Countries are encouraged to adapt the SNA according to their particular needs and abilities. Three possible ways of applying the SNA flexibility are described in the manuals.

The first way is by using the flexibility within the system itself to vary emphasis by:

- Using the SNA's classifications of sectors, industries, products, transactions, and sequence of accounts at varying levels of detail—including additional ones.
- Using different methods of valuation.
- Using different priorities and frequencies.
- Rearranging results.
- Introducing additional elements.

The second way is by using a social accounting matrix (SAM). The SAM is a presentation of the SNA in matrix terms that incorporates topics of special interest, such as the link between income generation and consumption. A SAM is usually prepared with emphasis on an item or a component of special interest to the user, indicating a greater degree of detail than shown in the SNA.

The third way is by using satellite accounts. Satellite accounts are recommended when alternative economic concepts need to be used or if the central framework would become overburdened with details in performing the analysis. Tourism is a good example. Various aspects of producing and consuming activities connected with tourism may appear in detailed classifications of activities, products, and purposes. However, specific tourism transactions and purposes appear separately in a very few cases; thus, satellite accounts can provide the needed detail.

Concluding Discussion of the SNA

This brief discussion is designed to present an overview of the SNA and does not convey its full richness. In fact, fully appreciating the comprehensiveness of the integrated accounts requires a careful study of the various definitions, concept tables, and accounting rules. The U.N. Manual includes chapters describing tools, the current accounts of the central framework, the accumulation accounts and balance sheets of the central framework, other accounts, and associated measures. Each of these topics is complex, but the crucial element is the integrated nature of the concepts and classifications applied to all of the accounts.

Understanding how an economic system functions requires an identification of the participants or transactors within the system and an understanding of the activities in which they engage. This is the essential objective of dealing with the questions mentioned earlier in which the entire system is a response to the fundamental links: "**Who** does **What**, by **What** means, for **What** purpose, with **Whom**, in exchange for **What**, with **What** changes in *stocks*?"

An earlier definition of institutional units illustrates that the fundamental units are entities capable of owning assets, incurring liabilities, and engaging in economic activities and transactions with other institutional units. Five types of institutional units identified earlier are mutually exclusive sectors of the economy. They, of course, may be further subdivided into subsectors for purposes of analysis and, as the SNA concept provides alternative methods of subsectoring, may be used for various purposes, so long as the total economy is the sum of the resident sectors.

In this global economy, it is also essential to deal with the rest of the world. In SNA terms, the rest of the world is comprised of all nonresident institutional units that enter into transactions or have economic links with resident institutional units. In fact, the framework provides for describing the rest of the world as though it is a sector. The Rest of the World Account shows the transactions in other flows between resident and nonresident units and the stocks of financial claims that each makes on the other. The Rest of the World Account is divided into current, accumulation, and balance sheet subaccounts. Thus, as noted earlier, it is appropriate to consider the Rest of the World Account as a sector of the system.

The integration of the SNA with the IMF balance of payment account is particularly crucial for analyzing the Rest of the World Account. As noted elsewhere in this report, the flows and assets in terms of global transactions require considerable work to take account of newly emerging data flows and transaction types. In the SNA framework, there are only two types of subaccounts. They are:

1. The external account of business services, which shows the exports and imports of goods and services and the resulting external balance of business services.

2. The external account for primary incomes and current transfers, which shows the compensation of employees, taxes less subsidies on production imports, property income (including reinvested earnings of direct foreign investment enterprises), and the current transfers receivable from or payable to nonresident units.

The System also provides for four accumulation subaccounts in the rest of the world sector and a balance sheet. The four subaccounts are:

1. The capital account, which shows capital transfers receivable and payable by nonresidents and the net acquisition of nonproduced, nonfinancial assets by nonresidents.

2. The financial account, which shows transactions in financial assets of all types with nonresidents, including the equity ownership of resident institutional units.

3. The other changes in volume of asset account, which includes such flows as uncompensated seizures of assets, write-offs of bad debts, and classification changes.

4. The reevaluation account, which shows the holding gains or losses on financial assets and liabilities of nonresidents.

The balance sheet that results shows the stocks, the financial assets issued by residents and held by nonresidents, and the liabilities of nonresidents to residents.

This integration of the national accounts with international flows is destined to be of growing significance with the evolving integration of the world economy.

Applications for Users

There are many concepts for elaborating and applying the SNA. The documents developed by the designers include several suggestions. To summarize from the earlier discussion, they include:

Functional applications. Four tables provide an alternative view of recording certain transactions—a classification by function. Outlays are classified by functional purpose for general government, producers, and nonprofit institutions serving households. Consumption (divided into individual consumption expenditure and social transfers in kind) is classified by purpose for individuals. This alternative view provides users with an expansion of analytical tools in selected areas.

Applications of the integrated framework to various circumstances and needs. Countries differ with respect to their stage of development, economic and social structure, legal organization, and so forth. The SNA is, consequently, constructed as a general framework that provides enough flexibility so that countries may use the framework to meet their specific requirements without departing from the standards that promote international comparability. Countries may utilize this flexibility to emphasize important sectors or activities, by using various levels of the SNA's classifications of transactions and transactors, by rearranging the results, or by introducing complementary classifications or additional levels of classifications. They may focus on an important activity by identifying it as a "key activity" and establishing accounts for a "key sector" in addition to those for the recommended sectors. This chapter in the U.N. Manual provides examples of how the integrated framework can be adapted to meet such specific needs, including a detailed analysis of the household sector. It also discusses special problems of accounting during periods of high inflation and includes an annex that provides an illustration of alternative treatments of nominal interest for economies that experience high inflation.

Social accounting matrices. A social accounting matrix (SAM) presents a sequence of accounts in a matrix that elaborates linkages between a supply-and-use table and sector accounts. It places special emphasis on interrelations between the structure of the economy and the distribution of income and expenditure among households. In a SAM, each account is represented by a row and column pair, with the convention that incomings are shown in rows and outgoings in columns. A transaction is represented by a single entry, which, in the case of an aggregate matrix, can be viewed as the grand total of a submatrix in which categories of transactors are presented.

As explained above, the detail shown in a SAM may be expanded or contracted as appropriate to the subject being considered; typical subjects include income flows by characteristics of recipient, employment by characteristics of population, and combinations of monetary and non-monetary data. SAMs may be constructed as, or in conjunction with, satellite accounts. The SAM approach, with its multiple sectoring, is useful for reconciling and integrating disparate but detailed basic source data, as well as allowing the introduction of a regional dimension where it is relevant and feasible. SAMs are also useful for policy analysis and modeling, in which the structural features of an economy play an important role, such as applied general equilibrium models.

Satellite analysis and accounts. Although the central framework of the SNA may be used in a flexible way, there are limits to this flexibility. Greater flexibility may be achieved through the use of satellite accounts, which permit the SNA to be expanded for selected areas of social concern without overburdening or disrupting the central framework. Satellite accounts generally make use of classification schemes and concepts that are complementary or alternative to the ones used in the central framework.

A section on satellite analysis illustrates by example various means of broadening the system. These examples include alternative classifications of products and concepts of production, enlarged concepts of transfers and disposable income, expanded concepts of capital formation, a broadened scope of assets and liabilities, and an expanded treatment of transactions by purpose. Another section presents in detail a framework for functionally originated satellite accounts. A final section discusses, as an example, how natural resources could be treated as capital. It is largely based on the United Nations System of Environmental Economic Accounts that will be presented in the *Handbook on Integrated Environmental and Economic Accounting*. It is just one of the frameworks in which environmental accounts could be developed.

CONCLUSION

Readers interested in the technical detail and sophistication of the new United Nations System of National Accounts should follow U.S. developments in this area as reported in the *Survey of Current Business* published by BEA. Those interested in the full detail should see the United Nations publication on the SNA; the technical papers of the major contributing organizations (the U.N., the Organization for Economic Cooperation and Development, the European Union, the World Bank, and the International Monetary Fund); and studies by other experts. A number of special studies of technical topics have been prepared by technical experts around the world. A sampling is provided in the Bibliography at the end of this text. A compilation of over 3,000 citations is available from the authors.

CHAPTER 8

GLOBAL INTERACTION

INTRODUCTION

The interdependence of the world economy has increased dramatically and will intensify in the future. Unquestionably, international commerce will be increasingly important. As noted in Figure 3 in chapter 1, the volume of trade in OECD countries has increased even in periods of economic weakness: evidence that major business organizations now approach inputs to production and marketing of products and services on a global basis.[1]

In a statistical sense, linkages among countries are captured in the balance of payments accounts of individual countries, which reflect trade, services, and capital flows. The United States has one of the most comprehensive systems of collecting data and plays a large role in helping other countries develop their programs of international statistics. With different legal systems for banking regulation, different taxation laws, and variations in trade policy, there are many difficulties in building the type of information system that will adequately meet the needs of public and private decision makers involved in international commerce.

U.S. balance of payments data, even with present shortcomings, are probably the most comprehensive in the world. Many other industrial countries also have sophisticated data collection procedures; whereas, data collection in the developing countries is often haphazard.

But the need for substantial improvement in international statistics is clear. For example, the individual categories in the world tabulation

---

[1]The authors wish to acknowledge the contributions of Marsha A. Kameron to this chapter.

of the balance of payments should, in principle, sum to zero (a $5 deficit in one country should be offset by surpluses equal to $5 in others). In fact, there are large imbalances in many categories, indicating errors or biases. The International Monetary Fund has addressed many of these questions in two major studies: *Report on the World Current Account Discrepancy*[2] and *Report on the Measurement of International Capital Flows*.[3]

As shown in Figure 56, when the current account of all the world's countries are added, this should net out to zero. The discrepancy in the current account topped $100 billion in 1990 and decreased somewhat in 1991. Errors of this magnitude indicate that many of the world's balance of payments tabulations are subject to considerable errors.

In this chapter, we will review some of the important challenges associated with understanding the global economy, especially as reflected in the U.S. system of statisics. However, it should be noted that equally important problems are evident in other countries, and the process of improving the international system is a major area calling for attention.

In the United States, numerous government agencies have responsibility for collecting and compiling the balance of payments statistics. That these agencies do not necessarily interact or cooperate poses a major obstacle to statistical reform. This chapter reviews some of the major shortcomings of the present system. Suggested improvements are presented in chapter 9.

FIGURE 56
Summary of World Balances

	1985	1986	1987	1988	1989	1990	1991
Current account	−80*	−66	−49	−60	−76	−112	−91
Long-term capital	16	46	30	−55	29	8	190
Short-term capital	21	46	97	79	25	106	−74
Errors and omissions	14	29	−19	−5	−15	26	−1

* All numbers represent billions of dollars.

[2]*Report on the World Current Account Discrepancy.* Washington, DC: International Monetary Fund, 1987.

[3]*Report on the Measurement of International Capital Flows.* Washington, DC: International Monetary Fund, 1992.

CURRENT ACCOUNT

I. Trade Statistics

This section focuses on the methodology of collecting international trade data. The discussion covers many problems that have been addressed in reviews during the past several years, and it highlights many of the present shortcomings of the data. Merchandise trade differs from other U.S. international transactions in several important respects: Its statistics are compiled from a full tabulation of all transactions, rather than with surveys, and much attention is placed on trade data. As a result, they are generally considered to be quite accurate.

Definitions
Merchandise exports and imports cover all movable goods sold, given away, or otherwise transferred from United States to foreign ownership and vice versa. It is assumed that goods moving through U.S. customs change ownership and that the physical position of the goods indicates ownership. For definition purposes, goods shipped between affiliated firms in the United States and abroad are assumed to change ownership even though the change-of-ownership rule may not strictly apply in a legal sense for some of those transactions.

Methodology
The U.S. Customs Service is responsible for collecting import and export documents at over 400 U.S. ports of entry and exit. It transmits the data to the Census Bureau via automated transactions and paper documents. The Census Bureau processes, compiles, and publishes trade statistics. The data are released to the public about 45 days after the end of the referenced month.

Exports
Within four days after merchandise has been exported, bills of lading containing information on quantities and destination, and a summary sheet must be submitted to the Customs Service. The carrier must also present a shippers' export declaration (SED), showing the commodity shipped and its value.

The Customs Service generally gives the SEDs little or no review for completeness or accuracy. They are forwarded to the Census Bureau for processing. This currently accounts for about 60 percent of the value of exports. SEDs are not required of the companies participating in the Census Bureau's Automatic Export Reporting Program (AERP). Computerized information is sent directly to the Census Bureau's Foreign Trade Division. This currently accounts for about 20 percent of the value of exports.

SEDs are generally not required for U.S. exports to Canada (20 percent of the value of total exports). The United States uses Canadian import data to compile U.S. exports to Canada. SEDs are also not required for export shipments under the U.S. military assistance program.

Imports

The majority of import transactions are transmitted directly by computer under the Census Bureau's Automated Broker Interface (ABI) Program. This accounts for 86 percent of the value of imports.

A small percentage of import data is still collected on Customs Form 7501. Importers must submit these forms within 10 days of receipt of the imports. The forms must be accompanied by commercial documents showing the required tariffs. This accounts for about 14 percent of the value of imports.

Formal quality control measures are applied in the processing stage. This includes a couple of different procedures:

1. A complete review by an import specialist is made of a 2 percent random sample.
2. The Census Bureau subjects high-value shipments to close scrutiny.

Recent Innovations and Changes

During the past several years, a number of changes have been made that substantially improved the quality of the trade statistics—especially import statistics, which are considered complete and accurate.

1. There has been a substantial rise in electronic filing. This streamlines compiling, although it does not eliminate the problems of nonfiling or errors in keyboard entry.
2. In March 1988, the Census Bureau increased by two weeks the time period in which monthly data are compiled. This has reduced the timing errors so that trade statistics accurately reflect the time period during which the transactions occurred.
3. In January 1989, the United States adopted the Harmonized System (HS) for classification of merchandise trade. This brought

the United States into line with most other countries using this classification system.

4. In January 1990, following several years of study, the United States and Canada began to use each other's import data to compile its export statistics.

Current Problems

Although import data are considered accurate, the quality of the export data needs further improvement. Methodological problems include the following:

1. Neither the Customs Service nor the Census Bureau has systematic controls to ensure that all documents are filed and received for processing.

2. Exporters have an incentive to understate sales to reduce their taxable income and to pay lower importer duties to importing countries.

3. Exporters do not report transactions that are restricted or banned under U.S. law. It is estimated that about 40 percent of all U.S. exports are subject to at least some type of restriction.

4. With the growing importance of trade among related parties, it is important to get better definition and quality control of data on such relationships.

Associated Trade

A great deal of trade occurs between parent and affiliated companies. As a result, a growing share of U.S. merchandise trade is transacted between affiliated parties. In 1990, trade between affiliated parties accounted for 63 percent of total exports and 43 percent of total imports. The high degree of intercompany transactions raises the question of whether goods are appropriately priced at the market or whether nonprice factors come into play. The data on the trade of multinational companies are summarized in Figure 57.

II. Services

The service accounts (referred to as invisibles) consist of these main categories: travel and tourism; transportation (including freight and port services); royalties and license fees; and numerous other services related to business. U.S. exports of services have nearly doubled over the past six

FIGURE 57
U.S. Merchandise Trade Associated
with U.S. Nonbank Multinational Companies

	1989	1990
U.S. exports of MNCs	236.4*	248.5
Shipped to affiliates	102.6	108.4
Shipped to other foreigners	133.8	140.1
Total U.S. exports	363.8	392.9
U.S. Imports—MNC associated	201.2	214.4
Shipped by affiliates	97.4	102.5
Shipped to other foreigners	103.8	111.9
Total U.S. imports	473.6	495.2

*All numbers represent billions of current dollars.

Source: *Survey of Current Business,* August 1992, p. 68.

years and account for 25 percent of the total exports of goods and services. Growth of imports of services has been slower, increasing 55 percent over the past five years and accounting for 16 percent of total U.S. imports of goods and services.

The service accounts are an important aspect of the current account that is often overlooked. The detailed service accounts are published with a considerable lag. For example, the 1991 detailed service accounts were published in the September 1992 *Survey of Current Business.* Quarterly estimates for the major categories are largely extrapolated from the previous year and are unlikely to capture significant changes that may be occurring.

Data collection for the service accounts has improved considerably, becoming more detailed during the past decade. The system in the United States is probably more comprehensive and sophisticated than in any other country. Nevertheless, data on trade in services are not as comprehensive, detailed, or timely as merchandise trade. Moreover, numerous questions about reliability suggest that coverage is incomplete, and the service accounts are probably understated. Since services are growing in importance and are little appreciated, the definition and estimation procedures for the four major accounts—Travel and Tourism, Transportation, Royalties and License Fees, and Other Private Services— are discussed in detail in Appendix C. The large diversity of the service accounts makes data collection complicated and often unreliable.

Figures 58–61 summarize the trends in the U.S. service accounts from 1986 to 1991.

FIGURE 58
U.S. Exports of Private Services

	1986	1987	1988	1989	1990	1991
Total private	77.1*	86.8	100.7	118.0	138.1	152.3
Travel	20.5	23.7	29.7	36.6	43.4	48.8
Overseas	15.7	18.0	22.3	26.9	30.8	34.5
Canada	2.7	3.3	4.2	5.4	7.1	8.5
Mexico	2.2	2.4	3.2	4.2	5.5	5.7
Passenger fares	5.5	7.0	8.9	10.5	15.1	15.6
Transportation other	15.8	17.3	19.5	21.1	22.9	23.6
Freight	4.7	5.1	5.9	6.3	7.2	7.2
Port services	10.6	11.6	12.8	13.9	14.7	15.3
Other	0.6	0.7	0.7	0.9	1.0	1.0
Total royalties and license fees	7.9	9.9	11.8	13.1	16.5	17.8
Affiliated	6.0	7.6	9.2	10.2	13.1	14.0
Unaffiliated	1.9	2.3	2.6	2.9	3.4	3.8
Other services	27.3	28.9	30.8	36.7	40.2	46.4
Affiliated	8.2	8.2	9.1	11.5	13.3	14.6
Unaffiliated	19.1	20.7	21.7	25.2	26.9	31.8

* All numbers represent billions of current dollars.

Source: *Survey of Current Business*, September 1992, p. 83.

INTERNATIONAL CAPITAL FLOWS

I. U.S. Capital Account

The U.S. capital account system was designed at a time when most transactions were conducted in conventional financial instruments and channeled through a few large banks and other financial institutions. Capital markets have changed dramatically since then, reflecting the deregulation of capital controls, new financial instruments, and the proliferation of transactions. The result is that the statistical problems faced by U.S. compilers have intensified and strained available resources.

The next section will focus on the concepts and methodology of the U.S. balance of payments as they relate to portfolio, direct investment, banking transactions, and nonbanking transactions.

A. Portfolio Capital Flows

During the past decade, large institutional investors such as pension funds, insurance companies, and investment trusts accounted for most of

FIGURE 59
U.S. Exports of Other Unaffiliated Private Services

	1986	1987	1988	1989	1990	1991
Total	19.1*	20.7	21.7	25.2	26.8	31.8
Education	3.5	3.8	4.1	4.6	5.1	5.7
Financial services	3.3	3.7	3.8	5.0	4.3	4.7
Insurance, net	2.0	2.3	1.5	1.6	1.8	2.2
Telecommunications	1.8	2.1	2.2	2.5	2.7	2.8
Business and Professional Services						
Total	4.4	4.3	5.4	6.2	6.8	10.4
Advertising	0.1	0.1	0.1	0.1	0.1	0.2
Computer & data processing	1.0	0.6	1.2	1.0	1.0	1.7
Database and information	0.1	0.1	0.2	0.2	0.3	0.4
R&D and testing	0.3	0.2	0.2	0.4	0.4	0.6
PR and consulting	0.3	0.3	0.3	0.3	0.3	0.3
Legal	0.1	0.1	0.3	0.4	0.5	1.2
Construction	0.8	0.7	0.8	0.9	0.7	1.3
Industrial engineering	0.1	0.3	0.3	0.2	0.5	0.5
Maintenance and repair	1.0	1.1	1.3	1.7	2.0	2.5
Other**	0.6	0.7	0.7	0.9	0.9	1.4
Other unaffiliated[†]	4.1	4.4	4.6	5.3	6.1	6.1

* All numbers represent billions of current dollars.
** "Other" consists of such services as accounting, auditing, bookkeeping, agricultural, mailing, management of health care facilities, medical services, personnel supply, sports, performing arts, and training services. Medical services is by far the largest category, comprising about half the "other" category.
† Includes mainly expenditures of foreign governments and international agencies in the U.S.

Source: *Survey of Current Business*, September 1992, p. 83.

the growth in international portfolio investment. Large investors shifted part of their assets to foreign managers and often bought and sold securities directly in foreign markets.

Methodology. Net U.S. purchases of foreign securities and net foreign purchase of U.S. securities are estimated by the Bureau of Economic Analysis (BEA) on the basis of data from the U.S. Department of the Treasury International Capital Reporting System (TICS). Only long-term stocks and bonds are reported. Filing is required for all banks, banking institutions, brokers, and dealers when total purchases or sales exceed $500,000 in any given month. The BEA adjusts the data to

FIGURE 60
U.S. Imports of Private Services

	1986	1987	1988	1989	1990	1991
Total private	64.5*	73.4	80.3	84.1	97.0	100.0
Travel	25.9	29.3	32.1	33.4	37.3	37.0
Overseas	20.3	23.3	25.3	25.7	28.9	28.1
Canada	3.0	2.9	3.2	3.4	3.5	3.7
Mexico	2.6	3.1	3.6	4.3	4.9	5.1
Passenger fares	6.5	7.3	7.8	8.3	10.6	10.6
Transportation other	16.7	17.8	19.5	20.7	23.4	23.3
Freight	10.8	10.7	11.7	11.7	12.6	11.9
Port services	5.2	6.4	7.1	8.2	9.9	10.4
Other	0.6	0.7	0.7	0.8	0.9	0.9
Total royalties and license fees	1.4	1.8	2.6	2.6	3.1	4.0
Affiliated	1.0	1.3	1.4	1.8	2.2	2.9
Unaffiliated	0.5	0.5	1.2	0.8	0.9	1.1
Other services	13.9	17.2	18.4	19.1	22.5	25.1
Affiliated	3.9	5.2	5.9	7.2	8.7	9.6
Unaffiliated	10.0	12.0	12.5	12.0	13.8	15.6

* All numbers represent billions of current dollars.

Source: *Survey of Current Business,* September 1992, p. 83.

exclude estimates of commissions, taxes, and other charges from the gross transactions. The activity of a large institution reflects the consolidation of many transactions made through the reporting institution. As a result, a small number of reporters account for a large share of the reported total.

Purchases and sales of U.S. securities by foreigners are reported by securities dealers in the United States. The reports of the dealers are supplemented by reports from corporations that sell bonds directly to foreigners, Eurobonds, for example. These are not regular reporters.

Problems.

1. *Incomplete or inaccurate data.* Money managers and large institutional investors are increasingly maintaining their own facilities for conducting business without dealing with a financial institution that must submit TICS forms.
2. *New financial instruments not reported.* Short-term marketable instruments and derivative instruments such as warrants, options,

FIGURE 61
U.S. Imports of Other Unaffiliated Private Services

	1986	1987	1988	1989	1990	1991
Total	10.0*	12.0	12.5	12.0	13.8	15.6
Education	0.4	0.5	0.5	0.6	0.7	0.7
Financial services	1.8	2.1	1.7	2.1	2.3	2.4
Insurance, net	2.2	3.2	2.6	0.8	1.8	2.6
Telecommunications	3.2	3.7	4.5	5.2	5.5	5.6
Business and Professional Services						
Total	1.3	1.3	1.8	2.0	2.0	2.6
Advertising	0.1	0.1	0.2	0.2	0.2	0.3
Computer & data processing	a	a	a	a	a	0.1
Database and information	a	a	a	a	a	0.1
R&D and testing	0.1	0.1	0.2	0.1	0.2	0.3
PR and consulting	0.1	0.1	0.1	0.1	0.1	0.2
Legal	a	0.1	0.1	0.1	0.1	0.2
Construction	0.3	0.2	0.3	0.4	0.3	0.3
Industrial engineering	0.1	0.1	0.1	0.1	0.1	a
Maintenance and repair	0.5	0.5	0.6	0.7	0.7	0.6
Other**	0.1	0.1	0.1	0.1	1.0	0.6
Other unaffiliated†	1.1	1.1	1.3	1.4	1.5	1.6

a = less than $50 million

* All numbers represent billions of current dollars.

** "Other" consists of such services as accounting, auditing, bookkeeping, agricultural, mailing, management of health care facilities, medical services, personnel supply, sports, performing arts, and training services.

† Includes mainly wages of foreign residents temporarily employed in the U.S. and of Canadian and Mexican commuters in the U.S. border area.

Source: *Survey of Current Business,* September 1992, p. 83.

puts, and calls are not ordinarily covered on the TICS forms. The TICS covers warrants and options only when the underlying security is a stock or long-term bond.

3. *Diffusion of reporting responsibilities.* As financial organizations are becoming increasingly complex and the responsibility for reporting becomes decentralized, the responsibility for reporting becomes obscured.

4. *Discrepancies due to foreign exchange conversion.* Transactions in foreign currencies are reported in terms of their dollar equiv-

alents converted at the prevailing exchange rate either at the time of the transaction or at the close of the last business day of the reporting month.

5. *Sales to third parties.* The geographic distribution of the reported data may not necessarily reflect the nationality of the ultimate foreign owner. Transactions in well-developed foreign financial markets are done on behalf of third-party customers or countries.

Foreign Direct Investment. During the past decade, there has been considerable concern about the growing globalization of world assets. In the United States, this was exemplified by the fear that Japan was buying out America. In other countries, there were worries about foreign interests exerting a disproportionate influence on domestic economic policies. Dismantled capital controls and large-scale mergers and acquisitions diversified the ownership of assets across national borders. Between 1986 and 1989, net direct investment flows more than doubled, to about $200 billion. The value of direct investment measured at book value exceeded $1,000 billion by the end of 1989. (Global data are compiled with a considerable lag.) Since direct investment is largely a function of economic growth, it is assumed that the growth of direct investment decelerated in the early 1990s.

The global presence of U.S. companies has grown dramatically over the past several decades. In 1990, worldwide assets of U.S. multinational companies amounted to $6,522 billion, of which $1,552 billion were assets of foreign affiliates.

B. U.S. Direct Investment Overseas
The U.S. system for collecting direct investment data is considered one of the most comprehensive systems in the world. Moreover, direct investment capital flows are considered more accurate than investment flows related to portfolio or banking flows.

Definition of Direct Investment. Outward investment or direct investment abroad: A direct investor is a U.S. person (or company) who has 10 percent or more ownership in a business enterprise located in a foreign country. Inward investment or direct investment in the United States refers to foreign ownership of more than 10 percent of a business enterprise located in the United States.

Methodology for Compiling U.S. Direct Investment.   The Bureau of Economic Analysis (BEA) conducts many surveys on both direct investment abroad and direct investment in the United States. Every five years, a benchmark survey is conducted, covering virtually all direct investment flows. Annual and quarterly surveys update information for inclusion in the balance of payments statistics.

U.S. Investment Overseas.   The latest benchmark survey covered data up through 1989 and was published in 1991. Reports were required from each U.S. parent and separately for each of its foreign affiliates with assets, sales, or net income greater than $3 million. Greater detail was requested for foreign affiliates that were majority owned.

On an annual basis, BEA collects key information on the operations of a sample of parent companies and their affiliates. Mandatory quarterly reports cover information required for balance of payments purposes.

Methodological Problems.

1. The quarterly and annual data are heavily skewed toward large companies and also toward investors with ownership of 50 percent or more. For example, the 10 largest U.S. parent companies, in terms of the assets of foreign affiliates, owned 32 percent of such assets. The 100 largest companies accounted for 72 percent of the total assets.[4]

2. Sizable revisions occur after quarterly reports are revised.

3. Ownership of less than 10 percent is excluded. Thus, if one party owns 11 percent and another owns 9 percent, the 11 percent is included but the 9 percent is excluded.

4. The distinction between direct investment and portfolio investment is often arbitrary. As noted above, direct investment implies that a person (company) has a lasting interest in the management of a business in another country, and this implies a long-term relationship. Portfolio investment reflects primarily short-term activity in financial markets, where the ability to shift funds between countries or financial investments is a major consideration.

---

[4]Anne Y. Kester, ed., *Behind the Numbers: U.S. Trade in the World Economy.* Washington, DC: National Academy Press, 1992, p. 161.

Foreign Investment in the United States.   The latest benchmark survey covered 1987. Complete reports covering financial, operating, balance of payments, and direct investment position data had to be filed if the U.S. affiliate of a foreign company had at least $1 million in assets, sales, or net income.

There are several problems with the surveys of foreign company affiliates. The following are some of the major problems:

1. Quarterly surveys are used for the most recent information. They are less comprehensive and only cover a sample of companies.

2. Some data are collected on a fiscal year basis and adjusted to a calendar year for use in the balance of payments.

3. Compliance with reporting requirements is not as good as it could be.

4. Late reporting is somewhat of a problem.

Impact on the U.S. Balance of Payments.   Direct investment has a sizable impact on both the current and capital accounts. Direct investment receipts and payments are captured in the current account as dividends, interest, and reinvested earnings. The capital account captures changes in the ownership of assets (net worth), including changes in owners' equity, intercompany accounts, and reinvested earnings.

The capital account has two major components. These are investment by U.S. citizens and organizations in businesses located in other countries, and investment in the U.S. by citizens and organizations from other countries.

U.S. Direct Investment Abroad.   Equity capital consists of changes in U.S. parents' equity in their foreign affiliates. Equity capital outflows are recorded at transactions values, based on the books of U.S. parents. Reinvested earnings of foreign affiliates are total earnings, including capital gains and losses, less distributed earnings. Intercompany debt flows consist of the increase in U.S. parents' net intercompany account receivables from their foreign affiliates during the year.

Foreign Direct Investment in the United States.   Equity capital consists of changes in foreign holdings of U.S. affiliates. Equity capital inflows are recorded at transactions values based on the books of U.S. parents. Reinvested earnings of U.S. affiliates are total earnings, including capital gains and losses, less distributed earnings.

Because of the special nature of the relationship between a direct investor and its affiliates, there may be cases in which goods, services, and technical know-how are provided from parent to the affiliate without any corresponding cash flow. It is estimated that these noncash transactions have increased in recent years.

Direct investment earnings are a major portion of the service account. Income on direct investment is the return that direct investors receive on their investment. The two major components of earnings are distributed earnings and reinvested earnings. Interest on intercompany accounts is a small fraction of earnings. Distributed earnings consist of U.S. parents' receipts less U.S. parents' payments. Data collection in this area presents two special difficulties:

1. *Confidentiality.* The BEA surveys are confidential, which poses a continuing problem in delivering specific industry information to the ultimate user. Data points are often suppressed because the cell is "dominated" by three or fewer firms.

2. *Classification.* All activities of foreign affiliates operating in the United States are consolidated and classified according to the primary activity of the affiliate. This method of classification overvalues the primary activity of the subsidiary and undervalues any secondary or other activities.

C. Bank Claims and Liabilities

Methodology. U.S. banks, depository institutions, international banking facilities, bank holding companies, brokers, and dealers are required to file TIC B forms. Reporting is mandatory. Data include information on loans, advances, overdrafts, and various other transactions. Data include operating transactions between U.S. banks and their foreign branches, as well as subsidiaries of foreign banks in the United States. Reports are required if total claims on, or liabilities to, foreigners are $15 million or more for any month-end closing balance. Reports are either monthly or quarterly, depending on the institution involved.

Data are generally assumed to be fairly accurate. Interbanking business between U.S. and foreign banks can be verified with the banking data collected by the Bank for International Settlements (BIS).

The following items are excluded from both claims and liabilities:

1. Long-term securities of foreign or U.S. issuers (reported on the ESE form).

2. Permanent capital invested in affiliated agencies.
3. Contingent claims and liabilities.
4. Gold, silver, or currency in transit to and from the United States.
5. Interest rate and foreign currency swaps associated with bank indebtedness.
6. Forward exchange contracts.

Problems. Several areas of problems need attention. They are:

1. *Omissions.* Some transactions are not included within the TIC B reporting system. These include direct transactions between non-financial lenders and borrowers, with financial intermediaries increasingly acting as agents or arrangers of the deal for a fee or commission.
2. *Accuracy of data.* There are large daily swings in banks' claims and liabilities vis-à-vis their own foreign offices, particularly between the last day of certain months and the first day of the next month. Swings of $10–$20 billion are not unusual.

    Data are end-month positions that must be converted to flows for use in the balance of payments accounts. Capital flows for banks are calculated from changes in asset positions. Balances in foreign currencies must be adjusted to reflect changes in various exchange rates. The currency composition of the accounts is not known.
3. *Data errors related to foreign banks.* The accuracy of data provided by U.S. affiliates of foreign banks has been subject to question. It is not clear whether filing instructions are always fully understood and properly acted upon.

D. Nonbanking Transactions

This is a small category made up of diverse transactions. Exporters, importers, and industrial and commercial firms are required to file TIC C forms on a quarterly basis. Transactions include financial claims or liabilities and commercial claims or liabilities related to the sale of goods and services in normal business operations.

Problems. Problems in this area cover the following areas:

1. *Nonreporting and reporting responsibilities.* TIC C reporters are not subject to the regulatory authority of the Federal Reserve

Bank, and they tend to be less cooperative about reporting. At present, it is believed that only a small fraction of the required transactions are reported. Nonbank transactions are a diverse group that includes individuals and businesses of many kinds. It is extremely difficult to measure transactions in this group.

In some respects, the TIC C reports are a residual report, catching transactions that are not reported elsewhere. They exclude direct investment transactions, securities, and custody items reported by banks, brokers, and dealers. As a result, there is confusion about reporting responsibilities.

For example, in September 1990, the TIC data on U.S. nonbank financial assets abroad amounted to $65 billion compared with $250 billion reported by the BIS and IMF. Similarly, the TIC data on U.S. nonbank financial liabilities was $80 billion compared with $235 billion reported by the BIS and IMF.

2. *Capital flight and money laundering.* There is a broadly held perception that private nonbank flows are seriously understated. Capital flight, money laundering, and illegal flows are often named as reasons for this problem.

3. *The use of the U.S. dollar abroad.* Foreign holdings of U.S. currency are not included in the balance of payments statistics. It has been estimated that from one- to two-thirds of all U.S. currency outstanding may be held by foreigners. In many foreign countries, the U.S. dollar is widely used as the most desirable medium of exchange because of hyperinflation, which makes the local currency worthless. The local currency is also not convertible for international trade purposes. The wide use of the U.S. dollar abroad is also a reflection of illegal drug traffic and eventual money laundering.

II. Other Aspects of International Capital Flows

The difficulties described in the U.S. capital accounts are compounded when analyzing global capital flows. The IMF Working Party "found that world capital account statistical systems are in a state of crisis."[5]

---

[5]*Report on the Measurement of International Capital Flows,* International Monetary Fund, September 1992.

Global integration of financial markets reflects the combination of a number of important changes over the past decade. These include dismantling capital controls, the increasing role of foreign banking in national markets, the internationalization of securities' markets, the development of new financial instruments, and the diversification of institutional investors. Global integration has been made possible because of technological advances.

Because of the growing globalization of capital flows, it is imperative to address questions related to the world financial reporting systems. As the reporting system becomes increasingly unreliable, the monitoring of international capital flows is becoming impaired.

Since relatively few countries account for the major part of world capital flows, these leading countries should be at the forefront of upgrading and harmonizing their capital account statistics. (About 10 countries account for 85 percent of the flows while Japan, the United States, the United Kingdom, and Germany together account for almost two-thirds of all transactions.)

Other Topics

Other aspects of international capital flows relate to offshore financial centers and the growth of the interbank market.

Offshore Financial Centers. Offshore Financial Centers (OFCs) are small economies that have set up systems to encourage or promote financial transactions among foreigners through domestic intermediaries. OFCs typically have special classes of business licenses that exempt holders from most forms of domestic regulation, provided they do not participate in the local economy and conduct only international business.

The transactions of offshore financial centers complicate the world balance of payments. OFCs do not necessarily report transactions; whereas, partner countries are more likely to report such transactions. There is a great deal of ambiguity as far as reporting, and it is likely that some portion of transactions are either not reported or misclassified.

For balance of payments purposes, capital flows are not usually recorded, since the transactions are not related to domestic activity. While OFCs omit such activities from their statements, partner countries report them in their own balance of payments as specific transactions with OFCs.

Often, transactions change form as they pass through OFCs. For example, they may enter as direct investment or interbank flows and leave as portfolio investment transactions.

The International Interbank Market.   There has been a tremendous expansion in the scale of net and gross capital transactions among the industrialized countries. The balance of payments capture the net transactions. An even more rapid expansion has occurred in the volume of capital transactions.

The progressive relaxation of capital controls, as well as the broader financial liberalization in the industrial countries, has brought about a growing integration and globalization of major offshore and domestic financial markets.

The development of financial instruments has led to increased linkages among financial markets domestically and internationally. The markets for short-term interest rate futures, swaps, forward rate agreements (FRAs), and interest rate options have emerged to complement and, in some cases, to substitute for the traditional interbank deposit and other cash markets. In essence, the interbank deposit markets now basically function as funding markets, while hedging and position taking have shifted to off-balance-sheet markets.

The derivative markets not only interact with the underlying cash market, but also are themselves deeply interconnected. For example, securities increasingly incorporate option elements or are swapped into payment flows involving different currencies. Bond issues with a menu of equity-linked elements have become increasingly common.

Figures 62–65 give an indication of the scope and size of the international capital markets.

The global interbank market more than tripled from 1983 to 1991 (Figure 62).

Off-balance-sheet assets have become an increasingly important part of interbank assets (Figure 63).

The growth in transactions and notional outstanding positions in derivative instruments had tended to outpace growth in other segments of the market. The outstanding notional volume of derivative contracts on interest rates and currencies as a proportion of international assets of BIS reporting banks has grown from around 25 percent at the end of 1986 to more than 100 percent at the end of 1991.

FIGURE 62

International Bank Positions—Amounts Outstanding at Year-End

Parent Country of Bank	Claims		Liabilities	
	1983	1991	1983	1991
Belgium	38.2*	135.1	39.6	133.1
Canada	112.9	110.1	115.2	121.2
France	191.4	565.4	185.8	630.4
Germany	114.5	640.4	131.7	489.2
Italy	80.9	397.5	78.9	427.5
Japan	456.9	1,935.1	414.7	1,828.1
Luxembourg	5.2	46.7	5.0	47.9
Netherlands	62.5	199.5	59.8	178.3
Sweden	18.2	128.9	17.2	126.1
Switzerland	79.9	408.9	67.2	398.6
United Kingdom	178.8	282.1	181.6	333.6
United States	605.5	650.7	544.4	683.1
Other	191.0	636.6	193.5	698.7
Total	2,165.9	6,137.0	2,034.1	6,095.8

* All numbers represent billions of dollars.

Source: *Recent Developments in International Interbank Relations,* Bank for International Settlements, October 1992, p. 43.

FIGURE 63

Comparison of On- and Off-Balance-Sheet Interbank Assets as a Percentage of Total Assets End of 1990

Parent Country of Bank	Total	On-Balance-Sheet	Off-Balance-Sheet
Belgium	11.0*	10.2	0.8
Canada	10.2	7.5	2.7
France	n/a	16.7	n/a
Germany	9.2	8.3	0.9
Italy	23.5	20.4	3.1
Japan	20.4	15.0	5.4
Luxembourg	30.0	29.2	0.8
Netherlands	20.6	18.3	2.3
Sweden	13.3	10.0	3.3
United Kingdom	30.7	21.5	9.2
United States	7.1	3.8	3.3

* All numbers represent billions of dollars.

Source: *Recent Developments in International Interbank Relations,* Bank for International Settlements, October 1992, p. 49.

FIGURE 64
Selected Derivative Instruments—Notional Principal Amounts Outstanding at Year-End

	1986	1987	1988	1989	1990	1991
Exchange Traded Instruments						
Interest rate futures	370*	488	895	1,201	1,454	2,159
Interest rate options	146	122	279	387	600	1,072
Currency futures	10	14	12	16	16	18
Currency options	39	60	48	50	56	59
Stock market index futures	15	18	28	42	70	77
Options on stock market	3	23	38	66	88	132
Total	583	725	1,300	1,762	2,284	3,518
Over-the-Counter Instruments						
Interest rate swaps	400	683	1,010	1,503	2,312	3,065
Currency and cross-currency interest rate swaps	100	184	320	449	578	807
Other derivative instruments	—	—	—	450	561	577
Total	500	867	1,330	2,402	3,451	4,449

* All numbers represent billions of dollars.

Source: *Recent Developments in International Interbank Relations,* Bank for International Settlements, October 1992, p.51.

CONCLUSION

The large statistical discrepancy in the U.S. balance of payments indicates there are serious data problems yet to be resolved. Theoretically, improvement of the U.S. balance of payments should be made as a coordinated effort by all the agencies charged with collecting and compiling data. In reality, this is not likely to happen. Over the next decade, cost considerations are expected to prevail, so allocation of new funding for improved data collection will be hotly debated. The improvement of the capital accounts should be a top priority.

The balance of payments is reasonably timely. With respect to the traditional trade-off between timeliness and accuracy, the trade and service accounts were not subject to significant revisions; whereas, the capital accounts showed considerable volatility.[6]

---

[6]This conclusion was supported, for example, in an evaluation of quarterly data for 1992.

FIGURE 65

Derivative Financial Instruments—Annual Number of Contracts in Millions

	1986	1987	1988	1989	1990	1991
Futures on short-term interest rate instruments of which:	16*	29	34	70	76	85
three-month Euro-dollar	12	24	25	47	39	42
Futures on long-term interest rate instruments of which:	75	116	123	131	143	150
U.S. Treasury bond	55	69	74	73	78	70
French bond	1	12	12	15	16	21
German bond	9	18	19	19	16	13
Currency futures	20	21	22	28	29	29
Interest rate options	22	29	31	40	52	51
Currency options	13	18	18	21	19	21
Total	146	214	227	289	319	336

* All numbers represent billions of dollars.

Source: *Recent Developments in International Interbank Relations,* Bank for International Settlements, October 1992, p.57.

Massive overhauls of the entire system are not being proposed here, but that should not be taken to imply that they are not needed. On the contrary, the growing importance of the global economy requires that a wide variety of perspectives be brought to bear on the task of constructing a system of statistics that will comprehensively and more perspicuously depict the global market. This chapter was designed primarily to invite that discussion. Some specific immediate recommendations are suggested in chapter 9.

CHAPTER 9

RECOMMENDATIONS—NATIONAL ACCOUNTS (THE SYSTEM OF NATIONAL ACCOUNTS) AND INTERNATIONAL STATISTICS

INTRODUCTION

This report has discussed the constraints to the reform of official statistics as well as current challenges and deficiencies. Where does this analysis lead us? In this chapter, we make a number of specific recommendations for improving national income accounting statistics and the closely related field of international trade and financial statistics. The earlier discussions of statistics about topics like energy, the environment, health, education, and general population statistics are not directly covered in these recommendations, although the improvements suggested in this chapter will provide a better framework for measurement in those areas as well.

The authors take an optimistic approach to developing an improved statistical system for the 21st century. It will be a complicated task, especially when seeking better statistics for all of the topics covered in this book. Yet, when we focus on the national income accounting system—one of the topics of this chapter—a number of recent developments offer important starting points:

- The culmination of a long effort to refine and update the United Nations System of National Accounts (SNA) was achieved when the United Nations Economic and Social Council approved the 1993 SNA revision in July 1993. This chapter outlines some of the elements required for implementation of the proposed revisions. In addition, it highlights improvements needed for major areas of the database used in preparing the national accounts.

- The National Academy of Sciences will soon publish a report on international financial flows as a companion to the highly regarded report *Behind the Numbers*.[1] This chapter summarizes key recommendations from the published report and makes independent recommendations in the area of international financial statistics aimed at redesign of the increasingly important global system of statistics about economic relations among nations.

- The Federal Economic Classification Policy Committee (ECPC)[2] is addressing a classification system that will reflect the economic structures of today and, hopefully, the future. The examination of economic structure and the resulting definition of a standard for industrial classification provides a unique opportunity to re-examine the needs for new statistical programs in response to these changing circumstances.

- Work is now underway to examine the structure and process for the population census to be taken in the year 2000. While funding for this effort is fragile (since some congressional cuts have been proposed in the current work plan), this fundamental review also provides a framework for addressing the needed improvements and for bringing about change.

While it is easy to be skeptical about fundamental changes emerging from these bureaucratic efforts, it should be noted that the professional statisticians supporting these efforts are competent and dedicated, and understand the deficiencies of the current system. Most impediments to change are broad in scope and not related to any specific proposal. They include:

- The resistance of administrators to become champions for causes that will not yield results on their watch.

- A reluctance of the executive branch to propose funding research and new statistical (overhead) programs in a time of chronic budget deficits.

---

[1] Anne Y. Kester, ed., *Behind the Numbers: U.S. Trade in the World Economy.* Washington, DC: National Academy Press, 1992.

[2] This committee is chaired by Jack Triplett of the Bureau of Economic Analysis. The Committee will report to the Office of Management and Budget with a target set of recommendations to be adopted in March 1996.

- Public resistance to supplying information to governments, including problems with the paperwork burden discussed earlier.[3]
- The tendency for legislative bodies to micromanage statistical agencies and to ignore the long-term effects of statistical program changes.
- The lack of a political constituency for statistical improvements.

With these well-defined and recognized barriers, why recommend improvement? We suggest several reasons.

First, we believe this report can be a starting point for the development of a practical "vision" of future directions. *If enough discussion and debate are fostered, the resulting consensus could be a starting point for building political pressure for change, not only within the statistical community but also, more importantly, in the user community (both public and private).* A cost-benefit analysis of improved data for better decisions versus status quo and weakening data for future needs should be a compelling case for change.

Second, the resistance of executive branch decision makers and legislators can be overcome if the case is presented in a long-range, well-documented manner. *We believe that trying to solve these issues incrementally has been a failure.* A comprehensive program is more likely to get attention and yield measurable and understandable results.

Third, the issues of "reporting burden" and public resistance to "big brother data banks" belong to another era. When available technology for electronic data interchange, encoding and protecting electronic files, and scanning and optical character recognition is combined with the rapid evolution of computer accessibility, enormous expansion of CPU power in desktop and handheld computers, and the availability of inexpensive data storage and telecommunications systems, *the opportunity to collect, analyze, and disseminate better information is at hand. We simply need to appreciate the opportunities and design new systems of collecting the information that is available throughout our society.*

Fourth, *a set of new and improved national statistics will invariably lead to a set of new and improved national goals.* For example, the current economic dogma places a high priority on balancing the trade deficit. Using alternative measures of international trade flows (as proposed in the satellite accounts of the SNA) should result in more pre-

---

[3]See discussion in chapter 1.

cise data, which may indicate that this goal is much closer to being achieved than previously recognized, or the data may uncover problems not currently appreciated. The power of economic statistics to shape economic policy recommendations can never be underestimated.

Further, other nations are already making rapid progress in these same areas. Their progress makes it important for the United States to show the path toward the 21st century with the recognition that this statistical framework can be replicated throughout the developed world and, later, in the developing world.

FUTURE DIRECTION FOR THE U.S. NATIONAL ECONOMIC ACCOUNTS

Key aspects of the U.S. national economic accounts need strengthening. This section recommends 18 major improvements to enhance the relevance of the accounts for use in economic analysis during the balance of the 1990s and into the 21st century.

These recommendations are based on a review of budget and technical papers of the Bureau of Economic Analysis (BEA), Bureau of the Census, Bureau of Labor Statistics (BLS), Internal Revenue Service (IRS), and the Office of Management and Budget (OMB).[4]

The papers contain actual and proposed improvements for economic statistics included in BEA, Census, BLS, and IRS budgets during the early 1990s through fiscal year 1994; reports and articles on technical subjects; and an accounting of the agencies' actions on the recommendations of the Creamer Report (the *Gross National Product Data Improvement Project Report*). Current programs, future plans, and new ideas were discussed with officials and staff of the above agencies. Discussion also focused on the new Joint Program in Survey Methodology of the Universities of Maryland and Michigan, and Westat, Inc. The Census, BLS, and IRS undertook a systematic review of their actions on the Creamer Report recommendations expressly for the review that served as background for this book; the BEA had previously done this. *Four of the 19 recommendations in this report are nonimplemented Creamer Report recommendations.*

---

[4]This review was undertaken by Norman Frumkin, currently an economic consultant and writer. He formerly worked as a consultant in the early 1970s to the *Gross National Product Data Improvement Project Report* (The Creamer Report), which was published in 1977.

The conceptual design of the accounts requires that a vast array of economic transactions be summarized into usable statistics for economic analysis, balanced by the limitations of data collection costs, by the lack of appropriate data in business records, and by reporting burdens involved in obtaining the necessary data to convert the concepts into actual statistical measures. *The conceptual evolution will continue in the second half of the 1990s when BEA converts the national income and product accounts (NIPA) to the United Nations System of National Accounts (SNA).* In preparing the accounts, BEA relies heavily on data from other federal agencies and, to a lesser extent, on data from private and international organizations.

The recommendations in this chapter address three broad areas:

1. The statistics underlying the accounts provided by the Census, BLS, and IRS that account for the bulk of the database.
2. The preparation of the accounts by BEA.
3. The infrastructure of economic statistics in the public and private sectors that affects the accounts.

The following includes specific recommendations for addressing problems with international statistics, which were dicussed in chapter 8, Global Interaction. There is some overlap in the SNA because it also deals with "rest of the world" interrelationships as discussed in chapter 7. Let us now turn specifically to recommendations concerning NIPA and the SNA.

SPECIFIC TOPICS OF THE NATIONAL ACCOUNTS

This section highlights four aspects of the national accounts: (1) quarterly gross domestic product; (2) price measurement and real output; (3) input/output tables; and (4) satellite accounts.

Quarterly Gross Domestic Product

The gross domestic product (GDP) estimates, prepared on a current basis every quarter, are the bedrock of the accounts. They are used in cyclical analyses of the economy and in formulating fiscal and monetary policies. Three GDP estimates are prepared every quarter. The "advance" figure is published roughly 25 days after the reference quarter ends, and subsequent revisions are published in the "preliminary" figure 55 days after the quarter and in the "final" figure 85 days after the quarter.

Two aspects of the quarterly estimates are discussed: new data collections and the statistical discrepancy.

New Data Collections

New data collections to improve the GDP database are recommended for the following components: personal consumption expenditures, purchases and total expenditures of state and local governments, employee compensation, and corporate profits.

Personal consumption expenditures. Quarterly personal consumption expenditures for services are based on extrapolating annual levels by the movement of wage payments in service industries from the monthly BLS survey of employer payrolls to estimate approximately 30 percent of total services expenditures. Personal service outlays totaled $2.3 trillion in 1992. The Census Bureau greatly expanded the annual and quinquennial coverage of service industries in its surveys and economic censuses during the 1980s. There is, however, no quarterly coverage of important service industries, such as health care and auto repair. Outlays for services are subject to wide cyclical fluctuations, contrary to the common notion that they move steadily in one direction.

Recommendation

Our recommendation is to eliminate the 85-day estimate. If a decision is made to continue publication of the 85-day estimates, the Census Bureau should collect quarterly data on sales of service industries for use in the final 85-day GDP estimates. In planning this survey of service industry establishments, Census should examine the ongoing Consumer Expenditure Survey of households that it conducts for the Bureau of Labor Statistics to determine if some outlays reported by households can be used to supplement the industry estimates.

State and local governments' purchases of goods and services and total expenditures. Government expenditures include purchases of goods and services that are part of the GDP. In addition to purchased goods and services, expenditures include transfer payments for income maintenance, interest, social insurance funds, subsidies, and other items. Expenditures are used in the derivation of government budget surplus/deficit positions in the national accounts.

There are several gaps in these data. First, quarterly data on purchases of goods and services other than for employee compensation and structures are not available. Thus, purchases totaling $118 billion in 1992 of equipment, supplies, utilities, and services for education, police, health, transportation, housing, welfare, utilities, and other governmental functions are judgmentally extrapolated from earlier annual levels for the subsequent quarterly GDP estimates. Additionally, these purchases are subject to cyclical fluctuation since they are in part governed by changes in tax revenues.

The second gap is in the quarterly estimates of state and local budgets. Here too, trend extrapolation of purchased goods and services is used for some transfer payments. Total expenditures were $822 billion in 1992. Quarterly data on receipts of state and local governments are available.

Third, quarterly source data are not available for about 10 percent of receipts, primarily contributions for social insurance, and for interest receipts, which are recorded in the NIPAs as negative expenditure. They amount to over $100 billion!

Recommendation

Our recommendation is to eliminate the 85-day estimate. If a decision is made to continue publication of the 85-day estimates, the Census Bureau should conduct a quarterly survey of expenditures of state and local governments for use in both the final 85-day GDP estimates and in the 85-day state and local budget estimates. The survey should cover compensation other than wage and salary compensation, which is the only component currently reported. This is a nonimplemented Creamer Report recommendation.

Compensation of employees. The employee compensation figures are composed of wages and salaries, social insurance (employer taxes for social security and unemployment insurance), and other labor income (mainly employer-paid private pension, health, and welfare plans). Wage and salary data are based on the monthly BLS survey of employer payrolls. The social insurance estimates are derived by multiplying the BLS wage data by social security and unemployment insurance tax rates. The other labor income figures are extrapolated from annual trends. Employee compensation was $3.5 trillion in 1992 ($2.9 trillion for wages and salaries, and $0.3 trillion each for social insurance and other labor income).

Recommendation

The Internal Revenue Service should tabulate data from a probability sample of the Employer's Quarterly Federal Tax Return (Form 941) on wages and social security payments for use in the final 85-

day GDP estimate. This is a nonimplemented Creamer Report recommendation.

Corporate profits. The corporate profit estimates for manufacturing, mining, and trade corporations are based on Census Bureau survey information in the *Quarterly Financial Report* (QFR). Quarterly corporate profits in the construction, transportation, utilities, finance, and service industries are based on stockholder and regulatory agency reports and extrapolating annual data using industry sales or other measures of industry activity multiplied by trended profit margins. Corporate profits before the payment of income taxes for this latter group of industries were $134 billion in 1991. Corporate profits are a cyclically volatile component of the GDP.

Recommendation

The Census Bureau should conduct a comprehensive review of the scope of the *Quarterly Financial Report* (QFR) in consultation with the Bureau of Economic Analysis to determine where it can feasibly remedy major data gaps in the quarterly estimates of corporate profits. Based on an assessment of the quality of the existing data sources used in estimating corporate profits, the review should include the benefits and costs of (a) expanding coverage to the construction, transportation, utilities, finance, and services industries; and (b) expanding the coverage to unincorporated businesses in those industries where sole proprietorships and partnerships are prominent. If some expansion of the QFR is warranted, research and pilot surveys will be necessary prior to operational surveys. The inclusion of banks in the survey would have to be coordinated with the banking regulatory agencies. The FY 1994 Census Bureau's budget included a request for funds to add the business services industries (SIC 73) to the QFR.

Statistical Discrepancy

The statistical discrepancy is a broad guide of the extent of statistical inconsistencies and statistical error in the national accounts. Specifically, the discrepancy is the GDP estimated from the product side (the sum of all *uses* of income) minus the GDP estimated from the income side (the sum of all *sources* of income). The product side comprises consumer expenditures, private investment, government purchases, and net exports. The income side comprises employee compensation, business profits, rental income, net interest, consumption of fixed capital, indirect business taxes, current surplus of government enterprises, subsidies, and business transfer payments. Conceptually, the sum totals of the product and income sides are equivalent since they both represent the nation's output, only viewed from different perspectives; the product side focuses on markets and the income side on production costs.

When the discrepancy is positive, the product side is larger than the income side; and when the discrepancy is negative, the income side is larger. Because the discrepancy is a net figure, it is smaller than the actual statistical inconsistencies and errors among the various items of the accounts because the positive and negative inconsistencies and errors are partly offsetting.[5] Other GDP measures with slightly different definitions or methodology are published: final sales of domestic product, gross domestic purchases, final sales to domestic purchasers, gross national product, and command-basis gross national product.

Figure 66 shows the GDP and the discrepancy during 1988–92 in current dollars. The discrepancy shifted from –$28.4 billion in 1988 to $33.4 billion in 1992, a swing of $62 billion over the period. The discrepancy was 0.6 percent of the GDP in 1992. It was primarily positive in the past five years, but before 1988 it was often negative and is likely

FIGURE 66
U.S. GDP and the Statistical Discrepancy

	1 GDP	2 Statistical Discrepancy	3 Percent of GDP (1)/(2) × 100
1988	4,900.4*	–28.4	–0.6
1989	5,250.8	1.1	0.02
1990	5,522.2	5.4	0.1
1991	5,677.5	21.9	0.4
1992	5,950.7	33.4	0.6

*All numbers in billions of dollars.

Source: Based on data in the *Survey of Current Business* (Spring 1993).

[5]Other reasons why the statistical discrepancy understates the error in the accounts can be found in Allan H. Young, "Evaluation of the GNP Estimates," *Survey of Current Business*, August 1987.

to become negative again because of the misreporting adjustments to wages, profits, and nonfarm proprietors' income, which now total over $300 billion. The 1977 benchmarks for these adjustments were rough approximations, and they are now being extrapolated by less reliable source data. There are no similar source data problems of this size on the product side.

Figure 67 shows the differences in annual rates of economic growth obtained when using the alternative product- and income-side GDP measures in constant dollars. The annual growth rates typically differed by no more than 0.2 percentage point during 1988–92, although the differential was 0.6 percentage point in 1989 due to the sharp change in the discrepancy between 1988 and 1989. The growth rates were usually higher for the product-side than for the income-side estimates because the discrepancy became increasingly positive; when the discrepancy becomes increasingly negative, the income-side estimate shows a greater growth rate. On a quarterly basis, the differentials in growth rates are sometimes larger than in these annual figures.

The disconcerting aspect of the discrepancy since 1990 has been the noticeable increases in 1991 and 1992. The increases may reflect problems with a few large items or with several small items. Furthermore, the nature of the discrepancy is that it only indicates changes in

FIGURE 67
U.S. Real GDP on the Product and Income Sides: Annual Growth Rates

	1	2	3	4	
				Percent Change from Previous Year	
	GDP Product	Statistical Discrepancy	GDP Income (1)–(2)	GDP Product (1)	GDP Income (3)
1988	4,718.6*	−27.4	4,746.0	3.9	4.0
1989	4,838.0	0.9	4,837.1	2.5	1.9
1990	4,877.5	4.9	4,872.6	0.8	0.7
1991	4,821.0	18.7	4,802.3	−1.2	−1.4
1992	4,922.6	27.9	4,894.7	2.1	1.9

*All numbers in billions of 1987 dollars.

Source: Based on data in the *Survey of Current Business* (Spring 1993).

the magnitude of statistical problems; it does not identify sources of the problems.

The discrepancy also may increase when particular improvements in the database affect the product side or the income side more than the other. This should not inhibit incorporating data improvements when they become available. It is impractical to wait for comparable improvements to be made simultaneously on the product and the income sides before incorporating the improvements in the national accounts simply to avoid increasing the discrepancy.

Recommendation

The Bureau of Economic Analysis (BEA) should examine possible sources of the large increases in the statistical discrepancy in 1991 and 1992 for (a) clues of problems that may be developing in the GDP database or in the BEA estimating procedures; and (b) the effect of incorporating new data improvements in the national accounts. If the increases in the statistical discrepancy are considered to reflect particular data problems, remedial action is necessary. To the extent the increases are considered to reflect the incorporation of new data improvements, no remedial action is warranted.

Recommendation

The Bureau of Economic Analysis should publish the GDP as estimated from the income side of the national accounts and the income-side growth rates. This will provide an immediate comparison with economic growth rates based on the product-side GDP. The income-side measure can be calculated using the data published on the statistical discrepancy. However, only sophisticated users are likely to perform this calculation and then also calculate the income-side growth rates. The income-side GDP has the same statistical validity as the product-side GDP.

Price Measurement and Real Output

Economic growth rates are based on movements of real GDP; that is, GDP in constant dollars. This section focuses on the price indices used to deflate GDP in current dollars to GDP in constant dollars. BEA recently enhanced the measures of economic growth with its new alternative constant-dollar measures in which alternative base-period prices provide different rates of economic growth.[6]

GDP in constant dollars is obtained primarily by using price movements from the Bureau of Labor Statistics' (BLS) consumer, producer, and import/export price indices to deflate GDP in current dollars. Other indices used in the deflation include the Census Bureau's price index of single-family new-housing construction, BEA's price index of multifamily new-housing construction and its hybrid price-cost index of defense purchases of goods and services, and the Census Bureau's construction cost indices for nonresidential structures.

Quality Change in High-Tech Products

In preparing price indices, it is critical to adjust for specification changes in the goods and services items being priced from one quarter to the next. Changes in the specifications of the size, durability, safety, performance, or other characteristics of a product are referred to as quality changes. When there is no change in the quality of a product from one period to the next, the percent change in the market price is incorporated in the price index with no adjustment. By contrast, when the quality is enhanced, an estimate of the cost of the enhancement is subtracted from the market price; and when the quality is lessened, an estimate of the quality deterioration is added to the market price. The percent change between this quality-adjusted price in the current period and the market price in the previous period is the price change incorporated in the price index.

Adjustments for quality change require estimates of the cost of the quality change from producers of the product. When estimates are not available, the adjustments made by the analyst in preparing the price index become more subjective. The assumption in this procedure is that quality enhancements are associated with price increases, and quality deterioration is associated with price decreases.

However, quality improvement is sometimes accompanied by price declines. Thus, the traditional method of using cost estimates of the quality change is problematic. BLS has changed its methodology of pricing computers in the producer price index to accommodate this phenomenon by estimating price changes due to changes in the quality of the product

---

[6]Allan H. Young, "Alternative Measures of Change in Real Output and Prices, Quarterly Estimates for 1959–92," *Survey of Current Business,* March 1993.

through statistical regressions. This is referred to as the hedonic method. The substitution of these new price indices for computers in the national accounts had a noticeable effect on the GDP growth rate. For example, the annual growth in real GDP during 1982–88 was revised from 3.8 percent to 4.1 percent due to the new method of pricing computers.

Recommendation
The Bureau of Labor Statistics should improve the measures of price change for various high-tech products in the producer, consumer, and import/export price indices. First, it should identify electronic and communications equipment, medical equipment, pharmaceuticals, and other high-tech products in which quality improvements have been accompanied by lower prices. Second, for these high-tech products, it should develop new methods for measuring quality change similar to the hedonic technique it uses for computers in the producer price index. Third, when the same high-tech products are included in two or more of the producer, consumer, and import-export price indices, the new procedures should be included in all of the affected indices.

Nonresidential Construction Price Indices
The Census Bureau provides cost indices for new construction of nonresidential structures—industrial, commercial, school, hospital, and other nonresidential buildings; and utilities, bridges, dams, and other nonbuilding structures. It also provides a price index for road building. The indices are prepared by other federal agencies and by private companies and are compiled by the Census Bureau.

A construction cost index is based on changes in the cost of materials, labor, and equipment inputs used in construction projects. Because it does not include the effect of changes in productivity and profit margins in the construction industries, it is an input index. This differs from a price index, which is an output measure and thus captures productivity and profit margin changes as well as the materials, labor, and equipment inputs. Currently, the only price indices for new construction are for single-family and multifamily housing and for road building.

Recommendation
The Census Bureau should develop price indices for new nonresidential building and nonbuilding structures. These should refine the presently used input-cost indices if feasible. However, it may be nec-

essary to develop completely new output-price indices for some types of structures. This is a nonimplemented Creamer Report recommendation. The FY 1994 Census Bureau's budget included a request for funds to develop a price index for nonresidential buildings.

Productivity of Government Workers

Government purchases of goods and services are composed of purchases from private industry and of wage and fringe benefit compensation of government workers. Purchases from private industry are deflated for specific items, using BLS producer and consumer price indices and average hourly wages in selected services industries, the Census Bureau's and BEA's construction cost and price indices noted above, and BEA's hybrid price-cost index of defense purchases.

Employee compensation accounted for 59 percent of government purchases in 1992—44 percent for the federal government purchases and 68 percent for state and local governments. The constant-dollar measure of employee compensation of government workers assumes that productivity for workers with the same level of education and experience is constant over time. The only allowance for productivity change is when there is a shift in the composition of workers toward those with more or less education and experience. Estimates of the education and experience of workers are based on the number of employees at different pay scales. If the proportion of employees in the higher-pay categories rises, it is assumed this represents more education and experience and thus a productivity increase; if the proportion of employees in the lower-pay categories rises, it is treated as a decline in education and experience and consequently in productivity; and when the proportion of workers in all pay categories is unchanged, there is no measured change in productivity.

These estimates are an input measure of the change in labor productivity. BEA uses this technique because it is difficult to quantify the output of government workers since it relies on presumed direct linkages of the amount of education and experience with productivity. Input measures do not allow for change in the quality of education, experience, and other factors affecting worker skills and know-how over time. By contrast, an output measure of labor productivity based on the goods and services produced by government workers would implicitly capture all factors contributing to worker efficiency. The currently used input measure probably lowers the growth rate of real GDP since it does not include improvements in worker skills and know-how other than those associated with greater amounts of education and experience. There are no estimates of the effect of this exclusion.

Recommendation

The Bureau of Economic Analysis should focus on developing output measures of the productivity of government workers. The Bureau of Labor Statistics' studies of the productivity in 28 federal government functions and services are a major data source for preparing federal government estimates. These studies may also be appropriate for estimating productivity in related state and local government programs. This is a nonimplemented Creamer Report recommendation.

Input/Output Tables

Input/output tables are used in two major ways: (1) in preparing the quinquennial benchmarks of the national accounts; and (2) in economic analysis, such as in projecting future employment associated with varying rates of anticipated economic growth and in quantifying the regional impacts of proposed military base closings. A benchmark input/output table is prepared at five-year intervals that coincide with the years of the economic censuses (1982, 1987, 1992, 1997, etc.). Abbreviated updated annual input/output tables are prepared in other years.

The benchmark table incorporates the maximum amount of fresh data for each cell of the input/output table largely on data from the economic censuses. By contrast, fresh data for the annual tables are confined to the rims of the table comprising each industry's total output and the final demand and value added quadrants of the table. The intermediate production quadrant is simulated from the most recent benchmark-year coefficients, which are then modified to equate the sum of the cells in each industry row and column to the industry output total.

The average completion time for the benchmark table is seven years after the reference year. This lengthened to over nine years for the 1982 table. BEA's goal is to reduce the completion time to five years. An abbreviated 1987 table was released in 1994 using fresh data from the economic censuses.

Three problems have contributed to the average lag of seven years. First, there is a high turnover of personnel in the input/output program, resulting in a high proportion of the staff with no experience in having worked on a previous input/output table. Second, the estimating procedures have not been sufficiently automated. Third, certain detailed data in the microdata files of the economic censuses, such as those for small companies and central administrative offices, have not been tabulated.

Recommendation

The Bureau of Economic Analysis should revitalize the input/output program to reduce the completion time of the benchmark tables to five years after the reference year. This includes motivating experienced employees to stay with the program and developing automated procedures for estimating the intermediate production quadrant cells of the table.

Recommendation

The Census Bureau should tabulate certain data from the microdata files of the economic censuses for use in preparing the benchmark input/output table. Examples of such tabulations are those for small companies and central administrative offices. The FY 1994 Bureau of Economic Analysis budget included a request for funds to reimburse the Census Bureau for such tabulations.[7]

Satellite Accounts

Satellite accounts are part of the United Nations System of National Accounts that BEA will adopt in the second half of the 1990s. Satellite accounts extend the national accounts by encompassing an entire field of economic activity. They may be prepared for a variety of activities, such as research and development, natural resources, pensions, housing, health, transportation, and education. Satellites enlarge and enrich the analytical framework for formulating public policies.[8]

Satellites differ from traditional national accounts in several ways, although they are statistically linked to them. For example, in the traditional accounts, elements of research and development are spread among the household, business, and government sectors. In the satellite accounts, these are brought together in one place to give a comprehensive accounting of the activity. The satellite accounts also allow for different definitions of particular activities. In the traditional accounts,

---

[7]An interesting discussion of issues of input-output is found in Robert L. Steiner, "Caveat/ Some Unrecognized Pitfalls in Census Economic Data and the Input-Output Accounts," *Review of Industrial Organization,* forthcoming 1995.

[8]Carol S. Carson and Bruce T. Grimm, "Satellite Accounts in a Modernized and Extended System of Economic Accounts," *Business Economics,* January 1991, pp. 58–63.

research and development are treated as a business expense, a government purchase, or a nonprofit institution consumption item; but in the satellite accounts, research and development is defined as capital investment, albeit intangible investment, with deductions for depreciation in future years. In addition, satellite accounts provide for more detail on the activity, including its subcategories, employment, and financing.

BEA has been working on satellite accounts for research and development and natural resources, and has proposed to add pensions as a third category. Much of the database required for the satellites is available from the traditional accounts and other existing data sources. BEA has not developed an inventory of new data needs for the satellites. These needs will become clearer as work progresses on the satellite estimates.

Recommendation

When it can be foreseen that existing data sources are inadequate to develop the satellite accounts further, BEA should prepare an inventory of high-priority data needs for these accounts. Because the satellites involve the program and statistical activities of other agencies, BEA should consult with these agencies in drawing up the data needs inventory through an interagency committee. Such an inventory will facilitate the planning of future statistical programs by putting them in an overall context.

INFRASTRUCTURE OF ECONOMIC STATISTICS THAT IMPACTS THE NATIONAL ACCOUNTS

This section identifies several underlying aspects of economic statistics that affect the accuracy and relevance of the national accounts. Although these topics are less direct, they have both tangible and intangible impacts that accumulate significantly over time. The topics are BEA consultation with users, the standard industrial classification system, funding for economic statistics, the reporting burden, college teaching of economic measurement, and private industry uses of the national accounts.

BEA Consultation with Users

The national accounts are designed and prepared by BEA. BEA refines and expands the concepts, scope, and definitions of the accounts over time to reflect changes in the economy and to enhance the use of the accounts for economic analysis. Recent examples of such enhancements are the alternative measures of real output introduced in 1993 and the ongoing development of satellite accounts noted previously.

Ideas for the further development of the national accounts originate with the BEA staff, from contacts with public and private users of the accounts, and from a general awareness of trends in the American economy. Occasionally, outside expert groups, such as the National Accounts Review Committee in the 1950s and the Advisory Committee on Gross National Product Data Improvement in the 1970s, are designated to study the accounts and recommend needed changes in them. BEA participates with other countries in developing the United Nations System of National Accounts (SNA); changes in the SNA generate changes in the U.S. national accounts, such as those that will be incorporated in the accounts in the second half of the 1990s.

While these sources of ideas will continue to be important in the future, BEA lacks a vehicle to consult with users on a regular basis. Such a vehicle would have major benefits. First, it would provide a forum for systematically obtaining a range of views on potential innovations in the accounts that originate with BEA or the users. Second, it would assist BEA in seeking advice on handling technical issues of definition, classification, and statistical estimation. Third, it would provide a general benefit from an interactive feedback on a variety of issues on a timely basis. Both the Census Bureau and the Bureau of Labor Statistics have advisory committees that provide a means for consulting with users on a regular basis.

Recommendation

The Bureau of Economic Analysis should convene a standing group of users of the national accounts with whom it consults on a regular basis.[9] The group should include representatives from the Council of Economic Advisers, Federal Reserve Board, Congressional Budget Office, universities, private industry, labor unions, and research organizations. The subjects would include conceptual innovations, technical issues, data presentation, or other aspects of the accounts.

---

[9]This idea has been endorsed by the Bureau. Carol Carson, Director of BEA, commented on the need for an advisory group in *Business Economics,* July 1993.

Standard Industrial Classification System

The Standard Industrial Classification (SIC) is a system for grouping industry data on a consistent basis. The SIC provides a code number for each industry that government and private organizations use in tabulating and presenting statistical data obtained from surveys, which in turn are incorporated in the national accounts. For example, data on the production, employment, prices, profits, and capital expenditures of the automobile manufacturing industry are always included in SIC 3711.

The SIC system is revised about once every decade to reflect the changing nature of American industry. The revisions typically involve adding new and growing industries, deleting or combining declining industries, and reclassifying industries to reflect more accurately the activities and organization of U.S. industries. The most recent SIC revision was in 1987. The SIC is adopted and published by the Office of Management and Budget after consultation with government agencies and the public.

A comprehensive review of the SIC is underway by the Economic Classification Policy Committee (ECPC). The ECPC is chaired by the Bureau of Economic Analysis, with members from the Census Bureau and the Bureau of Labor Statistics; the Office of Management and Budget is an ex officio member. The SIC will be revised in the 1990s based on the outcome of this review.

The ECPC issued a notice for private and governmental comment in March 1993 on two issue papers, "Conceptual Issues" and "Aggregation Structures and Hierarchies," with comments due by the end of May 1993. Additional issue papers were also prepared, regarding collectability of data, criteria for determining industries, time series continuity, service classifications, international comparability, and detailed product classifications. The work plan includes additional notices for public comment in 1994 and 1995, with OMB adoption of the revised SIC in March 1996.

This timing allows sufficient time for the Census Bureau to incorporate the revised SIC in the 1997 economic censuses, which will be mailed to respondent companies in January 1998. Data tabulations from the 1997 economic censuses will be available in 1999–2000. Monthly, quarterly, and annual survey data that are based on samples of companies drawn from the company lists used in the economic censuses, and which are benchmarked to the economic censuses, will be revised to be consistent with the new SIC codes in 1999–2000. If the targeted completion date of March 1996 for the revised SIC slips more than a couple of months, the new SIC codes will first be introduced in the 2002 economic censuses, with data first available in 2004–2005.

Contrary to previous SIC revisions, this one involves a reassessment of several principles underlying the SIC. One is the method of designating certain activities as industries. The current method primarily classifies industries according to the method of production, which is a supply-side definition; by contrast, an industry classification based on the markets for products would be a demand-side definition. In the current supply-side system, for example, sugar products such as granulated sugar and molasses made from cane sugar are classified in SIC 2061, while the same products made from beet sugar are classified in SIC 2063. Thus, even though the products are perfect substitutes, they are grouped in different industries based on their method of production. The question in this case is whether to maintain the current supply-side definition or to modify or supplement these definitions with demand-side classifications. Among the other issues to be addressed are the underrepresentation of detailed categories of services industries, the present concept of using business establishments of large companies that are located in specific geographic locations as the linchpin of industry designations, and the method of forming hierarchies of broadly similar products grouped in two-, three-, and four-digit SIC industries.

Recommendation
The Economic Classification Policy Committee composed of the Office of Management and Budget (ex officio), Bureau of Economic Analysis, Bureau of the Census, and Bureau of Labor Statistics should make a concerted effort to complete the ongoing revision of the Standard Industrial Classification system by its target date of March 1996. This will provide the required lead time for the revised system to be incorporated in the 1997 economic censuses. If there is a slippage of more than a couple of months in this completion date, the revised SIC would first be incorporated in the economic statistics of the 2002 economic censuses.

Funding for Economic Statistics

Economic statistics are the foundation for decision-making information. While information is important for formulating and evaluating public policies, its precise value is difficult to quantify. The federal government produces massive quantities of economic statistics, yet sometimes there are not enough data or data of the right kind. Or as policy makers say, "When we need a prompt answer to a question, relevant and accurate information is not always available."

Having good information is part of good government. Planning to provide for good information means forecasting the type of data that will be necessary to analyze the wide range of events that may occur in the future. The provision of information also costs money; but presidents, representatives, and senators are elected to improve the daily lives of the population, not to provide good information. Although the availability of good information may be a more certain way of devising successful policies that will help in reelection campaigns, elected officials are not typically staunch supporters of statistical programs.

Persuading elected officials of the need for better data is not easy. It is most convincing when the data are related to concrete problems or issues that currently exist or have a reasonable chance of occurring in the future.

Several recommendations in this paper to enhance the database and preparation of the national accounts will require additional funding for BEA, Census, BLS, and IRS. It means justifying the need for these improvements at four main phases of the federal government's budget process:[10]

1. Within the statistical agency.
2. Within each agency's department, such as the Commerce Department for BEA and Census, the Labor Department for BLS, the Treasury Department for IRS.
3. In review by the Office of Management and Budget and the president's final recommendations.
4. In the oversight and final recommendation of the House of Representatives and the Senate.

Recommendation
When submitting their budgets to the executive branch and to Congress, statistical agencies should give more attention to relating the need for the data to existing or potential problems and issues of the nation. Requests should provide an example of how the data will

---

[10]See Figure 4 and related discussion in chapter 1.

help address a concrete problem, in contrast to explaining the consequences of not having the information. This is particularly important in requests for a new program or to expand an existing one.

The Reporting Burden

One of the costs of producing economic statistics is the time and money spent by survey respondents in completing survey forms. These costs are borne by private and government respondents. In designing surveys, it is important to limit requests for information to necessary items, to have easily understood forms, and to use samples of the population to be surveyed (in contrast to the universe) when feasible. In the case of businesses, it is helpful to be familiar with their recordkeeping practices so that questions can be designed to minimize the burden on the businesses in compiling data. Such efforts in survey design help contain the reporting burden on the public, increase the cooperation of the public in responding to surveys, and raise the quality of the information reported. In addition, statistical agencies have instituted such automated reporting technologies as computer-assisted telephone interviewing and touch-tone data entry that reduces reporting burden.

The Office of Management and Budget oversees the containment of all federal paperwork through its required approval of each survey's forms, frequency, and sampling, the design of tax forms, and similar reviews of other information collections.

Despite these efforts to contain paperwork, there is a societal trend in the United States not to respond to surveys. For the most part, federal statistical surveys are voluntary, which means that public cooperation in responding to surveys is vital. The erosion of public participation in surveys diminishes the representativeness of survey data, and additional expense is incurred in recontacting the respondent or contacting higher-level people in the organization, finding replacement respondents, or imputing for missing respondents. In some cases, the inability to obtain responses prevents the survey from being based on a probability sample, and thus no measures of sampling error can be calculated. Examples of such nonprobability sample surveys are the Census Bureau's monthly Survey of Manufacturers' Shipments, Inventories, and Orders, and the Bureau of Labor Statistics' monthly survey of employer payrolls and employment, both of which are basic data sources used in preparing the national accounts.

The general decline in survey participation has been exacerbated in the economic statistics by the tendency of some businesses only to respond to mandatory surveys. This stems from the point of view that says:

1. Since there is no penalty for not responding, there is no requirement for me to cooperate.
2. If the government thought the survey was important, it would make responding mandatory.

Additionally, some companies state that one way to reduce costs—to accommodate their downsizing or when business is slack—is to eliminate survey reporting.

The policy of only responding to mandatory surveys endangers the representativeness of economic statistics. It is a no-win situation and needs to be stanched. There is a political risk associated with legislation to make certain surveys mandatory. If a few surveys are made mandatory, this only intensifies the response problem for the vast majority of surveys that remain voluntary, and in the end the statistical system suffers even more. We propose a positive response to the nonresponse issue on behalf of both the statistical agencies and the corporate respondents. Nearly all readers of this book can also play a role by encouraging others to cooperate in statistical surveys.

Recommendation
Federal statistical agencies should make broad-based efforts to raise the response rate on voluntary business surveys. One approach is for the agencies to convene regional or industry conferences of high-level company officials stressing the importance of the data for public policy and the direct or indirect benefits to the company. The officials should be encouraged to institute policies within their companies to ensure that survey forms are completed and that care is given in supplying accurate information. Such private industry groups as the National Association of Business Economists, U.S. Chamber of Commerce and local Chambers of Commerce, National Association of Manufacturers, and National Federation of Independent Business should work with the federal agencies in this effort.

College Teaching of Economic Measurement

The qualifications and abilities of economists and statisticians working in federal statistical agencies are key to the development of economic statistics. As in all fields, experience gained on the job in statistical agencies is vital to performing the ongoing work with increasing efficiency, dealing with problem areas, and designing changes in the content, methodology, and presentation of economic statistics to reflect the evolving changes in the economy. The knowledge and training that the economists and statisticians bring to the job are also critical to the level and quality of their work. Both job experience and education and training interact in determining the usefulness of the output of statistical agencies.

A long-standing weakness in college courses in economics and statistics is that at best they only superficially teach the properties and methodology of economic measurement. In economics courses, glancing reference is given to the concepts and meaning of economic indicators and to the data and estimation techniques used in preparing the indicators. These are treated as concepts learned on the job and, in general, as less important and uninteresting. In statistics courses, minimal attention is given to the process of survey design: conceptualizing a topic, designing a survey to collect information on the topic, collecting the data, analyzing the data, and drawing inferences from the analysis. The major emphasis is on analyzing the data through various tests of statistical significance.

The loss to economic intelligence from this lack of teaching economic measurement at the college level is that persons coming to work in statistical agencies do not have the training for sophisticated analysis of the implications of the data programs they work on. It affects their judgment in making everyday decisions, in deciding which problem areas are worthy of exploration, and in the content of research projects they undertake to investigate problem areas. The new Joint Program in Survey Methodology of the Universities of Maryland and Michigan, and Westat, Inc., is a model for a course program on survey methodology.

Recommendation

The federal statistical agencies should work with economics and statistics departments in universities to introduce meaningful courses in economic measurement. These may include interdisciplinary programs between the economics and statistics departments. It will involve convening conferences with college faculties, perhaps through professional organizations such as the American Economic Association and the American Statistical Association, to present the dimensions of the problem and to design appropriate course programs. Follow-up conferences should monitor the progress and modify or expand the teaching programs as experience is gained with them. The new Joint Program in Survey Methodology of the Universities of Maryland and Michigan, and Westat, Inc., would be an appropriate vehicle for organizing the conferences.

Private Industry Uses of the National Accounts

The national accounts primarily provide the federal government with the analytic basis for formulating and evaluating fiscal and monetary policies to promote maximum sustainable economic growth with minimum unemployment and inflation. Private industry use of the accounts is far less frequent. And within private industry, large companies are the primary users because they can relate the fortunes of their companies to national trends more readily than small- and medium-size companies that have more limited product and regional markets.

Companies use the annual data in the national accounts more than the quarterly estimates because the annual data provide more product- and income-side detail. This detail in the annual estimates allows some large companies to compare their performance on sales, profits, and labor costs with national product, industry, and labor markets. Less private industry use is made of the price measures in the national accounts because they do not provide sufficient product detail; far more product detail is available in the Bureau of Labor Statistics' producer, consumer, and import/export price indices. There also is little private industry use of the input/output tables. While the I/O tables provide considerable product detail, they are too out-of-date for relevant use.

Overall, private industry makes highly selective use of the accounts because of the weak statistical linkage between economy-wide trends and a company's performance and prospects. This does not mean the accounts are unimportant to private industry. The accounts are used to formulate and evaluate public policies that create a healthy climate for economic growth and thus have a weighty impact on business sales and profits.

Recommendation
Private industry companies should reverse their declining participation in government business surveys and ensure that the information they report is accurate. While industry makes only limited direct use of the national accounts, the economic well-being of businesses is significantly influenced by use of the accounts to formulate and evaluate fiscal and monetary policies. Government business

surveys are the lifeblood of the accounts, and the accounts under-lie basic policies used to create a climate of economic growth in which businesses prosper.

ACTIONS TAKEN ON THE CREAMER REPORT SUGGESTIONS

The Advisory Committee on Gross National Product Data Improvement completed the *Gross National Product Data Improvement Project Report* in 1977.[11] Daniel Creamer was the chairman of the advisory committee and staff director. The report contained over 150 recommendations affecting the Bureau of Economic Analysis (BEA), Bureau of the Census, Bureau of Labor Statistics (BLS), Internal Revenue Service (IRS), Departments of Agriculture, Defense, and Health and Human Services, and other federal agencies. It included a six-year plan to implement the recommendations during the period 1978–83. The highest-priority recommendations and those that were relatively easy to implement and required little or no additional funding were scheduled to begin in the earlier years. The total cost of the recommended improvements was roughly estimated at $25 million in 1976 prices.

The Creamer Report provided a coherent framework for shaping federal statistical programs. It is not another advisory report gathering dust. Considerable progress has been made in implementing its recommendations. Selected nonimplemented Creamer recommendations are included as recommendations in this paper, attesting to their continued relevance.

RECOMMENDATIONS—INTERNATIONAL STATISTICS

This book has stressed the emergence of an unprecedented level of global interaction. Statistics to meet the needs of the 21st century must have a special capability to deal with global issues. In Chapter 8, Global Interaction, some of the weaknesses in current data collection efforts are stressed. This section, while not dealing with all of the issues that have

---

[11]U.S. Department of Commerce, Office of Federal Statistical Policy and Standards, Report of the Advisory Committee on Gross National Product Data Improvement, *Gross National Product Data Improvement Project Report,* October 1977.

been raised, makes a number of key recommendations for improving international trade and financial statistics.[12]

The interdependence of the world economy can only intensify in the future. Relationships are captured in the balance of payments accounts of individual countries with respect to trade, services, and capital flows. Since the conceptual consistency of economic statistics across international boundaries is a principal objective of the statistical improvements suggested in this book, this consistency must start within the realm of international economic data.

The United States has one of the most comprehensive systems of collecting data of all types, particularly foreign trade information. For the balance of payments statistics, numerous government agencies have responsibility for collecting and compiling the data. That these agencies do not necessarily interact or cooperate with one another poses a major obstacle to statistical reform.

Merchandise Trade

Merchandise trade, in comparison with other U.S. international transactions, differs in several important respects. Its statistics are compiled from a full tabulation of all transactions rather than from surveys. A great deal of attention is placed on trade data and, as a result, they are generally considered to be quite accurate. Moreover, during the past several years, a number of changes have been made to improve substantially the quality of trade statistics.

Still, a number of problems remain. Trade statistics are presently based on the concept of *residence*. A resident is anyone or any business that has a center of economic interest in a given country and resides in the country for more than a year. Thus, for example, trade between a U.S. parent and its foreign subsidiary enters the balance of payments even though a U.S. company is the ultimate owner. When foreign direct investment was minimal and virtually all exports were made by domestic companies, there was little difference between the resident and the owner. With the tremendous growth of multinational companies and joint ventures, a growing percentage of trade involves multinational companies. A considerable portion of trade is not owned by the country in which it is manufactured.

---

[12]The authors wish to acknowledge the contributions of Marsha A. Kameron to this section as well as chapter 8.

Similarly, the present trade statistics do not differentiate between affiliated and nonaffiliated trade. Under the present methodology, trade statistics are compiled as merchandise crosses the border. Thus, trade between multinational companies and their affiliates abroad is included in the trade balance. No distinction is made between this type of trade and trade between unaffiliated, or unrelated, partners. In 1991, 46 percent of total U.S. imports were from related parties. Although export data are not publicly available, it is assumed that exports by related parties are also high.

Recommendation

Use a supplemental balance of payments framework that captures transactions between foreign affiliates of U.S. firms abroad and U.S. parents and foreign affiliates in the United States and their foreign parents. This supplemental framework would dramatically change a country's international trade balance.

For example, in 1987, the U.S. trade deficit was $148 billion; but computed under a supplemental framework, the deficit was $68 billion. For policy purposes and trade negotiations, this dramatically alters the position of the United States. A summary of the supplemental balance of payments is given in Figure 68.[13] There are, however, several difficulties in collecting these data.

First, sales by foreign affiliates are collected annually, but data on domestic purchases are not collected at all.

Second, data on foreign affiliates of U.S. firms and U.S. affiliates of foreign firms are based on data where ownership is only 10 percent or more. In the current pattern of interactions ranging from loose federations to controlling ownership, there is a need for more detailed definitions of the affiliated relations. This would require agreement on a new set of consistent definitions.[14]

---

[13] Anne Y. Kester, ed., *Behind the Numbers: U.S. Trade in the World Economy.* Washington, DC: National Academy Press, 1992, p. 182.

[14] BEA notes that its current definitions are consistent with the IMF and OECD 10 percent definition. BEA does publish more data on a majority-owned basis for foreign affiliates than for U.S. affiliates, but it says it can identify majority-owned affiliates of both types, and, in the major area of services, it has already addressed supplemental-framework-type issues. Further, although BEA does not publish separate data on affiliated-part trade in the main balance of payments, it does collect and publish annual data on affiliated party trade for exports and imports collected on its annual surveys of foreign affiliates of U.S. firms and U.S. affiliates of foreign firms.

FIGURE 68

Net Sales of Goods and Services by Americans to Foreigners, 1987—Cross-Border Sales to and Purchases from Foreigners by Americans

Exports to Foreigners	
+ U.S exports of goods and services	$336*
− U.S. exports to foreign affiliates of U.S. firms abroad	−87
− U.S. exports shipped by U.S. affiliates of foreign firms	−51
Total	198
Imports from Foreigners	
+ U.S. imports of merchandise and services	484
− U.S. imports from foreign affiliates of U.S. firms	−75
− U.S. imports shipped to U.S. affiliates of foreign firms	−143
Total	264
Exports minus imports equals net cross-border sales to foreigners	−68

*All numbers in billions of dollars.

Source: Anne Y. Kester, ed., *Behind the Numbers: U.S. Trade in the World Economy.* Washington, DC: National Academy Press, 1992, p. 182.

Recommendation

Incorporate the annual surveys of multinational companies into the balance of payments accounting. Also, incorporate data from the annual surveys of direct investment for more detailed data on affiliated trade.

Make a distinction between raw, intermediate, or final goods. Components for various products are often imported from various countries and then assembled for export. With the present statistics, it is not possible to derive a value-added component.

Recommendation

Use universal bar coding to track the components of trade. Such an automated system would produce information about the origin of various factors of production and assist in improved classification. Finally, although the present system for collecting trade data is extremely comprehensive, there are questions about the usefulness of the data.

Recommendation

Simplify the amount of data compiled. Although this might involve a loss of accuracy and completeness, the considerable cost savings that would be generated could be used to improve the collection of other international statistics, notably in the capital accounts. Methods for simplification include:

- Limiting publicly available trade data to the aggregate categories. More detailed category breakdowns would be available by special request, and the users could be charged for the information they request. Present data are unwieldy and often not in a usable format. Specialized requests could improve the quality and usability of the data.
- Shifting from a full tabulation system to a sample system to collect trade data. The trade-off between accuracy and cost would need to be evaluated.
- Adopting a data-sharing system that the United States and Canada presently use in which imports of one country are used to compile the exports of the other country.

The Invisibles and Service Accounts

The invisibles and service accounts are becoming an increasingly important component of the current account. U.S. exports of services have nearly doubled over the past six years and account for 25 percent of the total exports of goods and services. Although data collection for services has improved considerably during the past decade, data are not nearly as comprehensive, detailed, or timely as merchandise trade. It would be unrealistic to expect the data on the service account to ever approach the accuracy of the trade accounts since this sector is so diverse and much smaller than its merchandise counterpart. With the realization that service information is largely an "estimate," improvements should be made via statistical means to improve the accuracy of the samples.

Recommendation
Consistent estimation and sampling procedures need to be established. The framework developed by the United States should be coordinated with the major industrial countries to ultimately develop a consistent framework for use on a worldwide basis. Using estimates and simplifying the data collection process should be considered a reliable alternative to survey methods with considerable cost savings.

The largest service categories are travel, passenger fares, freight, and port services. There is room for improvement in the data collection from each of these categories. Tourist expenditures and revenues are calculated based on random surveys of travelers. This method is cumbersome and subject to serious inaccuracy.

Recommendation

Integrate Immigration and Naturalization Service (INS) data—which are already being collected at the Customs Service—with balance of payments statistics. Integrate computerized data from airlines on international travel for balance of payments accounting, including data on cost of airfare, number of passengers, and number of days abroad. A system needs to be developed to compile these data into a form usable for the balance of payments. Estimation procedures to determine other costs of international travel such as meals and hotels could be used.

For freight and shipping, the convention is to consider that all payments are paid by the importer. Problems arise because the flag of the carrier often differs from the residency of the operator and because the operator may not be accurately determined.

Recommendation

Data on imports need to track not only freight, but also the country of origin. A five-year benchmark survey would improve the statistical accuracy of these expenditures.

The Capital Accounts

World capital flows have increased tremendously during the past decades, reflecting innovation, deregulation of financial markets, and elimination of capital controls. At the same time, the resources in the United States for adequately collecting data have been shrinking due to budgetary constraints.

The United States has made a major effort to revise direct investment data to more accurately reflect market conditions. Portfolio and other capital flows are subject to considerable error in the balance of payments accounts. These errors reflect many factors, including purchase of securities directly overseas, use of financial instruments that are not captured in the present system, money laundering and the extensive use of the black market, and use of the dollar as a local currency in many countries throughout the world.

The U.S. system was designed when most transactions were conducted in conventional financial instruments and channeled through a few large banks and other financial institutions. Capital markets have changed dramatically since then, reflecting deregulation of capital controls, new financial instruments, and the proliferation of transactions. The statistical problems faced by U.S. compilers have intensified and strained available resources.

The concepts and methodology of the U.S. balance of payments as they relate to portfolio, banking transactions, and nonbanking transactions have been addressed in Chapter 8, Global Interaction.

Recommendation

It is widely acknowledged that these serious shortcomings exist in the present system as discussed in Chapter 8, Global Interaction.

There are three basic approaches to revising the entire system of capital accounts:

1. Make revisions and changes to improve the accuracy of the present system. These types of changes are the easiest to implement, but the usefulness of such a piecemeal effort is questionable. A marginal improvement in the accuracy of the capital flows would not necessarily be more reliable than what presently exists.

2. Restructure the domestic system entirely and change the method of reporting. This may involve a change to annual statistics via benchmark surveys. The quarterly data are presently so volatile and subject to such tremendous revision that they are of limited use. A more accurate framework that is produced annually would represent an improvement for users, although the intra-year changes in financial conditions could not be well tracked. It may be true that a full tabulation of international capital flows is not possible. Use sampling techniques that are less costly but just as accurate in tracking capital flows. Finally, any new system must have the flexibility to include new financial instruments.

3. Develop a worldwide system to monitor capital flows. In view of the tremendous linkages of global capital, it is becoming increasingly difficult for the United States or any single country to adequately monitor capital flows without international coordination and cooperation. As an alternative to the present methodology, a new system could be

developed by international monetary and financial agencies with consistent concepts and definitions. In developing a worldwide system, serious consideration should be given to whether the present classifications are meaningful. Of course, there would obviously be a number of difficulties and objections to a global system, such as enforcing compliance among participating countries, ensuring confidentiality, and managing the huge number of transactions.

Revisions to the present system, or development of a new system, must begin with clarifying and redefining important concepts for consistency. For example, there needs to be an improvement in the interaction between agencies assigned to collect, report, and analyze data. Innovations will require frequent adaptations of reporting systems. The definition of portfolio capital needs to be expanded to include derivative financial instruments.

Before new procedures can be developed, conceptual problems need to be addressed, including:

Defining residence: foreign vs. domestic. Under the present system, foreigners establishing a local address are no longer considered foreigners. Investors frequently find it convenient to lodge their securities with nominees when investing in overseas markets, and compilers have no way of knowing whether financial intermediaries correctly capture all transactions involving foreign accounts held in nominees' names.

Classifying transactions. The present classification system contains many overlapping elements and ambiguities. For example, it is becoming increasingly difficult to distinguish between banking and securities transactions. It is often hard to distinguish between short and long term because of the increasing liquidity of many financial instruments.

Timing. In principle, the sale and purchase of an asset should be recorded at the same time. In practice, countries may record transactions at different times.

Deriving flows from stock data. In many countries, outstanding claims and liabilities are used to derive capital flows. Stocks can change for a number of reasons not related to flows, including changes in market price of assets, changes in exchange rates, write-offs, and expropriations and uncompensated seizures.

Defining reporting responsibilities. As the distinctions between banking and the securities business become increasingly blurred, specific reporting responsibilities need to be defined.

Maintaining a balance of timeliness and accuracy. There obviously is a trade-off between timeliness and accuracy. There is nothing to be gained from a quick release of information that is not considered reliable and accurate. It would be far more useful to delay reporting for a reasonable amount of time after which the data are considered accurate. Data could include footnotes about confidence bands, eliminating the need for an endless revision of data that are seldom used.

Linking domestic data with the remainder of the global economy. Despite its shortcomings, the U.S. reporting system is one of the most comprehensive in the world. Most of the leading industrial countries have well-developed statistical systems; whereas, many of the statistics of developing countries lack timeliness and accuracy. International comparability is made more difficult in instances where developed countries have not implemented the most recent U.N. revisions of international economic classification.

The individual categories in the world tabulation of the balance of payments should, in principle, sum to zero. In actuality, there are large imbalances in many categories that indicate errors or biases. The IMF has addressed many of these questions in two studies: *Report on the World Current Account Discrepancy*[15] and *Report on the Measurement of International Capital Flows.*[16] The magnitude of the discrepancies involved in global balance of payments statistics implies that any interpretation and analysis should be done at one's own risk.

Recommendation

Under the present system, countries should adhere to the definitions in the International Monetary Fund's *Balance of Payments Manual* to achieve greater consistency, but there is no realistic way to enforce this. In the future, a total revamping of the international balance of payments is needed to improve timeliness and accuracy. The task of revamping the world's balance of payments system is highly complex and would require global coordination and cooperation. Changes in the United States could serve as a model for a new global system that reflects the linkages in the world economy.

---

[15]*Report on the World Current Account Discrepancy.* Washington, DC: International Monetary Fund, 1987.

[16]*Report on the Measurement of International Capital Flows,* Parts I and II. Washington, DC: International Monetary Fund, September 1992 (Part I) and December 1992 (Part II—Background Papers).

Because of the tremendous international linkages and instantaneous communications, there is widespread interest in the economic data of countries throughout the world. It is unclear, however, which international agency should spearhead this effort. The IMF is the best source of international economic and financial data. It publishes country data in a timely fashion but makes no attempt to assure comparability from one country to the next. For example, comparisons of inflation rates in different countries can be somewhat misleading because the methods of calculation differ in various countries. On the other hand, the Organization for Economic Cooperation and Development is an excellent source of comparative data for its member countries; it imposes a consistent definition for many of its statistics. While the OECD is making an effort to include data on the transition countries in Central and Eastern Europe, it does not provide coverage for developing countries.

The United Nations compiles a vast array of internationally comparable data through its use of consistent methodology and definitions, but these data lack timelessness and, hence, usefulness to decison makers. Although the United Nations has historically played a key role in the development and adoption of global data improvements, the developed countries in recent years have not been satisfied with U.N. leadership in this area.

CHAPTER 10

CONCLUDING REMARKS

The preceding chapter makes a large number of specific recommendations for improving the base data for economic statistics, both for the United Nations System of National Accounts and for knowledge of international interactions. These recommendations are intended to complement other recommendations that have been presented recently. Specifically, the excellent report on trade statistics, *Behind the Numbers,* and the forthcoming report from the National Academy of Sciences, *Following the Money: U.S. Finance in the World Economy,*[1] offer a considerable number of detailed suggestions for improving the basic series.

As we come to the end of this book, it is clear that our journey has not been a fast trip toward a preordained destination. It has been more like a series of separate exploratory paths that lead from the edges toward the center of a vast thicket of existing statistical systems—rather like a series of dirt roads a forester might make into a stand of old-growth trees. Our intent has been to explore, to clear away underbrush, and to establish a more rational and balanced system of future growth. Each of the preceding nine chapters in this book represents one such path. Along some of those paths, our primary purpose was to observe and classify; along others, it was to clear away the dead wood and the obscuring underbrush; along still others, we looked for places to plant anew.

As we said at the beginning, we do not start the reform of statistical systems from the ground up. Instead, we have inherited a vast, interconnected system of statistics, the reform of which must be undertaken prudently, conservatively, and in the spirit of evolution rather than revolution. As we undertake such change, we must be constantly mindful

---

[1]Anne Y. Kester and Panel on International Capital Transactions. *Following the Money: U.S. Finance in the World Economy.* Washington, DC: National Academy Press, forthcoming early 1995.

of the need both to preserve what is still valuable and to seek wide consensus for whatever changes are undertaken.

But there must be changes! The current system of statistics has fallen woefully behind the pace of change of the realities it purports to represent. While a conservative and incremental approach to that change must be the constant watchword, truly effective change can only come about if it is informed by a larger vision: a vision that is clear-sighted in its understanding of the current statistical system, bold in its projections of what a more adequate system will look like, and aggressive in its determination to move all affected and interested parties toward making that vision a reality.

Such a layered and comprehensive vision of the required changes to the statistical system will not—to be effective it *cannot*—spring full grown from the mind of any single individual, nor from any single agency, bureau, or institution. It must, however, be "housed" in one place that can serve as a sort of "clearinghouse" to accumulate, sort, and disseminate the best ideas among all interested parties. The role of that kind of "clearinghouse" will be not to preempt a wide-ranging conversation about needed reforms, but to facilitate it.

This is a job for the Office of Management and Budget (OMB). Such a task is not new for OMB. While we have noted frequently in these pages that OMB in recent years has lost the largest parts of its resources for economic statistics, there was a period—during the 1940s and 1950s—when OMB was willing and able to coordinate the gathering and analysis of statistics, devoting a full third of its staff to that task. We are suggesting that OMB should reprise that central role, a role that belongs in the federal government, which is simultaneously the biggest producer and the biggest user of statistics and has the longest history of any player in both those roles. Within the federal government, that task belongs in the Executive Office of the President.

Quite simply, it belongs in OMB. But that is not to say that it is the sole responsibility of the OMB. On the contrary, we have pointed out throughout this monograph the large and ever-increasing number of producers and users of statistical information. In fact, most large producers are also large users and vice versa. Each of them has a crucial stake, a unique perspective, and a valuable contribution to make to the discussion of how our statistical systems should be changed and improved. Besides the federal government, those stakeholders include:

- Both large and small private companies. (Special attention should be given to smaller businesses whose importance and input are still underrepresented in statistics despite their growing importance in the economy itself.)
- Academicians.
- State and local governments.
- Trade associations.
- Unions.
- Environmentalists.
- Interest groups.

This is but a very partial listing of the plethora of groups who have important interests and perspectives on the reform of our statistical system. They should all have a voice and a place at the table as reform efforts are considered and go forward. How can that be accomplished? Over the years, there have been many proposals for combining or reorganizing statistical agencies. The simple premise is that if all statistics were collected by a central agency, it would be easier to make them uniform in concepts, definitions, and implementation. We have argued in this book that the pluralistic system brings considerable strength to the statistical information base. Therefore, we believe that statistical reorganization is not the answer to improving the statistical system. Rather, work needs to be done on identifying what should be measured and how it should be measured, followed by periodic evaluation of the statistical activities (a recommendation that repeats work of the 1970 President's Commission on Federal Statistics).

We recommend the creation of a permanent advisory committee to consult on a continuous basis with the OMB. It should be comprised of representatives of each of the groups listed above, each of whom would have staggered but long-term tenure on it in order to preserve some institutional expertise and memory within it. While it would have no official power, this Committee would meet regularly—and publicly—to consider the broad range of suggestions for change and improvement. Its statutory powers would be nonexistent. Its powers of persuasion could be limitless.

There are a number of topics that could be addressed by this Advisory Committee in addition to the "vision" for the statistical system. First, It could assist in reviewing existing statistical programs to see if priorities can be altered to reallocate existing resources more efficiently.

Second, it should investigate issues of information policy as it relates to statistics, including questions of reporting burden, the role of statistical agencies in dissemination, and the development of mechanisms for fostering improved governmental and private-sector cooperation in the development of information systems.

Throughout *Statistics for the 21st Century,* there have been numerous comments about revisions and conflicting information. It is noted in Appendix A that the estimates of growth in gross domestic product show little change between the first, second, and third preliminary estimates (when compared with the more complete estimates provided by the July revisions).

We strongly endorse the recommendation of earlier studies, including Cole, Federal Reserve Bank of Boston, and Fleming, who have recommended that the early revisions be simplified to one. Specifically, we recommend publishing only the first (the 25-day) estimate and dropping the 55- and 85-day estimates. Instead, the resources of the Bureau of Economic Analysis could be better utilized in refinements that contribute to the July revisions.

The need for improvement is clear. No less clear is the need for mechanisms and motivation to involve all of those interested in the statistics that define us and shape our hopes for the future. That is the reason for this book—to sound a sentinel's early signal about the need for change and to invite others to join the process of reform.

The authors welcome—in fact, we *request*—your reactions to the topics treated in this book, as well as to the ways we have treated them. We intend here not to have the last word but to send a first signal, not to end the discussion but to begin it. Not only will we learn from your reactions and use them to improve our future efforts, we will also gladly send on your suggestions to OMB or to others who can benefit from them.

We have spoken of the institutional lethargy that can impede statistical reform. There is a counterpart in individuals: It is a sort of *psychological lethargy*—a tired pessimism that ruefully accepts the status quo as the best that can be done, a despairing sense that this is how things have to be, a feeling that no meaningful reform is possible, given budgetary restrictions and territorial disputes.

This book was written because we disagree with that pessimism; we passionately believe that meaningful change in our statistical systems is both necessary and possible. But such a book is only the first step.

The next steps are up to you.

APPENDIX A

ERRORS IN GDP ESTIMATES

INTRODUCTION

The struggle between timeliness and accuracy is illustrated in the quarterly estimates for Gross Domestic Product. The first estimate is published approximately 25 days after the end of the quarter, even though for many components the data available cover only the first or second month of the quarter. The preliminary estimate is then released after 55 days, and a so-called final estimate is published approximately 85 days after the end of the quarter. Further refinements of the estimates are published in the July revisions after the year is over. Subsequent July revisions are also introduced in later years with the five-year rebenchmarking (based upon the five-year cycle of the quinquennial censuses of business) when more detailed data are available.

These revisions have long been a subject of controversy. Many observers who do not understand statistical programs think that someone is "manipulating" the numbers, yet every analysis of the process reveals that these revisions are the final result of professional judgment based upon a deep understanding of available information. The classic study of the revisions was conducted by Rosanne Cole.[1] A more recent study was conducted by Stephen K. McNees of the Boston Federal Reserve.[2] More recently, Martin Fleming, Chairman of the Statistics Committee of the National Association of Business Economists, and

---

[1]Rosanne Cole, "Data Errors and Forecasting Accuracy," chapter 2 in *Economic Forecasts and Expectations: Analyses of Forecasting Behavior and Performance* (Jacob Mincer, ed.). New York: National Bureau of Economic Research, 1969.

[2]Stephen K. McNees, "Estimating GNP; The Trade-off between Timeliness and Accuracy," *New England Economic Review,* January/February 1986, pp. 3–10.

Allan Young, former Director of the Bureau of Economic Analysis, have also completed reviews of this topic.[3]

As part of the study for the present report, data were developed by the Bureau of Economic Analysis for Haver Analytics of New York. That database was used by Martin Fleming for his study. The data were also analyzed by George Feeney of Haver Analytics, as reported in this appendix (Figure 1A). The Feeney study used the third-year revision as an estimate of truth for the individual GDP components, while Fleming used the second-year revision as the benchmark for the "true" estimate. In the Feeney study, the early quarterly estimates (estimates 1, 2, and 3) and the first and second July revisions were compared with the third July revision (assumed truth) to see the pattern of variance. The results are presented in Figure 1A.

FIGURE 1A
Analysis of Variance of Quarterly Growth Rate Estimates (Assuming Third July Revision Equals Correct Final Estimate)

	25	55	85	First July Revision	Second July Revision	Third July Revision
Total GDP						
No. of qtrs	44	44	44	44	40	0
xbar	−0.42	−0.26	−0.20	−0.05	0.03	0.00
sigma	1.75	1.59	1.68	1.10	0.69	0.00
*Consumption (67%)**						
xbar	−0.15	−0.09	−0.11	−0.20	0.10	0.00
sigma	1.62	1.58	1.66	1.24	0.76	0.00
Durables (9%)						
xbar	−0.91	−0.64	−0.42	−0.46	−0.19	0.00
sigma	4.95	4.95	5.43	4.08	2.35	0.00
Nondurables (22%)						
xbar	−0.23	−0.21	−0.18	−0.28	0.14	0.00
sigma	2.39	1.99	1.94	1.60	1.14	0.00
Services (37%)						
xbar	0.11	0.17	0.03	−0.08	0.11	0.00
sigma	1.45	1.42	1.52	1.07	0.90	0.00

(continued)

---

[3]Fleming's report to the 1993 NABE Annual Meeting in Chicago was entitled "Measurement Error in the National Income and Product Accounts: Its Nature and Impact on Forecasts." Revised papers are entitled "The Impact of Measurement Error in the U.S. National Income and Product Accounts on Forecasts of GNP and Its Components" and "Macroeconomic Policy and Methodological Misdirection in the National Income and Product Accounts." At the time this book goes to publication, these reports are available only from Mr. Fleming. These papers present a lengthy discussion of many of the points summarized in this brief appendix.

FIGURE 1A *(continued)*

	25	55	85	First July Revision	Second July Revision	Third July Revision
Investment (14%)						
xbar	−0.54	−0.22	0.89	0.92	−0.11	0.00
sigma	12.09	11.13	11.13	8.40	5.56	0.00
Fixed Investment (15%)						
xbar	−0.61	0.51	1.00	0.82	0.30	0.00
sigma	5.46	4.73	4.47	3.60	2.89	0.00
Nonresidential (11%)						
xbar	−0.86	0.66	1.45	10.5	0.53	0.00
sigma	6.09	5.16	4.86	4.63	3.98	0.00
Structures (4%)						
xbar	0.68	1.14	1.24	1.19	0.10	0.00
sigma	9.52	8.04	7.94	7.11	7.41	0.00
PDE (8%)						
xbar	−1.78	0.30	1.36	0.78	0.55	0.00
sigma	6.78	5.93	5.30	5.71	4.48	0.00
Residential (4%)						
xbar	0.50	0.94	0.58	0.75	0.49	0.00
sigma	9.49	9.03	7.98	5.55	5.15	0.00
Exports (11%)						
xbar	−2.88	−2.06	−1.75	−1.03	−1.52	0.00
sigma	8.04	7.24	7.90	6.84	5.53	0.00
Imports (11%)						
xbar	0.93	0.98	1.44	0.83	−0.34	0.00
sigma	14.67	16.19	16.20	12.70	5.53	0.00
Government (19%)						
xbar	−0.52	−0.34	−0.61	−0.26	−0.08	0.00
sigma	4.07	4.35	4.04	2.93	1.90	0.00
Federal (8%)						
xbar	0.02	0.54	−0.12	0.54	0.20	0.00
sigma	9.08	9.78	9.19	7.05	4.59	0.00
State and Local (11%)						
xbar	−0.75	−0.84	−0.79	−0.71	−0.30	0.00
sigma	1.55	1.76	1.76	1.38	0.90	0.00

*Average percent of GDP.

(concluded)

Source: Haver Analytics, Inc., New York.

A table from Fleming's study is shown as Figure 2A; a graphic representation is shown in Figure 3A. The conclusions are similar to those statistically shown in Figure 1A. The estimates 1, 2, and 3 were below the final number in 1986, 1987, and 1988 and were higher than the final number in 1989 and early 1990. Most significantly, the error terms in Feeney's analysis are similar for estimates 1, 2, and 3, with the July revisions getting closer to the truth.

These two studies lead to our recommendation in chapter 10 that the first estimate be retained since it is as good as estimates 2 and 3, and that published revisions be limited to the July revisions. This would not reduce our understanding of the economy, and it would reduce confusion.

In a forthcoming book,[4] Allan Young discusses the reliability and accuracy of the quarterly GDP estimates in a very thorough manner. He notes that revi-

FIGURE 2A
Average Revision in Year-to-Year Change without Regard to Sign—
Annual Revisions Published from 1987 to 1991

	Most Recent Year	2nd Most Recent Year	3rd Most Recent Year
GDP	24.0*	6.6	6.1
PCE	26.7	7.0	5.8
Goods	12.0	5.0	3.8
Services	15.4	2.7	7.4
Fixed investment	9.5	3.5	1.4
Nonresidential structures	3.8	2.6	0.4
PDE	6.0	2.5	0.8
Residential structures	2.2	1.0	0.4
Change in business inventories	7.2	1.7	4.8
Net exports	2.8	0.7	4.1
Government	3.3	1.2	2.8
Federal	1.4	0.5	0.3
S & L	3.0	1.2	2.5

*All numbers in billions of dollars.

Source: Martin Fleming et al., "Measurement Error in the U.S. National Income and Product Accounts: Its Nature and Impact on Forecasts," Statistics Committee, National Association of Business Economists, September 15, 1993.

---

[4]Allan Young, "Reliability and Accuracy of Quarterly GDP Estimates: A Review," in *Socio-Economic Accounts: Development, Issues, Prospects* (John Kendrick, ed.). Amsterdam: Kluwer Academic Publishers, forthcoming 1995.

FIGURE 3A
U.S. GDP—Estimated Errors*

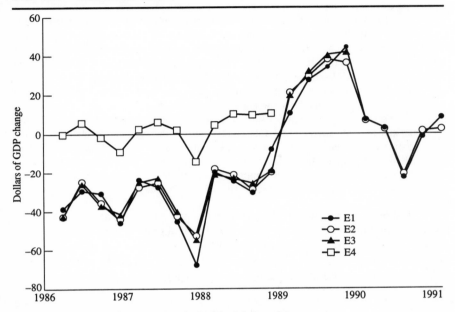

*Note: Actual value is assumed to be the 2nd July revision
E1—25-day estimate less 2nd July revision
E2—55-day estimate less 2nd July revision
E3—85-day estimate less 2nd July revision
E4—1st July revision less 2nd July revision

Source: Martin Fleming et al., "Measurement Error in the U.S. National Income and Product Accounts: Its Nature and Impact on Forecasts," Statistics Committee, National Association of Business Economists, September 15, 1993.

sions "come about for four reasons: (1) replacement of preliminary source data with later data, (2) replacement of judgmental projections with source data, (3) changes in definitions or estimating procedures, and (4) updating of the base year in the constant dollar estimates." He then goes on to describe the flow of the various revisions. Young describes the process as follows:

> GDP estimates for each quarter are prepared in the United States on a schedule that calls for three successive "current" estimates—"advanced," "preliminary," "final"—and for subsequent estimates prepared as part of annual and comprehensive NIPA revisions. The advanced estimate is prepared about twenty-five days after the end of the quarter. For most components, the estimate is based on source data for either two or three months of the quarter. In most cases, however, the

source data for the second and third months of the quarter are not final and are subject to revision by the issuing agencies. Where source data are not available, the estimate is based primarily on the estimator's judgment.

One month later, the "advanced" estimate is replaced by the "preliminary" estimate, which is typically based on source data for all three months of the quarter. However, in some instances, the source data used for the "preliminary" estimates, particularly the data for the third month of the quarter, are subject to further revision.

One month later, the "preliminary" estimate is replaced by the "final" estimate, which incorporates revisions in source data for the third month of the quarter and quarterly source data for some components.

Each quarterly estimate is subject to three successive annual revisions. The first annual revision incorporates further revisions in the monthly or quarterly source data and introduces some annual source data. The second and third annual revisions incorporate a broad range of annual source data. Each quarterly estimate is also subject to one or more comprehensive revisions, in which information from the economic and demographic censuses is incorporated.

It should be noted that these estimates and revisions are done for very detailed components. There are about 2,500 annual components and 1,000 quarterly components in the current U.S. GDP estimates published in the *Survey of Current Business.* Based upon a major study of the reliability of the expenditure-side estimates GDP completed in 1993,[5] Young now reports:

The most interesting finding in the 1993 study was that dispersion was about the same size in the advance estimates of GDP as in the preliminary and final current estimates. This was the case not only for total GDP but for the major components as well. This finding suggested that one or both of the later current estimates of GDP might be discontinued without much loss of information.

Thus, the recommendation first made by the authors in September 1993 has received considerable empirical support in other independent investigations.

---

[5]Allan Young, "Reliability and Accuracy of the Quarterly Estimates of GDP," *Survey of Current Business,* 73, October 1993, pp. 29–43.

APPENDIX B

STATISTICAL BUDGETS

Figure 1B shows the budgets in current dollars (excluding decennial census funds) for the main statistical agencies for the period 1977–1994. The agencies are:

1. Economic Research Service—U.S. Department of Agriculture (ERS)
2. National Agricultural Statistics Service—U.S. Department of Agriculture (NASS)
3. Bureau of Economic Analysis—U.S. Department of Commerce (BEA)
4. Bureau of the Census—U.S. Department of Commerce (Census)
5. Energy Information Administration—U.S. Department of Energy (EIA)
6. National Center for Education Statistics—U.S. Department of Education (NCES)
7. National Center for Health Statistics—U.S. Department of Health and Human Services (NCHS)
8. Bureau of Justice Statistics—U.S. Department of Justice (BJS)
9. Bureau of Labor Statistics—U.S. Department of Labor (BLS)

These numbers are taken from the annual reports prepared by the Office of Management and Budget as part of its responsibility for reporting on budgets for statistical activities. The latest report covers 1994.[1] While the budgets for these statistical agencies are less than 50 percent of the total funding available for statistical activities as is shown in Figure 2B, these major agencies are responsible for producing some of the more important data that are used to measure the performance of the economy, to describe the country's social situation, and to determine what federal government policies and programs are appropriate.

Given the impact of the statistics produced by these agencies on the government decision-making and budgetary processes, it is no wonder there is con-

---

[1]Executive Office of the President. Office of Management and Budget. *Statistical Programs of the United States Government, Fiscal Year 1994.* 1993.

FIGURE 1B
Nine U.S. Agency Budgets as a Percentage of the Total Statistical Budget*

	All Statistical Agencies		Main Statistical Agencies**	
	Total Statistical Budget (current dollars)	Nine Agency Budgets (current dollars)	Deflators (1990)	Constant 1990 Dollars (millions)
1994	2,637	1,048	127.03	825
1993	2,451	977	123.36	792
1992	2,491	1,003	117.57	853
1991	2,005	787	117.57	669
1990	1,824	719	100.00	719
1989	1,635	700	95.88	730
1988	1,527	692	91.61	755
1987	1,363	637	88.90	717
1986	1,459	594	86.46	687
1985	1,510	573	84.73	676
1984	1,418	530	81.75	648
1983	1,285	487	78.79	618
1982	1,245	458	75.40	607
1981	1,128	456	71.06	642
1980	1,073	449	63.00	713
1979	791	429	58.01	740
1978	755	402	53.98	745
1977	637	340	50.44	674

* Excluding decennial census funds.
** See Figure 2B for agency details.

Source: Various U.S. government budget appendices for the time period covered.

cern among users of these data when the level of agency funding is reduced (or does not grow in response to new demands), especially since statistical funding levels affect the amount and quality of data available.

This report is not an analysis of the adequacy of funding levels, nor is it a critique of statistical agency priorities. It is clear, as noted in previous reports of the National Association of Business Economists and others, that during the past two decades the statistical system has been faced with increasing demands and with reduced budgets in real terms.

One important initiative mentioned on page 16 is the Boskin Initiative. Progress on budget enhancements is shown in Figure 3B.

FIGURE 2B
Budgets for Main U.S. Statistical Agencies

	ERS	NASS	BEA	Census**	EIA	NCES	NCHS	BJS	BLS	Total
1995	53.7*	89.5	48.6	309.2	84.9	113.0	83.4	24.3	310.8	1117.4
1994	55.2	81.9	39.8	248.8	89.9	87.4	83.4	23.3	292.1	1001.8
1993	58.9	81.0	40.7	327.9	80.7	88.0	80.4	24.3	274.5	1056.4
1992	58.9	82.6	34.8	310.1	74.7	86.6	79.1	24.5	251.4	1002.7
1991	54.4	76.5	30.5	184.7	69.1	73.3	70.4	24.4	203.7	787.0
1990	50.6	66.8	25.6	181.9	64.1	48.7	66.1	22.7	192.6	719.1
1989	49.4	63.5	24.6	190.3	62.4	39.6	60.7	21.8	187.7	700.0
1988	48.1	61.2	23.6	216.6	61.4	29.2	54.4	21.8	175.3	691.6
1987	44.8	57.6	23.0	189.6	60.3	20.1	52.1	22.1	167.1	636.7
1986	44.6	56.1	21.2	146.0	57.7	17.3	44.4	19.9	186.6	593.8
1985	46.4	58.1	21.8	138.9	60.9	14.1	42.8	19.7	170.6	573.3
1984	43.7	54.4	21.0	139.8	55.6	14.1	46.0	18.6	136.3	529.5
1983	38.8	51.7	19.1	131.4	58.1	8.6	40.8	17.1	121.3	486.9
1982	39.3	51.2	18.0	96.5	77.8	8.5	37.7	17.7	111.6	458.3
1981		93.0	17.1	92.2	89.8	8.4	33.7	12.3	109.9	456.4
1980		90.2	15.8	81.3	88.2	9.9	43.3	17.8	102.9	449.4
1979		78.9	14.6	95.4	65.6	13.0	38.9	28.1	94.9	429.4
1978		77.1	14.0	95.5	50.7	13.9	37.3	29.4	83.8	401.7
1977		69.0	12.8	76.0	29.9	13.1	29.3	25.4	84.3	339.8

* All numbers in millions of dollars.
** Excludes decennial census funds.
1974–1992 figures are actual.
1994 figures are estimates.
1995 figures are from the president's budget request and therefore do not reflect congressional appropriation actions.

FIGURE 3B
Current Status of U.S. FY 1992 Economic Statistics Initiative*

Initiative	1991 Enacted	1992 President's Budget	1992 Enacted	1993 President's Budget	1993 Enacted	1994 President's Budget
Bureau of the Census (S&E)	111,249	132,484	125,290	138,406	123,955	140,798
Improve service sector data coverage and detail	900	1,400	1,400	3,122	0	1,363
Improve construction statistics	0	1,300	0	1,300	0	1,300
SIC research/monitor emerging industries	0	400	0	300	0	0
Improve corporate financial data	200	800	0	1,626	0	808
Develop model to measure underpricing of exports	0	400	0	500	0	0
Census Bureau totals	1,100	4,300	1,400	6,848	0	3,471
Economic and statistical analysis	36,360	43,494	40,380	56,427	46,953	49,802
Bureau of Economic Analysis (BEA)	30,865	37,807	34,699	50,534	41,473	44,232
Maintain GDP estimates	1,200	1,300	1,300	2,691	0	600
U.N. System of National Accounts transition	1,300	1,700	500	2,010	0	1,200
Improve quality of balance of payments data	700	1,500	500	1,952	0	400
Improve quality of international investment and services data	2,100	800	0	894	0	800
BEA totals	5,300	5,300	2,300	7,550	0	3,000

Bureau of Labor Statistics (BLS)

S&E	203,669	258,504	251,343	282,315	274,992	280,448
Trust Fund	51,488	50,399	49,799	51,539	48,907	50,227
Total BLS	255,157	308,903	301,142	333,854	323,899	330,675
Improve accuracy of labor force data	0	3,900	4,234	4,969	4,969	4,863
Improve coverage of service sector employment detail and service industry output measures	1,578	7,910	6,009	6,845	4,691	4,336
Separate quality and inflation changes in price data	0	1,340	946	1,108	857	857
Improve quality of service sector establishment list	0	1,400	543	576	76	76
Develop automated data collection techniques	0	3,000	2,171	1,237	1,237	1,237
BLS totals	1,578	17,550	13,903	14,735	11,830	11,369
National Agriculture Statistics Service (NASS)	76,465	86,866	82,601	87,087	81,004	82,479
Improve farm sampling frames	1,200	2,400	1,195	1,425	0	0
NASS totals	1,200	2,400	1,195	1,425	0	0
National Science Foundation						
Improve quality of federal statistics workforce	0	400	400	700	700	1,000
NSF totals	0	400	400	700	700	1,000
Totals	9,178	29,950	19,198	31,258	12,530	18,840

*This table describes statistical program recommendations developed under the leadership of Michael Boskin, Chairman of the Council of Economic Advisers of the Bush Administration.

Note: The above categories are estimates of program levels as described in various budget documents and other reports. This table illustrates the difference between budget requests and congressionally authorized spending levels.

APPENDIX C

SERVICES AND INVISIBLES— METHODOLOGICAL PROBLEMS

TRAVEL AND TOURISM

Data are compiled from a voluntary survey conducted by the U.S. Travel and Tourism Administration (USTTA). This survey is not necessarily a representative sample of travel abroad and may be subject to considerable inaccuracy. Missing data are supplemented by information from the Immigration and Naturalization Service (INS).

Tourism Definition. The tourism account covers purchases of goods and services by U.S. travelers abroad and by foreigners in the United States. Expenditures include food, lodging, recreation, gifts, and incidental items. A traveler is defined as a person who stays for less than one year in a country of which he or she is not a resident.

Estimations for receipts and expenditures are made on the basis of the following procedures.

Total, Except Canada and Mexico

Receipts and payments are derived from surveys taken by the USTTA. The survey is conducted aboard a random sample of scheduled flights departing the United States. It covers about 70 percent of U.S. carriers and 35 percent of foreign carriers. Travelers are asked about their expenditures for airfare, travel, hotels, meals, and miscellaneous expenses.

Since the results of the USTTA survey become available only after a considerable lag, the most recent quarters are estimated in the following manner:

1. The number of visitors is obtained from INS, from which the year-to-year change is calculated.

2. Price changes are approximated by the year-on-year change in the CPI.
3. Both these changes are applied to travel receipts and expenditures of the same quarter of the previous year.

There are a number of problems with this existing data collection methodology:

1. The USTTA survey is strictly voluntary. Many surveys are not turned in, while others are incomplete. The missing data items are treated as though the reply matched the average for completed cards.
2. Sampling techniques may lead to biases. There may be misrepresentation of particular destinations.
3. The sample size is small, about $\frac{1}{10}$ of 1 percent.
4. U.S. residents traveling abroad take the survey before they reach their destination. They must estimate their expenditures.
5. Other complications arise when U.S. residents travel to several destinations. The Bureau of Economic Analysis (BEA) uses the information about how many nights the traveler expects to spend at each destination to prorate total expenditures for each destination.
6. The sample from the USTTA is then expanded, using the number of people departing the United States, obtained from the Immigration and Naturalization Service (INS).
7. Results of the USTTA survey are available only with a lag.
8. Surveys such as these can be grossly inaccurate: Some people want to overestimate their expenditures while others want to "forget" or possibly downplay some of their expenditures.

Canada

For Canada, the procedures are different. In order to estimate U.S. receipts, estimates are derived from questionnaires distributed to Canadians returning from the United States. Estimates of expenditures by U.S. citizens in Canada are derived from monthly data on the number of U.S. residents visiting Canada, which are supplied by Statistics Canada by port of entry. The data are combined with average expenditure figures developed from BEA sample data in the BE 536.

Mexico

Since two-way traffic across the border between Mexico and the United States is enormous, the border area and the interior are treated separately.

For border data, U.S. estimates of receipts are derived from Bank of Mexico surveys of Mexicans returning from the United States. For estimates of U.S.

expenditures, the number of U.S. visits to the border area is compiled by the Immigration and Naturalization Service (INS). The number of border crossings is combined with average expenditures developed from BE 575 data.

For data on interior tourism, the number of Mexicans visiting the United States is based on monthly INS data. It is estimated that all Mexican air travelers and 60 percent of land and sea travelers visit the interior. Average expenditures are estimated by adjusting the average expenditure figure for the same quarter of the previous year by the change in the U.S. CPI. This is multiplied by the number of Mexican visitors. For estimating U.S. expenditures in the interior, the number of U.S. travelers is obtained from the Bank of Mexico, based on counts by Mexican immigration officials of alien arrivals by air and land. (Eighty percent of all visitors are U.S. residents.)

Estimates of travel costs for transportation vary by mode of transportation, and the methods vary by data sources in some countries. Fares paid by residents of one country to carriers of other countries are important in the balance of payments. Travel expenditures of passengers using their own country's carriers are not included in the balance of payments.

Since 1975, nearly all U.S. ocean passenger liners have been taken out of service. For air travel, the number of foreign visitors to the United States is tabulated from the INS entry documents, but these data are not available by flag of carrier. The proportion of foreign visitors arriving on U.S. carriers is estimated from the USTTA surveys. Cost of travel is obtained from USTTA surveys. Fare receipts of U.S. citizens traveling to foreign points are estimated based on BEA data obtained from the quarterly BE 37 survey, "U.S. Airline Operators' Foreign Revenues and Expenses."

TRANSPORTATION

Collection of data on freight and shipping is one of the oldest categories in the services area. For ocean shipping on the payments side, the convention is to assume that all payments are paid by the importer. Determining the total freight bill is relatively simple since imports are compiled on both cost-insurance-freight (c.i.f.) and free-on-board (f.o.b.) The difference is the freight and insurance. It is assumed that insurance comprises 1 percent of the total c.i.f. and that freight is 99 percent.

Transportation Cost Definition. This category includes all freight charges when shipping services are performed by residents of one country for residents of another country. It also includes operating expenses that transportation companies incur in foreign ports and payments for vessel charters and aircraft and car rentals. The residency of the *operator* must be determined because it may differ from the country of registry of the vessel.

Receipts are estimated with differing procedures in the alternate modes of transportation.

For ocean shipments the earnings of U.S. vessels carrying U.S. merchandise exports to foreign ports are calculated as follows:

1. Data on waterborne export tonnage carried by U.S. flag vessels are obtained from U.S. Waterborne Exports, Domestic and Foreign SM 704.
2. This figure is increased by an estimate of the share of export tonnage carried by U.S. operators of foreign-flag vessels.
3. The resulting total tonnage carried by U.S.-operated vessels is multiplied by an average freight rate per ton (quarterly BEA survey of U.S. carriers BE-30).
4. Receipts are adjusted to include subsidies paid by the U.S government to U.S. vessel operators on grain shipments under foreign aid programs and negotiated rates on grain shipments to Eastern Europe (data compiled by USDA).

The number of U.S. ocean carriers is relatively small—fewer than 50. It is believed that the coverage of U.S. carriers is comprehensive, but there are several problems. The SM 704 does not give residency of the operator. The share of foreign-flag shipping for U.S. exports is assumed to be the same as that for U.S. imports tabulated in U.S. Waterborne Imports SM 304.

For air carriers, it is important to estimate both the earnings of U.S. air carriers transporting U.S. exports and the earnings for transporting freight between foreign points. Data come from the U.S. Airline Operators' Foreign Revenues and Expenses (BEA survey BE 37). Reported earnings are increased 5 percent to compensate for small carriers that are exempt from reporting. The expansion factor is derived by comparing export freight tonnage as reported in BE 37 with tonnage data in the Census Bureau AM 754, U.S. Exports by Air.

Pipeline transportation requires estimates of the earnings of U.S. affiliates of Canadian pipeline companies for transporting oil and gas unloaded from tankers at Portland, Maine, to Canada. Transportation of oil through pipelines in the Northeast U.S. that eventually is headed to Canada is also included. Data are obtained quarterly from the four U.S. affiliates of Canadian companies.

For railroads, earnings are derived from:

1. U.S. rail carriers transporting Canadian exports to and imports from third countries through the United States.
2. U.S. exports from the U.S. customs frontier to other rail connections in Canada.
3. Goods within Canada transported on U.S. rail carriers' leased trackage in Canada.

Four U.S. rail carriers operate in Canada. They submit revenue data to the BEA annually. Quarterly estimates are made for Balance of Payments purposes.

For the Great Lakes region, earnings of U.S. ship operators transporting goods between U.S. and Canadian Great Lakes ports are derived in the following way: Tonnage is obtained from SM 704; total receipts are derived by multiplying export tonnage by estimates of average freight rates on BE 30.

Transportation earnings include port service receipts. A large portion of gross shipping revenue is spent in the ports of the importing countries. BEA collects this information on form BE 29, which is sent to U.S. agents of foreign shippers. They are asked to complete the form for 10 ports of call during the year. Data requested include the amount spent by the operators of the vessels and the shipping weight of the cargo. Since the total shipping weight of all imports is known, the figures derived from the sample in BE 29 are blown up accordingly.

Some problems with this method are:

1. Agents' responses may not be reliable.
2. Data for shipping weight are often missing.
3. Data for one of the most important elements, bunker fuel, is often incomplete.

Despite these problems of estimation, over the period 1980–1988, port expenditure receipts averaged 74 percent of the ocean freight payments, and there were no large year-to-year variations. Recent evidence suggests that port receipts are increasing. The ratio of port receipts to ocean freight payments from 1989 to 1991 was 81 percent, 76 percent, and 83 percent, respectively.

On the payments side, the following procedures are currently used. By convention, for ocean shipments, it is assumed that all freight payments are paid by the importer. Data on earnings of foreign ship operators carrying U.S. imports are derived from Census Bureau SM 304. This form gives data on import charges and shipping weights by the registered flag of the vessel. To determine residency of the operator, BEA uses Customs Forms 1400, Records of Vessels Engaged in Foreign Trade and Entered or Arrived Under Permit to Proceed. BEA takes a sample from SM 304 and redistributes import charges from a flag of vessel to residency of the operator basis.

Earnings of foreign air carriers for transporting U.S. imports from foreign countries to the United States are estimated on the basis of special surveys. The annual BE 36 survey is the source of the data. Annual estimates are increased by 5 percent to account for earnings by small carriers that are exempt from reporting. Quarterly estimates are made by distributing the annual estimate according to the shipping weight of imports as reported in Census Bureau AM 354.

Earnings of Canadian rail carriers transporting U.S. imports in transit through Canada and U.S. goods through Canada from one U.S. point to another are important in the area of rail transportation. Quarterly estimates are obtained from Statistics Canada.

Also on the expenditures side, data are collected on the earnings of Canadian carriers transporting goods from Canada to U.S. Great Lakes ports; expenditures of U.S. ship operators in foreign ports; U.S. airline expenditures abroad for fuel, wages, agents' and brokers' fees, repair and maintenance, and miscellaneous; expenditures of U.S. rail carriers in Canada for maintenance, repair, fuel, and so on; and several smaller categories of U.S. expenditures to suppliers from other countries.

ROYALTIES AND LICENSE FEES

This category involves transactions between U.S. residents and foreign residents involving intangible assets and proprietary rights. Royalties generally refer to payments for the utilization of copyrights or trademarks. License fees generally refer to payments for the use of patents or industrial processes. There is a distinction between affiliated and unaffiliated transactions, each having its own estimation procedures.

Affiliated Transactions

These are transactions between U.S. parent companies and their foreign affiliates or U.S. affiliates and their foreign parents. "Affiliated" is defined as ownership of at least 10 percent, either directly or indirectly. Affiliated transactions, for the past several years, averaged 75 percent of the total royalties and licenses.

Data for receipts and payments are obtained from a series of BEA benchmark studies and sample surveys of U.S. direct investors and U.S.–based affiliates of foreign direct investors. Receipts are proceeds from royalties and license fees, received or accrued, by U.S. parents from their foreign affiliates. Net receipts are calculated by subtracting payments by U.S. parents to their foreign affiliates from receipts by U.S. parents from their foreign affiliates, after deducting U.S. and foreign withholding tax.

On the payments side are net payments of royalties and license fees by U.S. affiliates to their foreign parents and other members of the foreign-parent group. Net payments are calculated by subtracting receipts of U.S. affiliates from the foreign-parent group from payments by U.S. affiliates to the foreign-parent group, after deducting U.S. and foreign withholding tax.

Unaffiliated Transactions

Data are obtained from the Annual Survey of Royalties, License Fees, and Other Receipts and Payments for Intangible Rights Between U.S. and Unaffiliated Foreign Persons, BE 93. Completion of the survey is mandatory. The list was developed from industry directories and includes persons who reported transactions with unaffiliated foreigners in previous surveys. Quarterly estimates are interpolations of the annual estimates. Amounts are reported net of taxes.

There have been serious problems involving international copyright infringement and nonpayments for licenses and royalties. U.S. receipts are likely to be understated, possibly to a considerable extent.

OTHER PRIVATE SERVICES

This category includes services not specifically covered in travel, passenger fares, other transportation, or royalties and license fees accounts. There are different data-collection procedures for affiliated and unaffiliated transactions as well as for the different categories.

Affiliated Transactions

Data for accounts covered in this category are obtained from a series of BEA benchmark and sample surveys of U.S. direct investors abroad and U.S.–based affiliates of foreign investors.

On the receipt side, it is necessary to estimate net receipts of U.S. parents from their foreign affiliates for service charges, fees for the use of tangible property, and film and television tape rentals. The data are based on the books of the U.S. parents and are reported as of the date the funds are either received from, or paid to, foreign affiliates, or entered into intercompany accounts with foreign affiliates, whichever occurs first. In 1991, affiliated transactions comprised 31 percent of total other services; this share has been relatively stable over the past five years.

The payment side includes net payments by U.S. affiliates to their foreign parents and other members of the foreign parent group for service charges, fees for the use of tangible property, and film and tape rentals. Affiliated transactions accounted for 38 percent of the total in 1991; the share has been relatively steady over the past five years.

Unaffiliated Transactions

These are transactions between U.S. residents and unaffiliated foreigners for services, including education, financial, insurance, business, professional, and technical services. Data are derived from various sources, including four annual mandatory BEA surveys, data provided directly to BEA, private organizations, foreign governments, and international organizations. This category is extremely broad, covering a vast array of services. The complexity of this category makes data collection difficult and often unreliable. Since 1986, when a new mandatory reporting system was put in place (first BE 20 and subsequently BE 22), data collection has improved considerably, though there are still many gaps. Reports are mandatory for individual transactions over $250,000.

There are also three other surveys:

1. BE 93 covers receipts and payments of royalties and license fees. The number of respondents is over 400.
2. BE 48 covers premiums earned and paid for insurance. The number of respondents is about 300.
3. BE 47 covers services related to construction and engineering operations. Although the number of respondents is fewer than 100, this is considered rather complete since there are a small number of firms operating in this area.

These miscellaneous categories contain many areas that are difficult to estimate.[1] Categories include:

1. *Education.* Expenditures of foreign students enrolled in institutions of higher education in the United States.
2. *Financial Services.* This category includes commissions and fees transactions associated with the stock and commodity transactions, and non-interest income of U.S. and foreign banks paid and received.
3. *Insurance.* This consists of net premiums received, less losses paid to the ceding companies or individuals abroad, less cancellations and commissions charged by the ceding company abroad.
4. *Telecommunications.* Receipts for telephone, private leased channel service, telex, telegram, electronic mail, and fax. It also includes repair and the launching of communications satellites.
5. *Business, Professional, and Technical Services.* Includes a broad range of services, including accounting, auditing, bookkeeping, advertising, agriculture, computer and data processing, legal, engineering and construction, public relations, and so on.
6. *Other.* Consists of expenditures associated with diplomatic activities, expenditures of agents of foreign governments, and expenditures for the construction of embassy buildings and related facilities.

---

[1]The authors have compiled a report on methods used for these categories. It is available upon request.

BIBLIOGRAPHY

Abbott, Thomas A.; Andrews, Stephen H. August 1990. "The Classification of Manufacturing Industries: An Input-based Clustering of Activity." In: *Proceedings of the 1990 Annual Research Conference;* 1990 March 18–21; Arlington, VA. Washington, D.C.: U.S. Department of Commerce. Bureau of the Census: 26–45.

Aborn, Murray. 1986. "Statistical Legacies of the Social Indicators Movement." In: *1985 Proceedings of the Social Statistics Section.* Papers presented at the annual meeting of the American Statistical Association; 1985 August 5–8; Las Vegas, NV. Washington, D.C.: American Statistical Association: 138–147.

Abramson, Bruce; Finizza, Anthony. 1991. "Using Belief Networks to Forecast Oil Prices." *International Journal of Forecasting.* 7(3):299–315.

Ahmed, Bashir; Robinson, J. Gregory. 1991. *Differences between Preliminary and Final Estimates of Percent Net Undercount.* Washington, D.C.: U.S. Bureau of the Census. Demographic Analysis Evaluation Project No. D10.

Alexander, Charles H. 1994. "A Prototype Continuous Measurement System for the U.S. Census of Population and Housing." For presentation at the 1994 annual meeting of the Population Association of America; 1994 May 5; Miami, FL.

Alexander, Charles H.; Taylor, Bruce M. August 1989. "New Directions for Some Household Surveys and Associated Research Needs: The National Crime Survey Redesign." In: *Proceedings of the Fifth Annual Research Conference;* 1989 March 19–22; Arlington, VA. Washington, D.C.: U.S. Department of Commerce. Bureau of the Census: 14–47.

Alexander, Charles H.; Wetrogan, Signe I. 1994. "Small Area Estimation with Continuous Measurement: What We Have and What We Want." For presentation at the 1994 Census Bureau Annual Research Conference; 1994 March 22; Arlington, VA.

Ambler, Carole A.; Mesenbourg, Thomas L. November 1992. "EDI [Electronic Data Interchange]—Reporting Standards for the Future." In: *Proceedings of the 1992 Annual Research Conference;* 1992 March 22–25; Arlington, VA. Washington, D.C.: U.S. Department of Commerce. Bureau of the Census: 289–310.

Anolik, Irwin; Hogan, Howard. 1992. "Non-Response Conversion: The Experience of the 1990 Post-Enumeration Survey." In: *1991 Proceedings of the Section on Survey Research Methods.* Papers presented at the annual meeting of the American Statistical Association; 1991 August 18–22; Atlanta, GA. Alexandria, VA: American Statistical Association: 658–663.

Armknecht, Paul A.; Weyback, Donald. 1988. "Adjustments for Quality Change in the CPI [Consumer Price Index]: An Update." In: *1987 Proceedings of the Business and Economic Statistics Section.* Papers presented at the annual meeting of the American Statistical Association; 1987 August 17–20; San Francisco, CA. Alexandria, VA: American Statistical Association: 620–625.

Ashley, Richard; Vaughan, David. 1986. "Measuring Measurement Error in Economic Time Series." *Journal of Business and Economic Statistics.* 4(January):95–103.

Bailey, Leroy; Jansto, Ann; Smith, Charlene. 1991. "Assessing the Effects of Imputed Data on Selected Results from the 1987 Economic Censuses." In: *1990 Proceedings of the Section on Survey Research Methods.* Papers presented at the annual meeting of the American Statistical Association; 1990 August 6–9; Anaheim, CA. Alexandria, VA: American Statistical Association: 249–253.

Bartelmus, Peter. 1987. "Beyond GDP—New Approaches to Applied Statistics." *The Review of Income and Wealth.* Series 33(4):347–358.

Bauer, Raymond A., ed. 1966. *Social Indicators.* Cambridge, MA: The MIT Press: 357.

Baumgartner, Thomas; Midttun, Atle, eds. 1987. *The Politics of Energy Forecasting: A Comparative Study of Energy Forecasting in Western Europe and North America.* New York: Oxford University Press: 314.

Beanlands, G. E.; Duinker, P. N. 1984. "An Ecological Framework for Environmental Impact Assessment." *Journal of Environmental Management.* 18:267–277.

Beaver, Ronald D.; Huntington, Hillard G. 1992. "A Comparison of Aggregate Energy Demand Models for Global Warming Policy Analyses." In: *1991 Proceedings of the Business and Economic Statistics Section.* Papers presented at the annual meeting of the American Statistical Association; 1991 August 18–22; Atlanta, GA. Alexandria, VA: American Statistical Association: 11–18.

Bell, Daniel. 1969. "The Idea of a Social Report." *The Public Interest.* 15(Spring):72–84.

Berndt, Ernst R.; Grilliches, Zvi; Rosett, Joshua G. 1993. "Auditing the Producer Price Index: Micro Evidence from Prescription Pharmaceutical Preparations." *Journal of Business and Economic Statistics.* 11(January):251–264.

Berndt, Ernst R.; Triplett, Jack E., eds. 1990. *Fifty Years of Economic Measurement: The Jubilee of the Conference on Research in Income and Wealth.* National Bureau of Economic Research Conference on Research in Income and Wealth, 50th Anniversary Conference; 1988 May 12–14; Washington, D.C.; *Studies in Income and Wealth,* Vol. 54. Chicago, IL: University of Chicago Press: 454.

Bianchi, Suzanne M. 1983. "Changing Concepts of Household and Family in the Census and CPS [Current Population Survey]." In: *1982 Proceedings of the Social Statistics Section.* Papers presented at the annual meeting of the American Statistical Association; 1982 August 16–19; Cincinnati, OH. Washington, D.C.: American Statistical Association: 13–22.

Biderman, Albert D. 1966. "Social Indicators and Goals." In: Bauer, Raymond A. *Social Indicators.* Cambridge, MA: The MIT Press: 68–153.

Biemer, Paul P. July 1988. "Evaluating the Effect of Matching Error on Estimates of Census Coverage Error." In: *Proceedings of the Fourth Annual Research Conference;* 1988 March 20–23; Arlington, VA. Washington, D.C.: U.S. Department of Commerce. Bureau of the Census: 67–80.

Bishop, Yvonne M.; Werbos, Paul J. 1983. "An Interagency Review of Time-Series Revision Policies." In: *1982 Proceedings of the Section on Survey Research Methods.* Papers presented at the annual meeting of the American Statistical Association; 1982 August 16–19; Cincinnati, OH. Washington, D.C.: American Statistical Association: 180–184.

Bonnen, James T. 1983. "Federal Statistical Coordination Today: A Disaster or a Disgrace?" In: *1982 Proceedings of the Social Statistics Section.* Papers presented at the annual meeting of the American Statistical Association; 1982 August 16–19; Cincinnati, OH. Washington, D.C.: American Statistical Association: 28–37.

Bonnen, James T.; Clemence, Theodore G.; Fellegi, Ivan P.; Jabine, Thomas B.; Kutscher, Ronald E.; Roberson, Larry K.; Waite, Charles A. 1980. "Improving the Federal Statistical System: Report of the President's Reorganization Project for the Federal Statistical System." *Statistical Reporter.* 80–82(May):197–212. Also reprinted in *American Statistician,* November 1981, 35(4):183–209.

Boruch, Robert F. 1985. "Research on the Use of Statistical Data." In: *1984 Proceedings of the Social Statistics Section.* Papers presented at the annual meeting of the American Statistical Association; 1964 August 13–16; Philadelphia, PA. Washington, D.C.: American Statistical Association: 52–59.

Boskin, Michael J. 1990. "Issues in the Measurement and Interpretation of Saving and Wealth." In: Berndt, Ernst R.; Triplett, Jack E., eds. *Fifty Years of Economic Measurement: The Jubilee of the Conference on Research on Income and Wealth.* National Bureau of Economic Research Conference on

Research in Income and Wealth 50th Anniversary Conference; 1988 May 12–14; Washington, D.C.; *Studies in Income and Wealth,* Vol. 54. Chicago, IL: University of Chicago Press: 159–183.

Boskin, Michael J. September 1991. "Improving the Quality of Federal Economic Statistics." In: *Proceedings of the 1991 Annual Research Conference;* 1991 March 17–20; Arlington, VA. Washington, D.C.: U.S. Department of Commerce. Bureau of the Census: 247–251.

Bowers, Norman; Horvath, Francis W. 1984. "Keeping Time: An Analysis of Errors in the Measurement of Unemployment Duration." *Journal of Business and Economic Statistics.* 2(April):140–149.

Brick, J. Michael. 1993. "Reinterview Program for the 1990 National Household Education Survey." In: *1992 Proceedings of the Section on Survey Research Methods.* Papers presented at the annual meeting of the American Statistical Association; 1992 August 9–13; Boston, MA. Alexandria, VA: American Statistical Association: 387–392.

Brown, Ann; Britney, Heather; Roumelis, Dan. September 1991. "Adjustment of Estimates from Establishment Surveys for Undercoverage Due to Frame Processing Lags." In: *Proceedings of the 1991 Annual Research Conference;* 1991 March 17–20; Arlington, VA. Washington, D.C.: U.S. Department of Commerce. Bureau of the Census: 313–326.

Bruns, D. A.; Wiersma, G. Bruce; Rykiel, Edward J., Jr. 1991. "Ecosystem Monitoring at Global Baseline Sites." *Environmental Monitoring and Assessment.* 17(1):3–31.

Bryant, Barbara E.; Miskura, Susan M.; Dinwiddie, James L. August 1992. "Strategic Issues for 2000 Census Design." For Presentation at the Joint Statistical Meetings; 1992 August; Boston, MA. Washington, D. C.: U.S. Bureau of the Census: 21.

Burnham, Clinton E.; Massey, James T. 1981. "Redesign of the National Health Interview Survey." In: *1980 Proceedings of the Section on Survey Research Methods.* Papers presented at the annual meeting of the American Statistical Association; 1980 August 11–14; Houston, TX. Washington, D.C.: American Statistical Association: 115–118.

Buss, Terry F.; Lundell, Allan; Popovich, Mark G. August 1990. "The Accuracy of ES202 Files in Locating New Businesses." In: *Proceedings of the 1990 Annual Research Conference;* 1990 March 18–21; Arlington, VA. Washington, D.C.: U.S. Department of Commerce. Bureau of the Census: 559–568.

Cain, Glen G. 1979. "Are We Counting the Labor Force Properly?" In: *1978 Proceedings of the Social Statistics Section.* Papers presented at the annual meeting of the American Statistical Association; 1978 August 14–17; San Diego, CA. Washington, D.C.: American Statistical Association: 1–3.

Caplan, Nathan; Barton, Eugenia. 1976. *Social Indicators 1973: A Study of the Relationship between the Power of Information and Utilization by Federal Executives.* Ann Arbor, MI: Institute for Social Research, University of Michigan.

Carson, Carol S.; Landefeld, Steven. 1994. "Accounting for Mineral Resources: Issues and BEA's Initial Estimates." *Survey of Current Business.* 74(April):50–72.

Carson, Carol S.; Landefeld, Steven. 1994. "Integrated Economic and Environmental Satellite Accounts." *Survey of Current Business.* 74(4):33–49.

Cartwright, David W.; Smith, Scott D. 1988. "Deflators for Purchases of Computers in GNP [Gross National Product]: Revised and Extended Estimates, 1983–1988." *Survey of Current Business.* 67(11):22–23.

Chakrabarty, Rameswar P. 1986. "Redesign of the National Health Survey." In: *1985 Proceedings of the Section on Survey Research Methods.* Papers presented at the annual meeting of the American Statistical Association; 1985 August 5–8; Las Vegas, NV. Washington, D.C.: American Statistical Association: 252–257.

Childers, Dan R.; Diffendal, Gregg; Hogan, Howard; Schenker, Nathaniel; Wolter, Kirk. 1988. "The Technical Feasibility of Correcting the 1990 Census." In: *1987 Proceedings of the Social Statistics Section.* Papers presented at the annual meeting of the American Statistical Association; 1987 August 17–20; San Francisco, CA. Alexandria, VA: American Statistical Association: 36–45.

Chiswick, Carmel U. 1988. "Labor, Leisure and Home Production: Implications of the New International Standards for Labor Statistics." In: *1987 Proceedings of the Business and Economic Statistics Section.* Papers presented at the annual meeting of the American Statistical Association; 1987 August 17–20; San Francisco, CA. Alexandria, VA: American Statistical Association: 1–5.

Christian, D. E. 1974. *Social Indicators, the OECD Experience.* Paris, France: Organization for Economic Cooperation and Development.

Chu, Wen-sen; Strecker, Eric W.; Lettenmaier, Dennis P. 1987. "An Evaluation of Data Requirements for Groundwater Contaminant Transport Modeling." *Water Resources Research.* 23(3):408–424.

Clark, Cynthia Z. F. 1985. "Comparability of Data from the Censuses of Agriculture." In: *1984 Proceedings of the Section on Survey Research Methods.* Papers presented at the annual meeting of the American Statistical Association; 1984 August 13–16; Philadelphia, PA. Washington, D.C.: American Statistical Association: 600–605.

Clark, Cynthia Z. F.; Vacca, Elizabeth Ann. 1994. "Ensuring Quality in U.S. Agricultural List Frames." Forthcoming in *Journal of Official Statistics.*

Clogg, Clifford; Massagli, Michael; Eliason, Scott. June 1986. "Population Undercount as an Issue in Social Research." In: *Proceedings of the Second Annual Research Conference;* 1986 March 23–26; Reston, VA. Washington, D.C.: U.S. Department of Commerce. Bureau of the Census: 335–343.

Cohen, Morris. 1983. "The GNP Data Improvement Project (The Creamer Report): Overview and Business Cycle Perspective." In: Foss, Murray F., ed. *The U.S. National Income and Product Accounts: Selected Topics.* National Bureau of Economic Research Conference on Research in Income and Wealth, Conference on National Income and Product Accounts of the United States; 1979 May 3–4; Washington, D.C.; *Studies in Income and Wealth,* Vol. 47. Chicago, IL: University of Chicago Press: 383–397.

Cohen, Philip; Alley, William M.; Wilber, William G. 1988. "National Water-Quality Assessment: Future Directions of the U.S. Geological Survey." *Water Resources Bulletin.* 24(6):1147–1151.

Commission of the European Communities; International Monetary Fund; Organisation for Economic Co-operation and Development; United Nations; World Bank. 1993. *System of National Accounts 1993.* New York: United Nations. ST/ESA/STAT/SER.F/2/Rev.4: 711.

Corby, Carol. 1989. "Issues on Processing Errors in Establishment Surveys." In: *1988 Proceedings of the Section on Survey Research Methods.* Papers presented at the annual meeting of the American Statistical Association; 1988 August 22–25; New Orleans, LA. Alexandria, VA: American Statistical Association: 326–330.

Corby, Carol; Miskura, Susan. 1985. "Evaluating Data Quality in the Economic and Decennial Censuses." In: *Proceedings of the First Annual Research Conference;* 1985 March 20–23; Reston, VA. Washington, D.C.: U.S. Department of Commerce. Bureau of the Census: 159–175.

Corwin, Arthur F. 1982. "The Numbers Game: Estimates of Illegal Aliens in the United States, 1970–1981." *Law and Contemporary Problems.* 45(2):223–297.

Cowan, Charles D.; Breakey, William R.; Fischer, Pamela J. 1987. "The Methodology of Counting the Homeless." In: *1986 Proceedings of the Section on Survey Research Methods.* Papers presented at the annual meeting of the American Statistical Association; 1986 August 18–21; Chicago, IL. Washington, D.C.: American Statistical Association: 170–175.

Cox, Brenda G.; Cohen, Steven B. 1985. *Methodological Issues for Health Care Surveys.* New York, NY: Marcel Dekker, Inc: 446.

Cox, Brenda G.; Folsom, Ralph E. 1985. "Evaluation of Alternate Designs for a Future NMCUES [National Medical Care and Utilization and Expenditure Survey]." In: *1984 Proceedings of the Section on Survey Research Methods.*

Papers presented at the annual meeting of the American Statistical Association; 1984 August 13–16; Philadelphia, PA. Washington, D.C.: American Statistical Association.

Crutsinger, Martin. July 5, 1990. "Economists Question Accuracy and Value of U.S. Statistics." *Washington Post;* Sect. D: 1, 5.

Curtin, Richard T.; Juster, F. Thomas; Morgan, James N. 1989. "Survey Estimates of Wealth: An Assessment of Quality." In: Lipsey, Robert E.; Tice, Helen Stone, eds. *The Measurement of Saving, Investment, and Wealth.* National Bureau of Economic Research Conference on the Measurement of Saving, Investment, and Wealth; 1987 March 27–28; Baltimore, MD; *Studies in Income and Wealth,* Vol. 52. Chicago, IL: University of Chicago Press: 473–548.

Dagum, Estela Bee; Hidiroglou, M. A.; Morry, Marietta. 1985. "The Use of Administrative Records to Estimate Wages and Salaries for Small Businesses in Small Areas." In: *1984 Proceedings of the Business and Economic Statistics Section.* Papers presented at the annual meeting of the American Statistical Association; 1984 August 13–16; Philadelphia, PA. Washington, D.C.: American Statistical Association: 472–477.

Dagum, Estela Bee; Morry, Marietta. 1984. "Basic Issues on the Seasonal Adjustment of the Canadian Consumer Price Index." *Journal of Business and Economic Statistics.* 2(July):250–259.

Daniel, Terry C. 1976. "Criteria for Development and Application of Perceived Environmental Quality Indices." In: Craik, Kenneth H.; Zube, Ervin H., eds. *Perceiving Environmental Quality: Research and Applications. Environmental Science Research.* vol. 9. New York: Plenum Press: 27–45.

David, Martin H., ed. 1983. *Technical, Conceptual, and Administrative Lessons of the Income Survey Development Program (ISDP).* New York, NY: Social Science Research Council: 318.

de Leeuw, Frank. 1990. "The Reliability of U.S. Gross National Product." *Journal of Business and Economic Statistics.* 8(April):191–204.

DeMaio, Theresa J.; Martin, Elizabeth A.; Sigman, Elizabeth Page. 1988. "Improving the Design of the Decennial Census Questionnaire." In: *1987 Proceedings of the Section on Survey Research Methods.* Papers presented at the annual meeting of the American Statistical Association; 1987 August 17–20; San Francisco, CA. Alexandria, VA: American Statistical Association: 256–261.

Denison, Edward F. 1971. "Welfare Measurement and the GNP." *Survey of Current Business.* 5(1):13–16, 39.

Dilullo, Anthony; Laliberte, Lucie. 1993. "Reconciliation of the U.S.–Canadian Current Account, 1991–92." *Survey of Current Business.* 73(10):44–51.

Dovi, V. G. 1991. "Inverse Modelling of Environmental Pollution: The Role of Statistics." *Environmetrics.* 2(3, Sept.):309–321.

Duncan, Joseph W.; Shelton, William C. 1978. *Revolution in United States Government Statistics, 1926–1976.* Washington, D.C.: U.S. Government Printing Office: 257. SUDOC: C 1.2:St2/10/926–76.

Dunn, Edgar S. 1974. *Social Information Processing and Statistical Systems— Change and Reform.* New York, NY: Wiley Interscience, John Wiley & Sons, Inc.

Eargle, Judith H.; Lamas, Enrique J. 1990. "An Evaluation of Wealth Data in SIPP [Survey of Income and Program Participation]." In: *1989 Proceedings of the Social Statistics Section.* Papers presented at the annual meeting of the American Statistical Association; 1989 August 6–10; Washington, D.C. Alexandria, VA: American Statistical Association: 385–390.

Early, John F. 1979. "Producer Price Indexes: A New Analytical Framework to Replace the Wholesale Price Index." In: *1978 Proceedings of the Business and Economic Statistics Section.* Papers presented at the annual meeting of the American Statistical Association; 1978 August 14–17; San Diego, CA. Washington, D.C.: American Statistical Association: 164–176.

Elliott, Emerson J.; Cowan, Charles D. 1988. "Redesigning the Collection of National Education Statistics." In: *1987 Proceedings of the Section on Survey Research Methods.* Papers presented at the annual meeting of the American Statistical Association; 1987 August 17–20; San Francisco, CA. Alexandria, VA: American Statistical Association: 132–137.

El-Shaarawi, A. H.; Damsleth, Eivind. 1988. "Parametric and Nonparametric Tests for Dependent Data." *Water Resources Bulletin.* 24(3):513–519.

Ericksen, Eugene P. 1989. "Bayes Estimates of Population Undercount for Local Areas." In: *1988 Proceedings of the Section on Survey Research Methods.* Papers presented at the annual meeting of the American Statistical Association; 1988 August 22–25; New Orleans, LA. Arlington, VA: American Statistical Association: 18–27.

Esterby, S. R. 1989. "Some Statistical Considerations in the Assessment of Compliance." *Environmental Monitoring and Assessment.* 12(2/3):103–112.

Farley, Reynolds. 1991. "Race, Ancestry and Spanish Origin: Findings from the 1980s and Questions for the 1990s." In: *1990 Proceedings of the Social Statistics Section.* Papers presented at the annual meeting of the American Statistical Association; 1990 August 6–9; Anaheim, CA. Alexandria, VA: American Statistical Association: 11–16.

Farrell, Michael G.; Konschnik, Carl A. 1983. "A Review of Industry Coding Systems." In: *1982 Proceedings of the Section on Survey Research Methods.* Papers presented at the annual meeting of the American Statistical Association; 1982 August 16–19; Cincinnati, OH. Washington, D.C.: American Statistical Association: 278–283.

Fay, Robert E. 1992. "Multiple Causes of Nonresponse: Analysis of the Survey of 1990 Census Participation." In: *1991 Proceedings of the Social Statistics Section*. Papers presented at the annual meeting of the American Statistical Association; 1991 August 18–22; Atlanta, GA. Alexandria, VA: American Statistical Association: 525–530.

Fay, Robert; Passel, Jeffrey S.; Robinson, J. Gregory. 1988. *The Coverage of Population in the 1980 Census. 1980 Census of Population and Housing Evaluation and Research Report.* PHC80-E4. Washington, D.C.: U.S. Government Printing Office. SUDOC: C 3.223/16:980/E C4.

Ferriss, Abbott L. March 1988. "The Uses of Social Indicators." *Social Forces.* 66(3):601–617.

Fienberg, S. E. 1978. "Victimization and the National Crime Survey: Problems of Design and Analysis." In: Nambodiri, N. D. *Survey Sampling and Measurement.* New York, NY: Academic Press: 89–106.

Fienberg, Stephen. June 1986. "Adjusting the Census: Statistical Methodology for Going Beyond the Count." In: *Proceedings of the Second Annual Research Conference;* 1986 March 23–26; Reston, VA. Washington, D.C.: U.S. Department of Commerce. Bureau of the Census: 570–577.

Fisher, Joseph L. 1967. "The Natural Environment." *The Annals of the American Academy of Political and Social Science.* 371(May):127–140. Special issue "Social Goals and Indicators for American Society," Vol. 1.

Fitzgerald, John; Zuo, Zuejin. September 1991. "Alternative Samples for Welfare Duration in SIPP: Does Attrition Matter?" In: *Proceedings of the 1991 Annual Research Conference;* 1991 March 17–20; Arlington, VA. Washington, D.C.: U.S. Department of Commerce. Bureau of the Census: 352–368.

Foss, Murray F., ed. 1983. *The U.S. National Income and Product Accounts: Selected Topics.* National Bureau of Economic Research Conference on Research in Income and Wealth, Conference on National Income and Product Accounts of the United States; 1979 May 3–4; Washington, D.C.; *Studies in Income and Wealth,* Vol. 47. Chicago, IL: University of Chicago Press: 438.

Friend, A. M. 1977. *Frameworks for Environmental Statistics: Experience of Statistics Canada.* Ottawa, Canada: Office of the Senior Adviser on Integration, Statistics Canada.

Frumkin, Norman. 1992. *Tracking America's Economy.* 2nd ed. Armonk, NY: M. E. Sharpe: 340.

Fuchsberg, Robert R. 1979. "The National Health Interview Survey: An Overview." In: *1978 Proceedings of the Section on Survey Research Meth-*

ods. Papers presented at the annual meeting of the American Statistical Association; 1978 August 14–17; San Diego, CA. Washington, D.C.: American Statistical Association: 570–574.

Gallagher, K.; Duggar, B. C.; Lewis, W. F. 1983. "Coverage of U.S. Hospitals by Discharge Abstract Services." *Journal of the American Medical Records Association.* 54:23–27.

Garcia, Victor. 1992. *Counting the Uncountable: Immigrant and Migrant, Documented and Undocumented Farm Workers in California.* Washington, D.C.: U.S. Bureau of the Census. Ethnographic Evaluation of the 1990 Decennial Census Report No. 12. Prepared under Joint Statistical Agreement 89-29 with Guadalupe Community Health Center, Inc.

Garnick, Daniel H.; Gonzales, Maria Elena. 1980. "Statistical Uses of Administrative Records: Where Do We Go from Here?" In: *1979 Proceedings of the Section on Survey Research Methods.* Papers presented at the annual meeting of the American Statistical Association; 1979 August 13–16; Washington, D.C. Washington, D.C.: American Statistical Association: 89–94.

Garrett, Joseph; Hogan, Howard; Pautier, Charles. June 1986. "Coverage Concepts and Issues in Data Collection and Data Presentation." In: *Proceedings of the Second Annual Research Conference;* 1986 March 23–26; Reston, VA. Washington, D.C.: U.S. Department of Commerce. Bureau of the Census: 329–343.

Gerald, Debra E. September 1991. "Toward Developing a Supply and Demand Model for Elementary and Secondary School Teachers." In: *Proceedings of the 1991 Annual Research Conference;* 1991 March 17–20; Arlington, VA. Washington, D.C.: U.S. Department of Commerce. Bureau of the Census: 213–238.

Gieseman, Raymond W. 1987. "The Consumer Expenditure Survey: Results Compared with Data from Other Sources." In: *1986 Proceedings of the Social Statistics Section.* Papers presented at the annual meeting of the American Statistical Association; 1986 August 18–21; Chicago, IL. Washington, D.C.: American Statistical Association: 10–17.

Gilbert, Ronald D. 1979. "Monetary Aggregates Versus Economic Indicators: Which Is the Better Predictor of Reference Cycles?" In: *1978 Proceedings of the Business and Economic Statistics Section.* Papers presented at the annual meeting of the American Statistical Association; 1978 August 14–17; San Diego, CA. Washington, D.C.: American Statistical Association: 207–209.

Goldberg, Edward D. 1989. "Information Needs for Marine Pollution Studies." *Environmental Monitoring and Assessment.* 11(3):293–298.

Green, George R.; Beckman, Barry A. 1993. "Business Cycle Indicators: Upcoming Revision of the Composite Indexes." *Survey of Current Business.* 73(10):44–51.

Greenspan, Alan. 1985. "Assessing the Usefulness of Current Economic Statistics." In: *Proceedings of the First Annual Research Conference;* 1985 March 20–23; Reston, VA. Washington, D.C.: U.S. Department of Commerce. Bureau of the Census: 147–150.

Gruberg, Richard E.; Hughes, Arthur L. 1993. "Estimating Drug Abuse Episodes from a Nonrandom Sample of Hospitals." In: *1992 Proceedings of the Section on Survey Research Methods.* Papers presented at the annual meeting of the American Statistical Association; 1992 August 9–13; Boston, MA. Alexandria, VA: American Statistical Association: 297–302.

Grzesiak, Thomas J.; Lent, Janice. 1989. "Estimating Business Birth Employment in the Current Employment Statistics Program." In: *1988 Proceedings of the Section on Survey Research Methods.* Papers presented at the annual meeting of the American Statistical Association; 1988 August 22–25; New Orleans, LA. Alexandria, VA: American Statistical Association: 597–602.

Hansen, LeRoy T.; Hallam, Arne. 1991. "National Estimates of the Recreational Value of Streamflow." *Water Resources Research.* 27(2):167–175.

Harris, Kenneth W.; Royston, Patricia; Givens, Jimmie D. 1988. "Factors Affecting the Use and Interpretation of Diagnostic Statistics from Seven NCHS Data Systems." In: *1987 Proceedings of the Social Statistics Section.* Papers presented at the annual meeting of the American Statistical Association; 1987 August 17–20; San Francisco, CA. Alexandria, VA: American Statistical Association: 340–345.

Harrison, Anne. 1989. "Environmental Issues and the SNA." *The Review of Income and Wealth.* Series 35(4):377–388.

Helfand, Sol D.; Natrella, Vito; Pisarski, Alan E. 1984. *Statistics for Transportation, Communication and Finance and Insurance: Data Availability and Needs.* Washington, D.C.: National Academy Press: 138.

Hendershott, Patric H.; Peek, Joe. 1989. "Household Saving in the United States: Measurement and Behavior." *Journal of Business and Economic Statistics.* 7(January):11–19.

Hinaman, Kurt C. 1993. "Use of a Geographic Information System to Assemble Input-Data Sets for a Finite-Difference Model of Ground-Water Flow." *Water Resources Bulletin.* 29(3): 401–405.

Hing, Esther. 1992. "Analysis of Survey Data on Nursing Home Patients by Mode of Data Collection." In: *1991 Proceedings of the Social Statistics Section.* Papers presented at the annual meeting of the American Statistical Association; 1991 August 18–22; Atlanta, GA. Alexandria, VA: American Statistical Association: 472–477.

Hipel, Keith W. 1992. "Multiple Objective Decision Making in Water Resources." *Water Resources Bulletin.* 28(1):3–12.

Hirsch, Robert M.; Alexander, Richard B.; Smith, Richard A. 1991. "Selection of Methods for the Detection and Estimation of Trends in Water Quality." *Water Resources Research.* 27(5):803–813.

Hogan, H.; Wolter, K. 1988. "Measuring Accuracy in a Post Enumeration Survey." *Survey Methodology.* 14:99–116.

Holloway, Thomas M. 1989. "Present NIPA [National Income and Product Accounts] Saving Measures: Their Characteristics and Limitations." In: Lipsey, Robert E.; Tice, Helen Stone, eds. *The Measurement of Saving, Investment, and Wealth.* National Bureau of Economic Research Conference on the Measurement of Saving, Investment, and Wealth; 1987 March 27–28; Baltimore, MD; *Studies in Income and Wealth,* Vol. 52. Chicago, IL: University of Chicago Press: 21–93.

Horn, Robert V. 1993. *Statistical Indicators for the Economic and Social Sciences.* New York, NY: Cambridge University Press: 227.

Hughes, Arthur L.; Gfroerer, Joseph C. 1991. "Analysis of Survey Data on Drug Experience by Mode of Data Collection." In: *1990 Proceedings of the Section on Survey Research Methods.* Papers presented at the annual meeting of the American Statistical Association; 1990 August 6–9; Anaheim, CA. Alexandria, VA: American Statistical Association: 401–406.

Iachan, Ronaldo. 1989. "Design Issues in Environmental Surveys." In: *1988 Proceedings of the Section on Survey Research Methods.* Papers presented at the annual meeting of the American Statistical Association; 1988 August 22–25; New Orleans, LA. Alexandria, VA: American Statistical Association: 144–152.

Iachan, Ronaldo. 1989. "Issues in Environmental Survey Design." *Journal of Official Statistics.* 5(4):323–335.

Ingham, Lindy H. 1991. "Natural Resource and Environmental Accounting in the National Accounts." *Journal of Official Statistics.* 7(4):499–513.

Jabine, Thomas B.; Scheuren, Fritz. 1985. "Goals for Statistical Uses of Administrative Records: The Next Ten Years." In: *1984 Proceedings of the Section on Survey Research Methods.* Papers presented at the annual meeting of the American Statistical Association; 1984 August 13–16; Philadelphia, PA. Washington, D.C.: American Statistical Association: 66–75.

Johnson, Robert; O'Brien, D. 1980. "International Cooperation on a Framework for the Integration of Social Demographic and Related Economic Statistics." In: Taylor, Charles L., ed. *Indicator Systems for Political, Economic, and Social Analysis.* Cambridge, MA: Oelgeschlager, Gunn & Hain, Publishers, Inc.: 65–85.

Johnston, Denis F.; Carley, Michael J. 1981. "Social Measurement and Social Indicators." *The Annals of the American Academy of Political and Social Sci-*

ence. 453(January):237–254. Special issue "America Enters the Eighties: Some Social Indicators."

Judge, John F. 1981. "An Evaluation of the Geographic Coding in the 1977 Economic Censuses: An Overview." In: *1980 Proceedings of the Section on Survey Research Methods.* Papers presented at the annual meeting of the American Statistical Association; 1980 August 11–14; Houston, TX. Washington, D.C.: American Statistical Association: 160–162.

Juster, F. Thomas. 1990. "The State of U.S. Economic Statistics: Current and Prospective Quality, Policy Needs, and Resources" [Unpublished paper]. Presented at the National Bureau of Economic Research 50th Anniversary Conference on Research in Income and Wealth; 1988 May 12–14; Washington, D.C.

Juster, F. Thomas; Kuester, Kathleen A. 1991. "Differences in the Measurement of Wealth, Wealth Inequality and Wealth Composition Obtained from Alternative U.S. Wealth Surveys." *The Review of Income and Wealth.* Series 37(1):33–62.

Juster, F. Thomas; Land, Kenneth C., eds. 1981. *Social Accounting Systems: Essays on the State of the Art.* New York, NY: Academic Press: 479.

Kalsbeek, William D.; Weigle, Kristen A.; Allred, Norman J.; Liu, Pao-Wen. 1992. "A Comparison of Survey Designs for Estimating Childhood Immunization Rates." In: *1991 Proceedings of the Section on Survey Research Methods.* Papers presented at the annual meeting of the American Statistical Association; 1991 August 18–22; Atlanta, GA. Alexandria, VA: American Statistical Association: 175–180.

Kalton, Graham; Kasprzyk, Daniel; Santos, Robert. 1981. "Some Problems of Nonresponse and Nonresponse Adjustment in the Survey of Income and Program Participation." In: *1980 Proceedings of the Section on Survey Research Methods.* Papers presented at the annual meeting of the American Statistical Association; 1980 August 11–14; Houston, TX. Washington, D.C.: American Statistical Association: 501–506.

Keith, Lawrence, ed. 1988. *Principles of Environmental Sampling.* Washington, D.C.: American Chemical Society: 458.

Kelly, Henry; Wyckoff, Andrew. 1989. "Distorted Image: How Government Statistics Misrepresent the Economy." *Technology Review.* (Feb./Mar.):52–60.

Kulka, Richard A.; Holt, Nicholas A.; Carter, Woody; Dowd, Kathryn L. September 1991. "Self-Reports of Time Pressures, Concerns for Privacy, and Participation in the 1990 Mail Census." In: *Proceedings of the 1991 Annual Research Conference;* 1991 March 17–20; Arlington, VA. Washington, D.C.: U.S. Department of Commerce. Bureau of the Census: 33–54.

Kwiatkowski, Roy E. 1991. "Statistical Needs in National Water Quality Monitoring Programs." *Environmental Monitoring and Assessment.* 17:253–271.

Laganier, Jean. 1984. "The Possible Impact of National Accounts and Balances on the Development of Frameworks for Environment Statistics." *Statistical Journal.* 2(1, Jan.):43–61.

Land, Kenneth C. 1976. "A General Framework for Building Dynamic Macro Social Indicator Models: Including an Analysis of Changes in Crime Rates and Police Expenditures." *American Journal of Sociology.* 82:555–604.

Landefeld, J. Steven; Hines, James R. 1985. "National Accounting for Non-Renewable Natural Resources in the Mining Industries." *The Review of Income and Wealth.* Series 31(1):1–20.

Layton, Allan P.; Moore, Geoffrey H. 1989. "Leading Indicators for the Service Sector." *Journal of Business and Economic Statistics.* 7(July):379–386.

Lehnen, Robert G. 1990. "Improving National Education Statistics for Policy Studies." In: *1989 Proceedings of the Social Statistics Section.* Papers presented at the annual meeting of the American Statistical Association; 1989 August 6–10; Washington, D.C. Alexandria, VA: American Statistical Association: 209–214.

Lehnen, Robert G.; Reiss, Albert J. 1979. "Some Response Effects of the National Crime Survey." In: *1978 Proceedings of the Section on Survey Research Methods.* Papers presented at the annual meeting of the American Statistical Association; 1978 August 14–17; San Diego, CA. Washington, D.C.: American Statistical Association: 374–377.

Levin, Michael J.; Farley, Reynolds. 1983. "Historical Comparability of Ethnic Designations in the United States." In: *1982 Proceedings of the Social Statistics Section.* Papers presented at the annual meeting of the American Statistical Association; 1982 August 16–19; Cincinnati, OH. Washington, D.C.: American Statistical Association: 4–12.

Levine, Bruce. 1981. "Improving Industry and Place-of-Work Coding in the Continuous Work History Samples." In: *1980 Proceedings of the Section on Survey Research Methods.* Papers presented at the annual meeting of the American Statistical Association; 1980 August 11–14; Houston, TX. Washington, D.C.: American Statistical Association: 472–477.

Lipscomb, Emanuel A.; Walter, Bruce C. 1979. "Impacts of Reporting Burden Reduction on the Quality of Export Statistics." In: *1978 Proceedings of the Business and Economic Statistics Section.* Papers presented at the annual meeting of the American Statistical Association; 1978 August 14–17; San Diego, CA. Washington, D.C.: American Statistical Association: 500–503.

Lipsey, Robert E.; Tice, Helen Stone, eds. 1989. *The Measurement of Saving, Investment, and Wealth.* National Bureau of Economic Research Conference on the Measurement of Saving, Investment, and Wealth; 1987 March 27–28; Baltimore, MD; *Studies in Income and Wealth,* Vol. 52. Chicago, IL: The University of Chicago Press: 861.

Liverman, Diana M.; Hanson, Mark E.; Brown, Becky J.; Merideth, Robert W., Jr. 1988. "Global Sustainability: Toward Measurement." *Environmental Management.* 12(2):133–143.

Loebl, A. S.; Cantor, S. 1982. "Energy Data Validation: An Overview and Some Concepts." In: *1981 Proceedings of the Section on Survey Research Methods.* Papers presented at the annual meeting of the American Statistical Association; 1981 August 10–13; Detroit, MI. Washington, D.C.: American Statistical Association: 186–191.

Lussier, R.; Bray, D. F. 1992. "Towards a Better Use of Health Records for Statistical Purposes." In: *1991 Proceedings of the Social Statistics Section.* Papers presented at the annual meeting of the American Statistical Association; 1991 August 18–22; Atlanta, GA. Alexandria, VA: American Statistical Association: 551–555.

Mark, Jerome A.; Waldorf, William H. 1983. "Multifactor Productivity: A New BLS Measure." *Monthly Labor Review.* 106(12):3–15.

McDonald, Richard J. 1984. "The 'Underground Economy' and BLS Statistical Data." *Monthly Labor Review.* 107(1):4–18.

McGuckin, Robert; Peck, Suzanne. 1992. "An Examination of Reclassified Manufacturing Establishments." In: *1991 Proceedings of the Business and Economic Statistics Section.* Papers presented at the annual meeting of the American Statistical Association; 1991 August 18–22; Atlanta, GA. Alexandria, VA: American Statistical Association: 333–338.

McKelvey, Karen; Clark, Cynthia Z. F.; Killion, Ruth Ann. 1990. "1985 and 1986 Census of Agriculture Tests." In: *1989 Proceedings of the Section on Survey Research Methods.* Papers presented at the annual meeting of the American Statistical Association; 1989 August 6–10; Washington, D.C. Alexandria, VA: American Statistical Association: 605.

McKenney, Nampeo R.; Farley, Reynolds; Leving, Michael J. 1984. "Direct and Indirect Measures of Ethnicity: How Different Definitions Affect the Size and Characteristics of Various Ethnic Groups." In: *1983 Proceedings of the Social Statistics Section.* Papers presented at the annual meeting of the American Statistical Association; 1983 August 15–18; Toronto, Canada. Washington, D.C.: American Statistical Association: 123–130.

McLeod, A. Ian; Hipel, Keith W.; Bodo, Byron A. 1991. "Trend Analysis Methodology for Water Quality Time Series." *Environmetrics.* 2(2, June):169–200.

McNeil, John M.; Lamas, Enrique J. 1989. "Year-Apart Estimates of Household Net Worth from the Survey of Income and Program Participation." In: Lipsey, Robert E.; Tice, Helen Stone, eds. *The Measurement of Saving, Investment, and Wealth.* National Bureau of Economic Research Conference on the Measurement of Saving, Investment, and Wealth; 1987 March 27–28; Baltimore,

MD; *Studies in Income and Wealth,* Vol. 52. Chicago, IL: University of Chicago Press: 431–462.

McNichols, Roger J.; Davis, Charles B. 1988. "Statistical Issues and Problems in Ground Water Detection Monitoring at Hazardous Waste Facilities." *Ground Water Monitoring Review.* 8(4):135–150.

McPherson, E. Gregory. 1993. "Monitoring Urban Forest Health." *Environmental Monitoring and Assessment.* 26(2–3):164–174.

Mulry, Mary H.; Spencer, Bruce D. July 1988. "Total Error in Dual System Estimates of Population Size." In: *Proceedings of the Fourth Annual Research Conference;* 1988 March 20–23; Arlington, VA. Washington, D.C.: U.S. Department of Commerce. Bureau of the Census: 48–66.

Mulry, Mary H.; Spencer, Bruce D. 1993. "Accuracy of 1990 Census Undercount Estimates for the Postcensal Estimates." In: *1992 Proceedings of the Section on Survey Research Methods.* Papers presented at the annual meeting of the American Statistical Association; 1992 August 9–13; Boston, MA. Alexandria, VA: American Statistical Association: 160–165.

Narayanan, A.; Sager, Thomas W. 1989. "A Comparison of Two Approaches to Classification of Air Pollution Data." *Journal of Official Statistics.* 5(4):375–389.

National Academy of Science. 1975. *Planning for Environmental Indices: A Report of the Planning Committee on Environmental Indices.* Washington, D.C.

National Association of Business Economists. October 1988. *Report of the Statistics Committee of the National Association of Business Economists.* Cleveland, OH: National Association of Business Economists. Summary reprinted in *Business Economics.* October 1988; 23(4):56–58.

National Association of Business Economists. September 1989. *Report of the Statistics Committee.* Washington, D.C.: National Association of Business Economists: 40.

National Research Council. Committee on AIDS Research and the Behavioral, Social and Statistical Sciences. 1989. *AIDS: Sexual Behavior and Intravenous Drug Use.* Turner, Charles F.; Miller, Heather G.; Moses, Lincoln E., eds. Washington, D.C.: National Academy Press: 589.

National Research Council. Committee on National Statistics. 1976. *Setting National Priorities: Report of the Panel on Methodology for Statistical Procedures of the Committee on National Statistics.* Washington, D.C.: National Academy Press: 172.

National Research Council. Committee on National Statistics. 1988. *The Aging Population in the Twenty-First Century: Statistics for Health Policy.* Gilford, Dorothy M., ed. Washington, D.C.: National Academy Press: 323.

National Research Council. Committee on National Statistics. 1988. *Income and Poverty Statistics: Problems of Concept and Measurement. Report of a Workshop.* Levine, Daniel B.; Ingram, Linda, eds. Washington, D.C.: National Academy Press: 23.

National Research Council. Committee on National Statistics. 1990. *Disability Statistics: An Assessment. Report of a Workshop.* Washington, D.C.: National Academy Press: 71.

National Research Council. Committee on National Statistics. May 20, 1994. *What Do We Need to Know Between One Census and the Next? (And How Should We Obtain the Information?)* Washington, D.C.: National Academy of Sciences. Volume Two. Seminar and Discussion of the 64th Meeting of the Committee on National Statistics.

National Research Council. Committee on National Statistics. Committee on Indicators of Pre-College Science and Mathematics Education. 1987. *Toward Understanding Teacher Supply and Demand. Priorities for Research and Development: Interim Report.* Washington, D.C.: National Academy Press: 143.

National Research Council. Committee on National Statistics. Panel on Decennial Census Methodology. 1985. *The Bicentennial Census: New Directions for Methodology in 1990.* Citro, Constance F.; Cohen, Michael L., eds. Washington, D.C.: National Academy Press: 404.

National Research Council. Committee on National Statistics. Panel on Foreign Trade Statistics. 1992. *Behind the Numbers: U.S. Trade in the World Economy.* Kester, Anne Y., ed. Washington, D.C.: National Academy Press: 297.

National Research Council. Committee on National Statistics. Panel to Evaluate Microsimulation Models for Social Welfare Programs. 1991. *Improving Information for Social Policy Decisions: The Uses of Microsimulation Modeling.* Citro, Constance F.; Hanushek, Eric A., eds. Washington, D.C.: National Academy Press. 2 vol. Vol. I is "Review and Recommendations"; Vol. II is "Technical Papers."

National Research Council. Committee on National Statistics. Panel to Evaluate the National Center for Education Statistics. 1986. *Creating a Center for Education Statistics: A Time for Action.* Levine, Daniel B., ed. Washington, D.C.: National Academy Press: 76. SuDoc: ED 1.102:St2/2.

National Research Council. Committee on National Statistics. Panel to Evaluate the Survey of Income and Program Participation. 1992. *The Future of the Survey of Income and Program Participation.* Citro, Constance F.; Kalton, Graham, eds. Washington, D.C.: National Academy Press: 284.

National Research Council. Committee on National Statistics. Panel to Review Productivity. 1979. *Measurement and Interpretation of Productivity [Rees Report].* Washington, D.C.: National Academy of Sciences: 449.

National Research Council. Committee on National Statistics [and] Committee on Indicators of Pre-College Science and Mathematics Education. 1987. *Toward Understanding Teacher Supply and Demand. Priorities for Research and Development: Interim Report.* Washington, D.C.: National Academy Press: 143.

National Research Council. Committee on Occupational Classification and Analysis. 1980. *Work, Jobs, and Occupations: A Critical Review of the Dictionary of Occupational Titles.* Miller, Ann R., ed. Washington, D.C.: National Academy Press.

Natrella, Vito; Popkin, Joel. 1987. "International Comparability of Industry Classification Systems." In: *1986 Proceedings of the Business and Economic Statistics Section.* Papers presented at the annual meeting of the American Statistical Association; 1986 August 18–21; Chicago, IL. Washington, D.C.: American Statistical Association: 13–16.

Norgaard, Richard B. 1990. "Economic Indicators of Resources Scarcity: A Critical Essay." *Journal of Environmental Economics and Management.* 19(1):19–25.

Norwood, Janet L. 1990. "Distinguished Lecture on Economics in Government: Data Quality and Public Policy." *Journal of Economic Perspectives.* 4(2):3–12.

O'Brien, Robert; Sinha, Bimal K.; Smith, William P. 1991. "A Statistical Procedure to Evaluate Clean-up Standards." *Journal of Chemometrics.* 5(3):249–261.

O'Conor, Karen; Wong, William. 1989. "Measuring the Precision of the Employment Cost Index." Monthly Labor Review. 112(3):29–36.

Organisation for Economic Co-operation and Development. 1991. *Environmental Indicators: A Preliminary Set.* Paris: OECD: 77.

Ostro, Bart D.; Anderson, Robert C. 1982. "Morbidity, Air Pollution and Health Statistics." In: *1979 Proceedings of the Business and Economic Statistics Section.* Papers presented at the annual meeting of the American Statistical Association; 1981 August 10–13; Detroit, MI. Washington, D.C.: American Statistical Association: 59–67.

Ott, M. Gerald; Norwood, S. K.; Cook, R. R. 1985. "The Collection and Management of Occupational Exposure Data." *The American Statistician.* 39(4, Pt. 2):432–436.

Parker, Robert P. 1983. "The GNP Data Improvement Project (The Creamer Report): A Bureau of Economic Analysis Perspective." In: Foss, Murray F., ed. *The U.S. National Income and Product Accounts: Selected Topics.* National Bureau of Economic Research Conference on Research in Income and Wealth, Conference on National Income and Product Accounts of the

United States; 1979 May 3–4; Washington, D.C.; *Studies in Income and Wealth,* Vol. 47. Chicago, IL: University of Chicago Press: 424–427.

Passel, Jeffrey S.; Woodrow, Karen A. 1985. "Growth of the Undocumented Alien Population in the United States, 1979–1983, as Measured by the Current Population Survey and the Decennial Census" [Unpublished paper]. Presented at the annual meeting of the Population Association of America, Boston, Massachusetts.

Penner, Rudolph G. 1990. "A Policy Users' Panel [on 'how well government statistical systems in the United States and Canada meet the need for policy-analytic data']." In: Berndt, Ernst R.; Triplett, Jack E., eds. *Fifty Years of Economic Measurement: The Jubilee of the Conference on Research on Income and Wealth.* National Bureau of Economic Research Conference on Research in Income and Wealth 50th Anniversary Conference; 1988 May 12–14; Washington, D.C.; *Studies in Income and Wealth,* Vol. 54. Chicago, IL: University of Chicago Press: 427–431.

Poe, Gail S. 1979. "Re-Evaluation of the Health Interview Survey." In: *1978 Proceedings of the Section on Survey Research Methods.* Papers presented at the annual meeting of the American Statistical Association; 1978 August 14–17; San Diego, CA. Washington, D.C.: American Statistical Association: 575–579.

Popkin, Joel. 1993. "An Alternative Framework for Analyzing Industrial Output." *Survey of Current Business.* 73(11):50–56.

Radermacher, Walter. 1994. "Sustainable Income: Reflections on the Valuation of Nature in Environmental-Economic Accounting." *Statistical Journal of the United Nations Economic Commission for Europe.* 11:35–51.

Repetto, R. 1989. *Wasting Assets: Natural Resources in the National Income Accounts.* Washington, D.C.: World Resource Institute.

Rice, Dorothy P. 1988. "Improvement of Data Resources for Policy Analysis for an Aging Population." In: *1987 Proceedings of the Social Statistics Section.* Papers presented at the annual meeting of the American Statistical Association; 1987 August 17–20; San Francisco, CA. Alexandria, VA: American Statistical Association: 22–26.

Roberts, Mark; Monahan, James. June 1986. "The Effects of Nonsampling Errors on the Development and Use of the Longitudinal Establishment Data (LED) File." In: *Proceedings of the Second Annual Research Conference;* 1986 March 23–26; Reston, VA. Washington, D.C.: U.S. Department of Commerce. Bureau of the Census: 131–146.

Root, Norman; McCaffrey, David. 1978. "Providing More Information on Work Injury and Illness." *Monthly Labor Review.* 101(4):16–22.

Ruggles, Richard. 1983. "The United States National Income Accounts, 1947–1977: Their Conceptual Basis and Evolution." In: Foss, Murray F., ed.

The U.S. National Income and Product Accounts: Selected Topics. National Bureau of Economic Research Conference on National Income and Product Accounts of the United States; 1979 May 3–4; Washington, D.C.; *Studies in Income and Wealth,* Vol. 47. Chicago, IL: University of Chicago Press: 15–96.

Sands, Mark S.; Smith, Julie A.; Kashihara, David. 1991. "The Quarterly Financial Report Survey—Redesign Research." In: *1990 Proceedings of the Business and Economic Statistics Section.* Papers presented at the annual meeting of the American Statistical Association; 1990 August 6–9; Anaheim, CA. Alexandria, VA: American Statistical Association: 138–143.

Schirm, Allen L.; Czajka, John L. 1993. "Weighting a Panel of Individual Tax Returns for Cross-Sectional Estimation." In: *1992 Proceedings of the Section on Survey Research Methods.* Papers presented at the annual meeting of the American Statistical Association; 1992 August 9–13; Boston, MA. Alexandria, VA: American Statistical Association: 303–308.

Schreiner, Irwin; Pennie, Karen; Newbrough, Jennifer. 1989. "Interviewer Falsification in Census Bureau Surveys." In: *1988 Proceedings of the Section on Survey Research Methods.* Papers presented at the annual meeting of the American Statistical Association; 1988 August 22–25; New Orleans, LA. Alexandria, VA: American Statistical Association: 491–496.

Schultz, Linda K.; Huang, Elizabeth T.; Diffendal, Gregg J.; Isaki, Cary T. 1987. "Some Effects of Statistical Synthetic Estimation on Census Undercount of Small Areas." In: *1986 Proceedings of the Section on Survey Research Methods.* Papers presented at the annual meeting of the American Statistical Association; 1986 August 18–21; Chicago, IL. Washington, D.C.: American Statistical Association: 321–325.

Shah, Reena. 1989. "Environment Statistics Programme of the United Nations." *Journal of Official Statistics.* 5(4):457–469.

Sheldon, Eleanor B.; Freeman, H. E. 1970. "Notes on Social Indicators: Promises and Potential." *Policy Sciences.* 1:97–111.

Silverberg, Arthur R. 1983. "An Approach to Evaluating the Accuracy of Energy Data Series." In: *1982 Proceedings of the Section on Survey Research Methods.* Papers presented at the annual meeting of the American Statistical Association; 1982 August 16–19; Cincinnati, OH. Washington, D.C.: American Statistical Association: 309–313.

Simpson, Gloria; Keer, David; Cynamon, Marcie. 1993. "Plans for the 1993–94 National Health Interview Survey on Disability." In: *1992 Proceedings of the Section on Survey Research Methods.* Papers presented at the annual meeting of the American Statistical Association; 1992 August 9–13; Boston, MA. Alexandria, VA: American Statistical Association: 411–415.

Sims, Christopher A. 1985. "Can We Measure the Benefits of Data Programs?" In: *1984 Proceedings of the Social Statistics Section.* Papers presented at the annual meeting of the American Statistical Association; 1984 August 13–16; Philadelphia, PA. Washington, D.C.: American Statistical Association: 60–67.

Sinclair, James; Catron, Brian. 1990. "An Experimental Price Index for the Computer Industry." *Monthly Labor Review.* 113(10):16–24.

Sindermann, Carl J. 1988. "Biological Indicators and Biological Effects of Estuarine/Coastal Pollution." *Water Resources Bulletin.* 24(5):931–939.

Smith, D. G. C. 1989. "Combination of Forecasts in Electricity Demand Prediction." *Journal of Forecasting.* 8(3):349–356.

Spencer, Bruce D. 1985. "Towards Conducting Benefit-Cost Analysis of Data Programs." In: *1984 Proceedings of the Social Statistics Section.* Papers presented at the annual meeting of the American Statistical Association; 1984 August 13–16; Philadelphia, PA. Washington, D.C.: American Statistical Association: 46–51.

Steiner, Robert L. 1994. "Caveat! Some Unrecognized Pitfalls in Census Economic Data." Draft April 4, 1994. Forthcoming *Review of Industrial Organizations.*

Steuerle, C. Eugene. 1994. *Economic Effects of Health Reform.* Washington, D.C.: AEI Press: 25.

Stone, Richard. 1981. "The Relationship of Demographic Accounts to National Income and Product Accounts." In: Juster, F. Thomas; Land, Kenneth C., eds. *Social Accounting Systems: Essays on the State of the Art.* New York, NY: Academic Press: 307–376.

Taylor, Stephen. 1989. "World Payments Imbalances and U.S. Statistics." In: Lipsey, Robert E.; Tice, Helen Stone, eds. *The Measurement of Saving, Investment, and Wealth.* National Bureau of Economic Research Conference on the Measurement of Saving, Investment, and Wealth; 1987 March 27–28; Baltimore, MD; *Studies in Income and Wealth,* Vol. 52. Chicago, IL: University of Chicago Press: 401–428.

Thiébaux, H. Jean. 1991. "Statistics and the Environment: The Analysis of Large-Scale Earth-Oriented Systems." *Environmetrics.* 2(1, March):5–24.

Thompson, John H.; Woltman, Henry F.; Clark, Jon R.; Whitford, David C. 1994. "Sampling and Estimation for the 1995 Census Test." Presented at the Joint Advisoy Committee Meeting [U.S. Bureau of the Census]; 1994 April 14–15; Suitland, MD.

Trelogan, Harry C. 1976. "Toward More Accurate Farming Data." *Agricultural Economics Research.* 28(2):79–81.

Triplett, Jack E. 1975. "The Measurement of Inflation: A Survey of Research on the Accuracy of Price Indexes." In: Earl, Paul H., ed. *Analysis of Inflation.* Lexington, MA: Lexington Books: 19–82.

Triplett, Jack E. August 1990. "The Theory of Industrial and Occupational Classifications and Related Phenomena." In: *Proceedings of the 1990 Annual Research Conference;* 1990 March 18–21; Arlington, VA. Washington, D.C.: U.S. Department of Commerce. Bureau of the Census: 9–25.

Triplett, Jack E. 1991. "The Federal Statistical System's Response to Emerging Data Needs." *Journal of Economic and Social Measurement.* 17:155–177.

Triplett, Jack E. 1992. "Economic Theory and BEA's Alternative Quantity and Price Indexes." *Survey of Current Business.* 72(4):49–52.

Triplett, Jack E. 1993. "Economic Concepts for Economic Classifications." *Survey of Current Business.* 73(11):45–49.

United Nations. 1992. *Integrated Environmental and Economic Accounts (An Interim Report).* New York, NY: United Nations. Handbook on National Accounts Series.

United Nations Economic Commission for Europe. 1982. "Heath Accounts." *Statistical Journal of the United Nations Economic Commission for Europe.* 1:187-202. Based on a paper prepared for the Third Joint ECE/WHO Meeting on Health Statistics, 1982 February 15–18, Geneva.

U.S. Bureau of the Census. February 1994. "The 1995 Census Test. A Plan Based on Census Bureau Research and Critical Review by Stakeholders." Washington, D.C.: U.S. Department of Commerce. Bureau of the Census.

U.S. Congress. Office of Technology Assessment. 1988. *Statistical Needs for a Changing U.S. Economy.* Washington, D.C.: U.S. Government Printing Office. SUDOC: Y 4.Ec 7:P 94/29.

U.S. Department of Commerce. Bureau of Economic Analysis. 1988. "Gross Product by Industry: Comments on Recent Criticisms." *Survey of Current Business.* 68(7):132–133.

U.S. Department of Commerce. Bureau of Economic Analysis. 1991. "Improving the Quality of Economic Statistics: The 1992 Economic Statistics Initiative." *Survey of Current Business.* 71(3):4–5.

U.S. Department of Commerce. Office of Federal Statistical Policy and Standards. October 1977. *Gross National Product Data Improvement Project. Report of the Advisory Committee on Gross National Product Data Improvement.* Washington, D.C.: U.S. Government Printing Office: 204.

U.S. Department of Education. National Center for Education Statistics. September 1991. *Education Counts: An Indicator System to Monitor the Nation's Educational Health. Report of the Special Study Panel on Education Indicators to the Acting Commissioner of Education Statistics.* Washington, D.C.: U.S. Government Printing Office: 123. SUDOC: ED 1.102:M 74.

U.S. Department of Education. National Center for Education Statistics. May 1993. *Programs and Plans of the National Center for Education Statistics.*

Washington, D.C.: U.S. Department of Education. National Center for Education Statistics: 135.

U.S. Department of Education. National Center for Education Statistics; Bobbitt, Sharon A.; Quinn, Peggy; Dabbs, Patricia. November 1992. *Filling the Gaps: An Overview of Data on Education in Grades K Through 12.* NCES 92–132. Washington, D.C.: U.S. Government Printing Office: 62.

U.S. Department of Health and Human Services. National Center for Health Statistics. 1988. *Health of an Aging America: Issues on Data for Policy Analysis.* Vital and Health Statistics, Series 4: Documents and Committee Reports No. 25. Washington, D.C.: U.S. Government Printing Office: 188. SUDOC: HE 20.6209:4/25.

U.S. Department of Health and Human Services. National Center for Health Statistics. May 1992. *The National Committee on Vital and Health Statistics, 1991.* Hyattsville, MD: U.S. Department of Health and Human Services. National Center for Health Statistics. DHHS Publication No. (PHS) 92-1205: 139.

U.S. Department of Health and Human Services. Public Health Service. 1991. *Healthy Children 2000: National Health Promotion and Disease Prevention Objectives Related to Mothers, Infants, Children, Adolescents, and Youth.* Washington, D.C.: U.S. Government Printing Office: 244. SUDOC: HE 20. 9202:H 34/4.

U.S. Environmental Protection Agency. Office of the Administrator. 1990. *Environmental Investments: The Cost of a Clean Environment.* Washington, D.C.: U.S. EPA Office of Policy, Planning and Evaluation in cooperation with the Environmental Law Institute. EPA 230-119-0083: 511. NTIS: PB 91-153-783.

U.S. Environmental Protection Agency. Quality Assurance Management Staff. October 6, 1993. *Guidance for Planning for Data Collection in Support of Environmental Decision Making Using the Data Quality Objectives Process.* Washington, D.C.: U.S. Environmental Protection Agency. EPA QA/G-4; Interim Final.

U.S. Executive Office of the President. Office of Management and Budget. 1987. *Standard Industrial Classification Manual 1987.* Washington, D.C.: U.S. Government Printing Office: 705. SUDOC: PrEx 2.6/2:In 27/987.

U.S. General Accounting Office. November 4, 1987. *Education Information: Changes in Funds and Priorities Have Affected Production and Quality.* Gaithersburg, MD: U.S. General Accounting Office. GAO/PEMD-88-4; Chapter Report: 121.

U.S. General Accounting Office. October 1989. *Foreign Investment: Federal Data Collection on Foreign Investment in the United States.* Gaithersburg, MD: U.S. General Accounting Office. GAO/NSLAD-90-25BR: 18.

U.S. General Accounting Office. November 1989. *Air Pollution. National Air Monitoring Network Is Inadequate.* Gaithersburg, MD: U.S. General Accounting Office. GAO/RCED-90-15: 50.

U.S. General Accounting Office. August 1991. *Waste Minimization: EPA Data Are Severely Flawed.* Gaithersburg, MD: U.S. General Accounting Office. GAO/PEMD-91-21: 9.

U.S. National Commission on Employment and Unemployment Statistics. 1979. *Counting the Labor Force.* Washington, D.C.: U.S. Government Printing Office: 312.

U.S. Office of Management and Budget. Office of Information and Regulatory Affairs. Statistical Policy Office. July 1988. *Quality in Establishment Surveys.* Washington, D.C.: U.S. Office of Management and Budget. Statistical Policy Working Paper 15: 105.

Waite, Charles A. 1987. "Census Bureau Economic Statistics—Data Quality, Budget Austerity, and Other Dimensions of Change." In: *1986 Proceedings of the Business and Economic Statistics Section.* Papers presented at the annual meeting of the American Statistical Association; 1986 August 18–21; Chicago, IL. Washington, D.C.: American Statistical Association: 3–6.

Ward, Robert C.; Loftis, Jim C.; McBride, Graham B. 1986. "The 'Data-Rich But Information-Poor' Syndrome in Water Quality Monitoring." *Environmental Management.* 10(3):291–297.

Westman, W. E. 1978. "Measuring the Inertia and Resilience of Ecosystems." *BioScience.* 28:705–710.

Woldt, W.; Bogardi, I. 1992. "Ground Water Monitoring Network Design Using Multiple Criteria Decision Making and Geostatistics." *Water Resources Bulletin.* 28(1):45–62.

Wolfson, Michael C. November 1992. "POHEM—A Framework for Understanding and Modeling the Health of Human Populations." In: *Proceedings of the 1992 Annual Research Conference;* 1992 March 22–25; Arlington, VA. Washington, D.C.: U.S. Department of Commerce. Bureau of the Census: 261–282.

Wolter, Kirk; Monsour, Nash. June 1986. "Conclusions from Economic Censuses Evaluation Studies." In: *Proceedings of the Second Annual Research Conference;* 1986 March 23–26; Reston, VA. Washington, D.C.: U.S. Bureau of the Census: 41–53.

Woolsey, Theodore D. 1990. "The Value of Studying Uses of Data: Some Examples from Health Statistics." In: *1989 Proceedings of the Social Statistics Section.* Papers presented at the annual meeting of the American Statistical Association; 1989 August 6–10; Washington, D.C. Alexandria, VA: American Statistical Association: 41–45.

Worden, G. 1986. "Company Reporting for Segment of Business: Improving Industrial Statistics" [Unpublished paper]. Presented to the Census Advisory Committees of the American Marketing Association and the American Economic Association at the Joint Advisory Committee Meeting.

Yetley, E. A.; Rosenthal, S. A. 1990. "Nutrition Policy: How Have Data Made a Difference?" In: *1989 Proceedings of the Social Statistics Section*. Papers presented at the annual meeting of the American Statistical Association; 1989 August 6–10; Washington, D.C. Alexandria, VA: American Statistical Association: 46–50.

Young, Allan H. 1993. "Reliability and Accuracy of the Quarterly Estimates of GDP [Gross Domestic Product]." *Survey of Monthly Business.* 73(10):29–43.

INDEX